CARMELITE MONASTERY

W9-CLJ-132

1. *In the True Light of Vatican II*

RELIGIOUS LIFE
IN THE LIGHT OF
VATICAN II

RELIGIOUS LIFE IN THE LIGHT OF VATICAN II

Alberione
Anastasio
Antoniutti
Bea
Cushing
Gambari
Häring
John XXIII
Lalande
M. Ignatius
Mc Carthy
Paul VI

Pius XII
Poage
Sheen
Sr. M. Emil
Sr. R. Barrett
Sr. Teresa M.
Spellman

Compiled by the
Daughters of St. Paul

GLORY TO GOD   PEACE TO MEN

ST. PAUL EDITIONS

NIHIL OBSTAT:

    Rev. Shawn G. Sheehan
    Diocesan Censor

IMPRIMATUR:

    + Richard Cardinal Cushing
    Archbishop of Boston

May 3, 1967

Grateful acknowledgement is made to the following for use of selections in this book:

Centro Studi "U.S.M.I. (Union of Major Superiors of Italy); Scuola "Mater Divinae Gratiae," Rome.

Häring, Rev. Bernard, C.SS.R.

N.C.W.C. Documentary Service.

Newsletter of the Pontifical Office for Religious Vocations.

Rivista delle Religiose, Centro Studi "U.S.M.I."

Sheen, Most Rev. Fulton J.

Sister Formation Bulletin.

Sister Formation Proceedings.

Sisters Today.

The Pope Speaks Magazine, Washington, D.C.

248.894

Library of Congress Catalogue Card Number: 67-24029

Copyright, 1967, by the *Daughters of St. Paul*

Printed in U.S.A. by the *Daughters of St. Paul*
50 St. Paul's Ave., Jamaica Plain, Boston, Mass. 02130

The Daughters of St. Paul

dedicate this volume

to His Holiness

Pope Paul VI,

the Vicar of Christ

to whom all Religious

profess love, devotion

and complete submission.

THE MESSAGE OF VATICAN II
TO RELIGIOUS

Each of the twenty-one Ecumenical Councils in the history of the Church has had characteristics all its own. The Council of Trent, for instance, has been called the Council of faith because it defined essential points of Catholic doctrine and established salutary norms for both the clergy and the laity. The First Vatican Council stands out as the Council of the papal primacy. The Second Vatican Council will go down in history as the Council of love, the Council "of the Church."

There were no condemnations, no definitions; there was no bitterness, no discord. Rather, the Church revealed herself as a Mother. Yet another time she pointed out the way of salvation to those who have lost the way and are walking in darkness.

"The Church has gathered herself together . . . to probe more deeply still the mystery, the plan and the presence of God above and within herself; to revitalize in herself that faith which is the secret of her confidence and of her wisdom, and that love which impels her to sing without ceasing the praises of God." PAUL VI, CLOSING SPEECH OF VATICAN II

This Council which spoke on peace and hunger, on unity and religious freedom, on the laity and the clergy; this Council which dealt with every social question to provide light and guidance on the right course to be followed—how could this Council fail to guide and wisely enlighten the life of religious, who form the most distinguished part of the People of God. In fact, as the Constitution, *Lumen Gentium*, affirms, it fulfills this role by right:

"It is the duty of the ecclesiastical hierarchy to regulate the practice of the evangelical counsels by law, since it is the duty of the same hierarchy to care for the People of God and to lead them to most fruitful pastures. The importance of the profession of the evangelical counsels is seen in the fact that it fosters the perfection of love of God and love of neighbor in an outstanding manner"... (n. 45).

Thus in this same Constitution, the Council presents the theological foundations of religious life. It points out practical ways of realizing them in the Decree, *Perfectae Caritatis,* on the Adaptation and Renewal of Religious Life, and in a few paragraphs of *Christus Dominus,* the Decree on the Pastoral Office of Bishops in the Church.

The main points covered in Chapter VI of the Dogmatic Constitution on the Church, *Lumen Gentium,* are:

1. The evangelical counsels, considered in themselves

2. The nature of religious life as a consecration to God and the Church

3. The dependence of the religious state on Church authority

4. The spiritual freedom of consecrated religious

5. Perseverance and sanctity in religious life.

The Decree, *Christus Dominus,* on the Pastoral Office of Bishops in the Church, emphasizes the relationship between religious and ecclesiastical authority.

The Decree, *Perfectae Caritatis,* instead lays down prescriptions

"Meant to state only the general principles of the adaptation and renewal of the life and discipline of Religious orders and also ... of societies of common life without vows and secular institutes" (n. 1).

Thus it is a matter of adapting and renewing religious life, of treating the needs and modern requirements of the various institutes and of the apostolates they carry out.

The basic meaning of religious life is highlighted and the profession of the three vows of chastity, poverty and obedience. Aggiornamento is discussed, together with religious formation and the apostolate each institute performs according to its individual spirit, keeping in mind its usefulness to the Church universal and to the dioceses. Also handled are relationships between congregations and the problem of vocations.

So it is that through these documents, the Church clarified, specified and deepened its teaching on religious life.

In the present volume the norms for implementing the decree on religious life, as given in the Apostolic letter, *Ecclesiae Sanctae,* have been placed after the respective sections of the decree. The vital points of the various sections of Chapter 6 of *Lumen Gentium* and of *Perfectae Caritatis* are herein discussed for our profit and guidance by our Holy Father, and by authorities such as Cardinal Antoniutti, Prefect of the Sacred Congregation of Religious, various Council Fathers, Superiors General, and modern authors.

It is the hope of the compilers of this volume that it may prove a real help to both masculine and feminine communities updating their lives according to the mind, heart and will of the Church.

"All of us have to update as the decrees, pronouncements and constitutions of the Council dictate," writes Very Rev. J. Alberione, S.S.P. "Not all that is being said or printed in books and magazines today is to be followed. We religious have to know and follow the mind of the Church."

DAUGHTERS OF ST. PAUL

Contents

The Message of Vatican II to Religious - D.S.P. 9

THE EVANGELICAL COUNSELS

DOGMATIC CONSTITUTION ON THE CHURCH, N. 43, 44,
    45, 47 23
DECREE ON THE MINISTRY AND LIFE OF PRIESTS,
    N. 6 25
The Religious Meaning of Consecrated Lives 26
    - *Paul VI*
The Nature and Dimensions of Religious Life 30
    - *D.S.P.*

RELIGIOUS

DECREE ON THE ADAPTATION AND RENEWAL OF
    RELIGIOUS LIFE, *Perfectae Caritatis*, N. 1 45
A Spiritual Fact of Mysterious Significance - *Paul VI* 46
Origin and Development of Religious Life 49
    - *D.S.P.*

WHAT THE CHASTITY OF RELIGIOUS ENTAILS

DECREE ON THE ADAPTATION AND RENEWAL OF
    RELIGIOUS LIFE, N. 12 59
The Christian Virgin - *John XXIII* 61
The Value of Chastity - *Paul VI* 70

The Sphere of Chastity - *Bernard Haring, C.SS.R.* 72
An Undivided Love - *Bernard Haring, C.SS.R.* 74
Jesus Christ, Master and Teacher of Chastity 78
    - *James Alberione, S.S.P., S.T.D.*
Crisis over the Vows - *James Alberione, S.S.P., S.T.D.* 90

WHAT THE POVERTY OF RELIGIOUS ENTAILS

DECREE ON THE ADAPTATION AND RENEWAL
    OF RELIGIOUS LIFE, N. 13 95
On Poverty - *Ecclesiae Sanctae* 97
The Virtue of Poverty - *Paul VI* 98
Love for Poverty - *Paul VI* 100
Monastic Work - *Pius XII* 102
The Value of Work in Contemplative Life - *Pius XII* 103
Poverty, Dependence and Destitution 106
    - *Sister Teresa Margaret, O.C.D.*
The Witness of Collective Poverty 118
    - *Pius XII, Most Rev. Andrew Sol, James
     Alberione, S.S.P., S.T.D.*
Jesus Christ, Master and Teacher of Poverty 120
    - *James Alberione, S.S.P., S.T.D.*

WHAT THE OBEDIENCE OF RELIGIOUS ENTAILS

DECREE ON THE ADAPTATION AND RENEWAL
    OF RELIGIOUS LIFE, N. 14 139
Obedience and the Council - *Paul VI* 141
The Ecclesiastical Magisterium - *Paul VI* 147
The Superior-Servant - *Paul VI* 149
The Twofold Problem of Authority and Obedience 154
    - *Paul VI*
A Holocaust of the Will - *Paul VI* 156
Superiors Cannot Shed Responsibility - *Pius XII* 157
The Exercise of Authority 170
    - *Hildebrand Cardinal Antoniutti*

Obedience, Dialogue, and the Superior's Role 180
    - *James Alberione, S.S.P., S.T.D.*
The Reward of Obedience 182
    - *James Alberione, S.S.P., S.T.D.*
Obedience—A Scriptural View 186
    - *Sister Mary Ruth Barrett, S.N.D.*

RELIGIOUS VOWS AND PERSONALITY

DOGMATIC CONSTITUTION ON THE CHURCH, N. 46 195
Personality - *James Alberione, S.S.P., S.T.D.* 196
An Exchange—Not a Giving Up 197
    - *Most Rev. Fulton J. Sheen*
The Tensions of the Middle-Aged Sister and the Role
    of the Superior - *Sister M. Emil, I.H.M.* 199

COMMON LIFE

DECREE ON THE ADAPTATION AND RENEWAL
    OF RELIGIOUS LIFE, N. 15 223
Living the Common Life - *Ecclesiae Sanctae* 225
Community Life in Theory and Practice 227
    - *James Alberione, S.S.P., S.T.D.*
Family Spirit - *James Alberione, S.S.P., S.T.D.* 238
Community Life in the Light of the
    Council of Love - *Rev. Mother Ignatius, D.S.P.* 247

THE RELIGIOUS STATE AS WITNESS

DOGMATIC CONSTITUTION ON THE CHURCH, N. 31, 46 253
Your Life Means Christ Lived and Witnessed 254
    - *Paul VI*
Witness to Offset Materialism 258
    - *Father Germaine-Marie Lalande*

THE RELIGIOUS VOCATION: EXCEPTIONAL CHOICE OF SERVICE TO GOD AND THE CHURCH

DECREE ON THE ADAPTATION AND RENEWAL
OF RELIGIOUS LIFE, N. 5, 6 261
Mortification - *Ecclesiae Sanctae* 263
Mental Prayer - *Ecclesiae Sanctae* 263
What *Is* Religious Life? - *Paul VI* 264
For Religious, A Special Place in the Church
Community - *Paul VI* 268
"The Church Needs Your Sanctity" - *Paul VI* 271
Religious Must Always Live and Feel with the Church .. 276
- *Augustine Cardinal Bea*

RELIGIOUS AND THEIR FELLOWMEN

DOGMATIC CONSTITUTION ON THE CHURCH, N. 46 279
The Field of Action of Consecrated Virgins - *Pius XII* 280

RENEWAL—WHAT IT ENTAILS

DECREE ON THE ADAPTATION AND RENEWAL
OF RELIGIOUS LIFE, N. 2 285
The Criteria of Renewal and Adaptation 287
- *Ecclesiae Sanctae*
Religious in the Post-Conciliar Era - *Paul VI* 288
Guidelines for Renewal - *John XXIII* 292
The Founder's Spirit and Rule of Life - *Paul VI* 308
How Have You Accepted Renewal? - *Paul VI* 311
Perfect Charity—Ideal of Religious Life - *Paul VI* 314
The Importance of Knowing Christ through Scripture 317
- *Paul VI*
Know, Imitate and Live Jesus - *Paul VI* 321
Principal Motivator for Renewal 322
- *Anastasio of the Holy Rosary, O.C.D.*

Sacred Scripture in Our Lives 323
    - *James Alberione, S.S.P., S.T.D.*
Caution Must Be Observed in Renewal 326
    - *Francis Cardinal Spellman*
A Return to Primitive Fervor 327
    - *Anastasio of the Holy Rosary, O.C.D.*
Knowledge of the Times We Live In 328
    - *Anastasio of the Holy Rosary, O.C.D.*
Three Dangers Connected with Aggiornamento 330
    - *James Alberione, S.S.P., S.T.D.*

PRACTICAL ASPECTS OF RENEWAL

DECREE ON THE ADAPTATION AND RENEWAL
    OF RELIGIOUS LIFE, N. 3, 4 339

The Manner of Promoting the Adaptation and
    Renewal - *Ecclesiae Sanctae* 341
True Renewal - *Pope Pius XII* 347
Adaptation and Renewal of Constitutions 349
    - *Elio Gambari, S.M.M.*
The Relationship of Religious to Their Constitutions 353
    - *Elio Gambari, S.M.M.*
Conformity to Our Constitutions 355
    - *James Alberione, S.S.P., S.T.D.*
Revising and Adapting Community Prayer Manuals 360
    - *Elio Gambari, S.M.M.*

THE RELIGIOUS HABIT

DECREE ON THE ADAPTATION AND RENEWAL
    OF RELIGIOUS LIFE, N. 17 365

"A Sign of Consecration" 366
    - *Pius XII and Paul VI*
Motives Behind Renewal 368
    - *Richard Cardinal Cushing*

Updating and the Habit 370
    - *Anastasio of the Holy Rosary, O.C.D.*

RENEWAL AND THE APOSTOLATE

DECREE ON THE ADAPTATION AND RENEWAL
    OF RELIGIOUS LIFE, N. 20 373
Conciliar Directives on the Exercise of the
    Apostolate - *Decree Concerning the Pastoral*
    Office of Bishops in the Church - Decree on
    the Mission Activity of the Church 374
United Forces - *Paul VI* 381
How Great are Your Accomplishments - *Paul VI* 382
Religious Life Is Apostolic by Nature 383
    - *Anastasio of the Holy Rosary, O.C.D.*

THE VARIOUS FORMS OF RELIGIOUS LIFE

The Contemplative Life

DECREE ON THE ADAPTATION AND RENEWAL
    OF RELIGIOUS LIFE, N. 7, 16 387
The Cloister of Nuns - *Ecclesiae Sanctae* 389
The Church Today Still Needs Contemplatives 390
    - *Paul VI, John XXIII, Pius XII*
"You Are Chosen Souls but not Separated" - *Paul VI* 392

Communities Devoted to the Apostolic Life

DECREE ON THE ADAPTATION AND RENEWAL
    OF RELIGIOUS LIFE, N. 8 399
Apostolic Energy and Love Comes from Prayer 400
    - *Paul VI*
The Soul of the Apostolate 407
    - *James Alberione, S.S.P., S.T.D.*

The Monastic Life

DECREE ON THE ADAPTATION AND RENEWAL
OF RELIGIOUS LIFE, N. 9 408

Religious Life a Following of Christ - *Paul VI* 409

Secular Institutes

DECREE ON THE ADAPTATION AND RENEWAL
OF RELIGIOUS LIFE, N. 11 416

A Cry in the Wilderness 417
  - *Thomas P. McCarthy, C.S.V.*

Perfection To Be Exercised and Professed in the
World - *Pius XII* 418

Living in Christ and of Christ 419
  - *James Alberione, S.S.P., S.T.D.*

VOCATIONS TO THE RELIGIOUS LIFE

DECREE ON THE ADAPTATION AND RENEWAL
OF RELIGIOUS LIFE, N. 24 423

Conciliar Directives for Vocation Recruitment 424
  - *Decree on Priestly Training*
  - *Decree on the Ministry and Life of Priests*

There Are Still Vocations in Our Century 427
  - *Paul VI*

Four Pointers on Recruitment - *Paul VI* 433

How to Present Religious Life - *Paul VI* 438

Indispensable for Spiritual Training - *Pius XII* 440

Why the Vocation Decline? - *Godfrey Poage, C.P.* 441

The Vocation Problem Deserves First Place 443
  - *James Alberione, S.S.P., S.T.D.*

Vocation Clubs—Best Recruiting Technique 447
  - *Godfrey Poage, C.P.*

The Need of Prayers - *Fulton J. Sheen* 458

An Exemplary Recruiter - *Newsletter, Pontifical
Office for Vocations* 451

What One Pastor Did - *Newsletter, Pontifical Office
for Vocations* 454

Everything Depends on the Choice and Formation of
  Vocations - *Pius XII* 455
Point Out the Renunciations - *Paul VI* 456
Mediocrity, Not Sacrifice, Repels Youth 457
  - *Hildebrand Cardinal Antoniutti*
Why They Come to Religious Life 460
  - *James Alberione, S.S.P., S.T.D.*

UPDATING AND RELIGIOUS FORMATION

DECREE ON THE ADAPTATION AND RENEWAL
  OF RELIGIOUS LIFE, N. 18 465
The Training of Religious - *Ecclesiae Sanctae* 466
Formation for Interior Life and Apostolic Adaptation 468
  - *Paul VI*
What Today's Young Adults Want - *Paul VI* 470
Formation Personnel - *Elio Gambari, S.M.M.* 471
Juniorates, or Post-Novitiate Formation 472
  - *Elio Gambari, S.M.M.*

CONFERENCES OF MAJOR SUPERIORS

DECREE ON THE ADAPTATION AND RENEWAL
  OF RELIGIOUS LIFE, N. 23 474
On Conferences or Unions of Major Superiors of Men
  and Women - *Ecclesiae Sanctae* 475
Joining Forces - *Pius XII* 476
Unions of Chosen Souls 477
  - *James Alberione, S.S.P., S.T.D.*

CONCLUSION

DECREE ON THE ADAPTATION AND RENEWAL
  OF RELIGIOUS LIFE, N. 25 479

The

Evangelical

Counsels

The evangelical counsels of chastity dedicated to God, poverty and obedience are based upon the words and examples of the Lord. They were further commended by the apostles and Fathers of the Church, as well as by the doctors and pastors of souls. The counsels are a divine gift, which the Church received from its Lord and which it always safeguards with the help of His grace. Church authority has the duty, under the inspiration of the Holy Spirit, of interpreting these evangelical counsels, of regulating their practice and finally to build on them stable forms of living.

Dogmatic Constitution on the Church, n. 43

The faithful of Christ bind themselves to the three aforesaid counsels either by vows, or by other sacred bonds, which are like vows in their purpose. By such a bond, a person is totally dedicated to God, loved beyond all things. In this way, that person is ordained to the honor and service of God under a new and special title. Indeed through Baptism a person dies to sin and is consecrated to God. However, in order that he may be capable of deriving more abundant fruit from this baptismal grace, he intends, by the profession of the evangelical counsels in the Church, to free himself from those obstacles, which might draw him away from the fervor of charity and the perfection of divine worship. By his profession of the evangelical counsels, then, he is more intimately consecrated to di-

vine service. This consecration will be the more perfect, in as much as the indissoluble bond of the union of Christ and His bride, the Church, is represented by firm and more stable bonds.

Ibid., n. 44

The hierarchy, following with docility the prompting of the Holy Spirit, accepts the rules presented by outstanding men and women and authentically approves these rules after further adjustments. It also aids by its vigilant and safeguarding authority those institutes variously established for the building up of Christ's Body in order that these same institutes may grow and flourish according to the spirit of the founders.

Ibid., n. 45

From the point of view of the divine and hierarchical structure of the Church, the religious state of life is not an intermediate state between the clerical and lay states. But, rather, the faithful of Christ are called by God from both these states of life so that they might enjoy this particular gift in the life of the Church and thus each in one's own way, may be of some advantage to the salvific mission of the Church.

Ibid., n. 43

The state which is constituted by the profession of the evangelical counsels, though it is not the hierarchical structure of the Church, nevertheless, undeniably belongs to its life and holiness.

Ibid., n. 44

Let each of the faithful called to the profession of the evangelical counsels, therefore, carefully see to it that he persevere and ever grow in that vocation God has given him. Let him do this for the increased holiness of the Church, for the greater glory of the one and undivided Trinity, which in and through Christ is the fount and the source of all holiness.

Ibid., n. 47

Priests should remember that all Religious, both men and women, who certainly have a distinguished place in the house of the Lord, deserve special care in their spiritual progress for the good of the whole Church.

Decree on the Ministry and Life of Priests, n. 6

THE RELIGIOUS MEANING
OF CONSECRATED LIVES

Pope Paul VI

What marks Religious life is that it aims at the perfection of divine love by means of the evangelical counsels. St. Thomas remarks that there are two ways of loving God perfectly: the first is that of the blessed in heaven, who are ceaselessly in the act ("actualiter") of bearing their hearts to God ("perfectio patriae"). The second is the "perfectio viae"— that of travelers such as we are, who endeavor to bear their hearts in a habitual way ("habitualiter") to God, avoiding what would be contrary to this love. The perfection to which the counsels aim, St. Thomas adds, is like a middle way between these two estates: it is the way of one who tears himself away as much as he can from even legitimate temporal things which occupy the soul and prevent it from making progress actually (in act) toward God (St. Th. Summa Theol., IIa, IIae, q 44, art. 4, 2, 3).

This is your perfection. It is the perfection which you must inculcate in the souls of those who entrust themselves to you. It implies something absolute, total ("totalitas quaedam"), a unique love to which the heart gives itself completely and to which one must ceaselessly refer in order to live the Religious life in depth and in truth.

In a world which aims to set itself free from absolute imperatives and to regard all values as relative, the consecrated soul, fixed on God through the vows, appears as it were anchored in the absolute. It is in this light that the "religious" character properly so-called is perhaps best manifest in that same life.

It may be dedicated, by vocation as well as by obedience, to external works of teaching, charity, welfare. What will make its activities valuable is the inner charity which inspires them, that is, the value of its union with God.

This means, beloved daughters, that a certain degree of contemplative life, of an inner dialogue of love between the soul and its God is inherent in every form of Religious life. This is what is authoritatively affirmed by the decree *Perfectae Caritatis* when it exhorts all consecrated souls to live for God alone: "soli Deo vivant." It is necessary, it adds, that "members of every community, seeking God solely and before everything else, should join contemplation, by which they fix their minds and hearts on Him, with apostolic love, by which they strive to be associated with the work of redemption and to spread the Kingdom of God" (n. 5).

How, you will say, can the primacy of contemplation be inculcated in our Religious in the anxious present-day world?

First of all, you will be concerned with ensuring the external conditions which make it possible. You will endeavor to encourage meditation according to methods which may change from institute to institute but which must in any case provide for places and periods of silence. This is a point to which the conditions of modern life compel us to give the greatest attention.

The liturgy is and must remain together with Sacred Scripture one of the substantial nourishments of contemplation. That contrived argument was rightly denounced (J. and R. Maritain: "Liturgy and Contemplation"—Desclee de Brouwer, 1959)which creates a dichotomy between the public prayer of the Church and mental prayer. These two great supernatural realities must be associated and not divided. Liturgical prayer, especially now when each can take part in it more fully, is a valuable aid to contemplative souls in their spiritual ascent.

Because of a kind of mutual causality, nothing disposes the soul to participate fruitfully in liturgy better than a habitual interior life.

The same can be said of that which is the very object of the apostolate of most of your Religious families. By serving the poor, the sick, the children, by giving itself to the service of the Church, the consecrated soul grows in the love of God, in the desire to possess Him more fully. In its turn, this ardent desire to love and to possess God is the best stimulant to activities—of whatever kind—in the service of our fellow men.

Lastly, the very form of community life offers consecrated souls a permanent opportunity to grow in love and to dispose themselves to contemplation. This is true for those who exercise authority as well as for those who are subject to it, since in Religious life both obedience and authority refer to the love of God which inspires them and at the same time is nourished by them. Thus understood community life is a permanent witness to the love of God, a demonstration in a way of what a perfect life in this world can and must be.

This witness, however, can be intelligible only if it is manifested outwardly in ways of living and of being which are not opposed—as is sometimes the case—to the spirit of the Gospel, particularly regarding poverty. We know that many among you are concerned with this. We congratulate them and encourage them paternally along this path. As we have said on other occasions, the personal practice of Religious poverty is not enough: it is necessary that the entire community bear such witness in a manner clearly evident to modern men.

Address to International Union of Superiors General of
Religious Congregations of Women, March 7, 1967

THE NATURE AND DIMENSIONS
OF RELIGIOUS LIFE

In the Second Vatican Council, the Church concerned herself with the life of her children, neglecting no one. United heart and soul, the Pope and the Bishops directed their thoughts to all of us, their one desire being to make it easier for us to live our marvelous though difficult life with greater drive. Thus they pointed out the straight path to its goal, which will be both the culmination and the bliss of that life.

So it was that the Church considered yet another time the nature, the value, and the goals of our religious life. We might say that she wanted to reveal to us again its original beauty coming from God—that beauty that has been dimmed by human weakness. The Church desired to gain back the primordial vigor of religious life, prodding us on to new virtue and to a more vital, responsible awareness of our vocation.

THE NATURE OF RELIGIOUS LIFE

The basic structure, the nature of religious life is unchanging. Although the dimensions of the human situation may change from one age to the next, still all that flows from the very nature of the evangelical counsels retains its full force, which can in no way be diminished.

Aware, however, of the preoccupying decrease in vocations and increase in the number of those being dismissed or leaving voluntarily, the Church proposes the nature of religious life for an in-depth examination on our part—an honest, courageous scrutiny.

"We think that it is a duty today," wrote Pope Paul VI, in *Ecclesiam Suam,* "for the Church to deepen the awareness that she must have of herself, of the treasure of truth of which she is heir and custodian and of her mission in the world." Likewise, it is a duty for religious to deepen their awareness of their particular life, of the end to which it is directed, of the mission that has been given to them in the Church and in the world. Vocations will be better disposed to respond to God's call if they know the beauty of the life to which God is inviting them. And perseverance, at least humanly speaking, will come easier when minds are filled with an appreciation of the worth of the mission to which they are asked to devote their efforts freely and totally.

How did the Church once again define religious life?

I. Religious life is the same supernatural life to which we were reborn in Baptism, for it is the fullest and most perfect expression of the baptismal consecration: It "constitutes a special consecration, which is deeply rooted in that of baptism and expresses it more fully" (*Perfectae Caritatis,* n. 5). "Through Baptism, a person dies to sin and is consecrated to God. However, in order that he may be capable of deriving more abundant fruit from this baptismal grace ... by the profession of the evangelical counsels in the Church, ... he is more intimately consecrated to divine service" (*Lumen Gentium,* n. 44).

The profession of the evangelical counsels builds on the consecration of self in Baptism and completes it as a special consecration. For through it, the Christian not only dies to sin, but renounces the world. "He offers and consecrates himself entirely to God, making his whole life an exclusive service of the Lord" (Pope Paul VI). The comparison between Christian life and religious life may be expressed in these terms: "With his Baptism, every Christian is consecrated to God and must therefore live as a Christian. Religious life entails a different consecration, one regarding poverty, chastity, and obedience. One makes it in order to live the Christian life more perfectly" (Very Rev. James Alberione, S.S.P.).

Essentially, then, religious life is a life publicly consecrated to God. This is indeed the first effect of profession. For this reason, the person of a religious is sacred. Profession also produces particular supernatural effects in the soul.

Essentially again, religious life is a triple gift: a gift of God, a gift of the one consecrating himself, and a gift to the Church and from the Church. Just as Baptism presupposes the gift of faith, likewise the religious profession presupposes the gift of a special call on God's part. In fact, the Lord disposed everything in our regard before He created our soul. Vocation does not "come" at the age of ten, fifteen or twenty, but at the origin of life, when the soul is created. Vocation comes from our Heavenly Father. Every child is born with his own vocation, with his own destiny. Secondly, we can speak of profession as a gift to God, for the religious gives himself for a lifetime. And finally, it is a gift to and from the Church: "The religious life . . . [is] a particular gift in the life of the Church." "The evangelical counsels of chastity dedicated to God, poverty and obedience are . . . a divine gift, which the Church received from its Lord and which it will always observe with the help of His grace" (*Lumen Gentium,* n. 43).

The Church truly views religious as her gift to God. On the Feast of the Nativity of Our Lady, after speaking of Mary's role in leading men to God, Pope Paul offered her all the religious of the Church with these words: "See, Mary, what we are offering you—the most beautiful flowers of Holy Church!"

The tremendous value and supernatural character of religious life is evident, then, from these considerations, even though there are some who would like to see the religious state reduced to a purely lay life, to a merely natural way of life.

"Is it not perhaps true that often the young clergy or indeed even some zealous religious moved by the good intention of penetrating the masses or particular groups, tend to get mixed up with them instead of remaining apart, thus sacrificing the true efficacy of their apostolate to some sort of useless imitation? The great principle enunciated by Christ presents itself again both in its actuality and in its difficulty: To be in the world, and not of the world" (*Ecclesiam Suam,* n. 47).

To renew and restore religious life, then, means to live by the supernatural spirit! Religious life must be directed in the light provided by faith.

II. Because religious life is a lifelong donation to God, to the Church, and in the Church, it is God-centered, Christ-centered, and Church-centered.

The life of a religious, then, is God-centered: "It is necessary that the members of every community seek God solely and before everything else . . ." (*Perfectae Caritatis,* n. 5). "Let those who make profession of the evangelical counsels seek and love above all else God who has first loved us" (*Ibid.,* n. 6). "By such a bond, a person is totally dedicated to God, loved beyond all things" (*Lumen Gentium,* n. 44).

Thus constitutions and rules invariably exhort religious to live in charity towards God and neighbor, which is the supreme law of the Christian and of the religious life. Love for God is to find its highest expression in our profession.

No religious can live a horizontal life, flat and smooth. Ours must be a vertical, progressive life, ascending steadily toward heaven. "Let all religious, therefore, be rooted in faith and filled with love for God and neighbor, love of the cross and the hope of future glory" (*Perfectae Caritatis,* n. 25).

This theological character finds its place in the very nature of religious life—a consecration completing the baptismal consecration. If Baptism makes the believer a child of God, it follows that profession calls us to live our divine sonship even on this earth, to the point of consummation.

In his encyclical, *Ecclesiam Suam,* Pope Paul VI says that the Council awakened

"the desire to preserve and increase in Christian life its character of supernatural authenticity and reminded all of their duty of effectively and deeply imprinting that character in their own personal conduct, thus leading the weak to be good, the good to be better, the better to be generous, and the generous to be holy" (n. 43).

In this way, we shall feel our spirits testifying that we are indeed sons of God!

Religious life, then, entails living on this earth that perfect love which qualifies as filial love of God. This is a consequence not only of the fact that religious life perfects Baptism, but above all, because it is the perfect imitation of the life of the Son of God—indeed, it is a share in His life.

Next, religious life is Christ-centered. It means "following Christ with greater freedom, and imitating Him more closely through the practice of the evangelical counsels" (*Perfectae Caritatis,* n. 1). It means binding one's self "to the Lord in a special way, following Christ, who chaste and poor, redeemed and sanctified men through obedience even to the death of the Cross" (*Ibid*). It means living for Christ and enthusiastically uniting one's self to Him, so as to "share in Christ's emptying of Himself and His life in the Spirit" (*Ibid.,* n. 5). Religious arc people with one love—Christ! Rightly does the Decree, *Perfectae Caritatis,* state that the religious life "draws its origin from the doctrine and example of the Divine Master" (n. 1).

Hence the spiritual life of religious should be built around the study, imitation and love of Jesus, the Divine Master, who is the Way, the Truth and the Life, so as to make true progress in wisdom, grace and virtue, after His example, loving God with the whole mind, will, heart and strength. This kind of piety will lead to "Christification."

The more Christ-centered it is, in fact, the more perfect religious life is. The life of Christ is a life of love, for God is love. Religious life is Christ's life in us, the life of the Son living in us, and unceasingly loving the Father in us. Hence, the vows themselves must be permeated with this love. What is the poverty of Christ if not the poverty of the Son dependent on His Father for everything? What is His obedience if not the effort to do the will of Him Who sent Him? What is His virginity if not absolute freedom to love His Father above all else?

To increase Christ's life in us, the Church recommends that religious read the Holy Bible daily and take part in liturgical prayer, especially the Holy Mass. Where in fact do we find the Divine Master? Where can we approach Him if not in Sacred Scripture and in the Holy Eucharist, the Sacrament of His presence among us? Where does Christ make Himself our Way, Truth and Life if not in these two sources of authentic Christian spirituality?

Finally, religious life is Church-centered. "Since the Church has accepted their surrender of self, they should realize they are also dedicated to

its service." "They live more and more for Christ
and for His body which is the Church" (*Perfectae
Caritatis* n. 5, 1). They correspond to their divine
vocation and to the task given them in the Church.

Religious life is not Church-centered because
we labor in the Church; rather, we have to labor in
the Church because our life is essentially an ecclesial life. What is expected of us is not simply a
personal witness but—"Religious should carefully
keep before their minds the fact that the Church
presents Christ to believers and non-believers alike
in a striking manner daily through them" (*Lumen
Gentium*, n. 46).

Whence comes this relationship to the Church?
From the public consecration of which we have already spoken: "This consecration will be the more
perfect, inasmuch as the indissoluble bond of the
union of Christ and His bride, the Church, is represented by firm and stable bonds" (*Lumen
Gentium*, n. 44).

The public form of profession specifies this
bond with the Church and specifies, too, the particular mission in the Church which we are called upon to carry out.

We do not belong to the hierarchical structure
of the Church, but to her life and her holiness by an
act of the Church herself: "The Church not only
raises the religious profession to the dignity of a
canonical state by her approval, but even manifests
that this profession is a state consecrated to God by
the liturgical setting of that profession... accom-
panying their self-offering by the Eucharistic Sacrifice" (*Lumen Gentium*, n. 45).

Moreover, as a canonical state, the discipline of the religious life is provided for by the Church through special laws in this regard; our life is a state of religion. Rightly then can we say that the difference between the life of any community and the life of a religious community is the book of rules, the Constitutions. It is the Constitutions that bind religious to the Church, for it is the Church which gives them to religious when she approves them.

VALUE AND DIMENSIONS OF RELIGIOUS LIFE

By the value or worth of religious life, we mean its nature viewed functionally. Religious life is valuable from both an earthly and a heavenly viewpoint, from the human and the divine aspect.

It helps keep the Church equipped for every good work. For religious keep their contemporaries before their minds with the tender concern of Christ, and with them, they collaborate spiritually to build up the earthly city which is founded on the Lord and governed by Him.

The religious state offers greater glory to the Trinity, in and through Christ. Religious adorn the Church with their various gifts, so that she appears as a bride adorned for her husband and shows forth the manifold wisdom of God.

Because the People of God have no lasting city here below, but look forward to one that is to come, religious life appears as a splendid sign of the Kingdom of Heaven "which can and ought to attract all the members of the Church to an effective and prompt fulfillment of the duties of their Christian vocation" (*Lumen Gentium*, n. 44).

Following Christ, who redeemed and sanctified men, religious glorify with Christ our Father who is in heaven, producing fruits of salvation, spreading the kingdom of God and thus associating themselves with the work of redemption.

Religious place themselves completely at the service of the Church's mission. Throughout the world they spread the "good news" of Christ.

The dimensions of the religious life are boundless. They are all-embracing. Profession formulae might well be summed up in a statement like this: "I give my entire being for all the interests of God, for a total following of Jesus Christ, the Divine Master, for the needs of the Church and of all men. And this for my whole life, and even for eternity, unto the consummation of the kingdom of heaven."

THE GOAL OF RELIGIOUS LIFE

Life naturally tends to grow and develop. Every nature is destined to reach a determined goal. This end is the joy and crowning of a life.

The supernatural life which we received at Baptism and which is continually being perfected in our religious life through the practice of the evangelical counsels, tends toward final perfection as a seed tends to become a tree, to spread out its branches and bear fruit.

The goal of religious life is the perfection of Christian life—sanctity. There is no higher good in any life, for everything else is but a means to this end. For a religious, moreover, it is not only the supreme good but also that for which he has publicly agreed to aim. So when we pronounce vows or renew them, this thought should impress us ever more deeply and urge us on. May the yearning for holiness grow steadily within us!

Sanctity means glorification of God, our own transfiguration in Christ, and the carrying out of our specific apostolate in the Church. It is clear, then, that the goal of religious life is none other than its nature lived to the point of perfection.

It is often said that the end of religious life is love, and this is true. What is sanctity if not development of the grace that is in us so as to attain to perfect love of God? What is sanctity if not a rejection of all else for the love of Christ, a total commitment to the service of the Church in fraternal love for its members?

There is little need to speak at length of the purpose of religious life, since it is familiar to all of us and is clearly proclaimed in our Constitutions. In fact, all the rules are nothing else than a development of the principal ones dealing with the general and specific purpose of the Congregation.

The general purpose obviously must be the same for all religious, but the special purpose will vary from institute to institute, according to the specific task each is to carry out for the benefit of the Mystical Body:

"The evangelical counsels which lead to charity join their followers to the Church and its mystery in a special way. Since this is so, the spiritual life of these people should then be devoted to the welfare of the whole Church. From this arises their duty of working to implant and strengthen the kingdom of Christ in souls and to extend that kingdom to every clime. This duty is to be undertaken to the extent of their capacities and in keeping with the proper type of their own vocation. This can be realized through prayer or active works of the apostolate. It is for this reason that the Church preserves and fosters the special character of her various religious institutes." (*Lumen Gentium,* n. 44)

Although some need of the Church might require religious to move into a field of action created by circumstances for a period of time, the Church herself, through the words of the Pope and the Council documents, advises religious to avoid those activities which do not correspond to the essential scope of the institute as envisioned by the Founder.

*

These brief thoughts on the nature, value, dimensions and goal of religious life might be compared to drops of water which, as the reader proceeds through the various sections ahead, will expand to form a sea of incomparable breadth and beauty.

Daughters of St. Paul

Religious

Religious

From the very beginning of the Church men and women have set about following Christ with greater freedom and imitating Him more closely through the practice of the evangelical counsels, each in his own way leading a life dedicated to God. Many of them, under the inspiration of the Holy Spirit, lived as hermits or founded religious families, which the Church gladly welcomed and approved by her authority. So it is that in accordance with the Divine Plan a wonderful variety of religious communities has grown up which has made it easier for the Church not only to be equipped for every good work (cf. Tim. 3:17) and ready for the work of the ministry—the building up of the Body of Christ (cf. Eph. 4:12)—but also to appear adorned with the various gifts of her children like a spouse adorned for her husband (cf. Apoc. 21:2) and for the manifold Wisdom of God to be revealed through her (cf. Eph. 3:10).

Decree on the Adaptation and Renewal of Religious Life, n. 1

A SPIRITUAL FACT OF
MYSTERIOUS SIGNIFICANCE

Pope Paul VI

The ecumenical council tells us that the religious life is defined by a basic requirement, the fullness of love for God, thus for Christ, for the Church, for fellowman, for every human being (as St. Francis had). This is a fullness beyond all measure—there comes to mind the well known formula of St. Bernard, "Modum esse diligendi Deum, sine modo diligere," there is only one measure to the love of God, to love Him without measure, (De diligendo Deo, c. 6, n. 16; P. L. 182, 983)—a love that knows no obstacles. This is the releasing sense of the religious vows which are aimed precisely at removing every impediment, even though natural or legitimate, to the sole, the utmost, the complete love of God.

Not without reason does the council decree that refers to the religious life begin with, and therefore bear the title, "Perfectae caritatis ... prosecutionem," the pursuit of perfect charity.

This is known. What we must draw attention to is the call to the loving character of the religious life, a character that distinguishes, qualifies, gives finality to the religious life, not in a purely juridical, conventional, exterior manner, but in an intimate, profound, total, exclusive, intense, absolute manner.

This absolute aspect of love proper to the religious life recurs often in the new and sovereign
legislation of the council. Let us be content at present with a single citation: "The members of each
community should recall above everything else that
by their profession of the evangelical counsels they
have given answer to a divine call to live for God
alone, not only by dying to sin (cf. Rom. 6:11) but
also by renouncing the world. They have handed
over their entire lives to God's service in an act of
special consecration which is deeply rooted in their
baptismal consecration and which provides an am-
pler manifestation of it" (Perfectae caritatis, 5).

Everything is clear and obvious. However,
such a confirmation of the nature, aim and essential means of the religious life gains great importance in reference, first of all, to historical and
spiritual tradition. Here, then, the constituent
concepts of this kind of life come to us intact, almost
regenerated because they are derived from their
purest and most authoritative sources, from the
Gospel and from the effort of faithfulness and sanctity that traverses the centuries of Christianity by
means of the consecration and organization of souls
pervaded by the charity of Christ and by anxiety to
possess and irradiate it in accordance with its own
laws, in other words, toward that perfection which
is conceived as union with God and the imitation of
Christ.

It is a spiritual fact of mysterious significance;
we must seek its secret in the active presence of the
Holy Spirit; it is a paradoxical phenomenon before
the eyes of the world that observes and in the face

of it undergoes the most varied reactions; those of surprise, of repulsion, of disdain, of attraction and curiosity, of trust and veneration.

This occurs especially today when the religious motivation of souls is enfeebled and is almost socially lacking.

And it is here that the religious vocation in modern society, especially in the world of women, despite its quiet reserve, its desired humility, appears clearly in the eyes of everyone as a most singular episode of freedom, of courage, of awareness, of generosity, of spirituality, and we can say even of fortitude and beauty.

Address to Major Superiors of Women's Religious Institutes of Italy, January 12, 1967

ORIGIN AND DEVELOPMENT
OF RELIGIOUS LIFE

Religious life has been described by Fr. Anastasio, Superior General of the Discalced Carmelites, as a "divine reality." In his addresses to Superiors and Novice Mistresses, under the auspices of the Sacred Congregation of Religious, this expert on the spiritual life spoke of it thus:

"The evangelical counsels are a divine gift which brings with it transcendent, supernatural aids for becoming perfect Christians. This gift belongs to the order of charisms and hence to the order of permanent realities which the Church possesses that she may the better be what she is and do what she has to do. . . .

"Religious life, as we have said, is a divine gift, and divine gifts are God's. It is a gift overflowing with values in the order of grace, and grace is from God. It is a charismatic reality, and charisms come from God. He is their Author. Therefore, the religious life exists in the Church not as the sociological product of a historical period, but as the effect of the divine munificence of Christ, the Founder of His Church, the Spouse of His Church. Precisely in this sense and in this perspective is religious life a divine reality, as is the Gospel."

from *La Vita Religiosa nella Chiesa*

From apostolic times, the Church has had holy women consecrated to God, active in serving the Church and in doing good to their neighbor.

The "widows" and "virgins" of whom St. Paul speaks in his epistles (I Tim. 5:9-11; 3:9-11; Rom. 16:1) are none other than these holy women, for in a broad sense they constitute the first stage in the organizational development of the consecrated life.

The fourth century ushered in organized religious life. When the three centuries of persecutions came to an end, a relaxation in spirit and dedication began to set in among Christians. The challenge of the arena was no more.

This situation disturbed those elect souls who desired to live the evangelical counsels fully. They found a solution in the desert and there began the life of the monks. From the very beginning, it followed two paths: the life of the hermits, who prayed, practiced penance and worshipped God in utter solitude; and the regulated life of the cenobites, who lived in community, serving God with common religious practices.

The monastic foundations were laid by St. Anthony, then by St. Pachomius, the first cenobitic legislator, and then by St. Basil, the father of Greek monasticism.

In these first centuries, other rules were drawn up by St. Augustine, St. Vincent of Lerins, St. Caesarius of Arles, and by St. Benedict, the father of western monasticism.

Pachomius' sister, St. Mary; Benedict's sister, St. Scholastica; and Caesarius' sister, St. Caesaria of Arles; St. Brigid of Kildare, and many other holy ab-

besses directed devout women in the practice of
monastic life. Cloister grew more strict during the
fifth and sixth centuries and was rigidly enforced
during the eighth century, in a natural reaction to
the spirit of laxity which had swept over the Church
at that time.

From the sixth to the ninth centuries, monasticism reached its highest stage of development. It
declined during the following centuries, owing to
the anarchy of the times. But one must note also in
this dark age the great Cluniac reform of the Bene-
dictines and the institutions of the orders of Canons
Regular.

Religious life flourished anew in the eleventh
century with St. Bernard of Clairvaux, and in the
twelfth century with the Friars, St. Francis of Assisi
and St. Dominic de Guzman.

In the twelfth century and later, the Poor
Clares and the Second Order Dominicans, spiritual
daughters of St. Francis and St. Dominic, entered
into cloistered life to offer a continual holocaust of
praise and adoration for the fruition of the Franciscan and Dominican apostolates. And similarly, the
Carmelites, the Canonnesses of St. Augustine, and
the Brigittines devoted themselves to the life of
penance and contemplation.

One must here give special mention to St.
Teresa of Avila, the great saint of the Carmelite
Nuns, because of her tremendous work for reform of
religious life and for her sublime mystical writings.

At the same time there sprang up the popular
"third orders"—the Dominicans, the Franciscans,
and later the Augustinians, Carmelites, Mercedar-

ians and Trinitarians. One might say that these "third orders" constituted the Catholic Action of the time, for the apostolate of the laity was not a discovery of the twentieth century. They worked to restore the Christian sense to an unfortunately materialistic Renaissance society. St. Catherine of Siena, St. Rose of Lima and St. Rose of Viterbo are typical examples of members of the "third orders."

Next to these sisters who occupied a position midway between the cloister and the world, one may also note the feminine congregations dedicated to the service of the poor, sick and infirm—the Black Nuns and the Grey Nuns, who were established in northern France in the second half of the fourteenth century. Thus, next to the enclosed life of the cloister during the Middle Ages, place was also found for another form of feminine religious life of a genuine apostolic activity.

The period from the fifteenth to the seventeenth century was a complicated era for religious life. The two guiding fundamentals were initiatives aimed at making apostolic and charitable activity more fruitful on the one hand, and on the other a firm adherence to the reformative decrees of the Council of Trent.

The general practice was that all nuns should pronounce solemn vows and live in cloistered communities. The Ursulines, founded by St. Angela Merici (1474-1540) are an example of this. St. Angela, with an innovating spirit, founded the Company of St. Ursula, composed of young women who would dedicate themselves to any apostolate without common life, without a habit, and without dwelling in strict cloister. Chastity was the only vow which united them.

But eventually the daughters of St. Angela Merici had to follow the general practice of wearing a religious habit and of living in common within a cloister. In their new life the Ursulines were still able to dedicate themselves to the instruction of girls, and the daughters of St. Angela Merici became outstanding pioneers of the apostolate of teaching.

The Visitation Nuns, founded by St. Jane Frances de Chantal, experienced a similar development.

But the seventeenth and eighteenth centuries witnessed a new type of feminine religious life, institutes devoted in a special way to charitable, apostolic and missionary activities. Such congregations of nursing and teaching nuns multiplied and spread throughout the Catholic world. Among the modern congregations of religious sisters who originated at this time, are the Daughters of Charity, founded by St. Vincent de Paul, the Sisters of St. Joseph, the Sisters of St. Paul of Chartres, the Sisters of St. Alexius, the Daughters of Wisdom and many others.

On the eve of the French Revolution, in 1789, there were at least 30,000 sisters in France alone. The revolution, in its attempt to destroy all religious activity, sent several of the nuns, contemplative and active, to the guillotine. The anti-religious laws of the revolution and the materialism and secularism which were their consequences threatened the very idea of religious women, whether cloistered, nursing or teaching. As a consequence, the many institutes of religious women founded in the nineteenth and twentieth centuries pronounced simple vows.

The modern period, from the end of the French Revolution to the present day, may be considered a golden age of feminine religious life, both in regard to numerical development and to varied forms of apostolic endeavor.

Sisters work devotedly in elementary and secondary schools, charitable institutions, re-education programs, orphanages, homes for the aged, programs of assistance and catechetical instructions. Religious women have contributed incalculable services to the Church in this modern secular and materialistic era.

The number of teaching congregations founded during this century and a half is truly astonishing. Just as inspirational are the congregations which were founded to devote themselves to the charitable work of the Church; such would be the Little Sisters of the Poor and the Little Sisters of the Assumption.

During this epoch, the institutes of the contemplative nuns also shared the development; not only multiplying in Europe and the United States but also establishing convents of prayer and penance in the mission lands.

However, in recent times the feminine religious life has undergone crises, both in regard to the recruitment of vocations, and the activities of the apostolate.

These times are dark and difficult for the religious life; examination of the problems is called for, and possibly new initiatives in the apostolate are to be sought. Today we are witnessing the efforts of the great, old religious orders to renew themselves while retaining the spirit of their particular vocation. We are also witnessing the starting of new forms of religious life, which are aimed at working more directly in the world and reaping fruitful harvests, yet all the while keeping faithful to fundamental traditions.

The Pious Society of St. Paul and and the Daughters of St. Paul, founded by Rev. James Alberione in 1915, are marvelous examples of the fusion of the traditional religious life with the utilization of the swiftest and most fruitful means which human progress furnishes, means which the necessities and conditions of the times require. The apostolate of the media of social communication which they pursue is, in the words of their Founder, "the same as the oral preaching of Jesus Christ Himself, the kerygma of the apostolic era, of the Fathers of the Church, of the mendicant friars, adapted and directed to the needs of our own times. These religious cooperate in fulfilling the mandate which Christ gave His successors: 'Go and teach all nations.' They do not simply look backward, but endeavor to draw upon the universal message of Christ and transmit it in its entirety to men of the twentieth century, 'that through the Church there may be made known the manifold wisdom of God' (Eph. 3:10)."

Daughters of St. Paul

What the

Chastity of

Religious Entails

The chastity "for the sake of the kingdom of heaven" (Matt. 19:12) *which religious profess should be counted an outstanding gift of grace. It frees the heart of man in a unique fashion (cf. 1 Cor. 7:32-35) so that it may be more inflamed with love for God and for all men. Thus it not only symbolizes in a singular way the heavenly goods but also the most suitable means by which religious dedicate themselves with undivided heart to the service of God and the works of the apostolate. In this way they recall to the minds of all the faithful that wondrous marriage decreed by God and which is to be fully revealed in the future age in which the Church takes Christ as its only spouse.*

Religious, therefore, who are striving faithfully to observe the chastity they have professed must have faith in the words of the Lord, and trusting in God's help not overestimate their own strength but practice mortification and custody of the senses. Neither should they neglect the natural means which promote health of mind and body. As a result they will not be influenced by those false doctrines which scorn perfect continence as being impossible or harmful to human development and they will repudiate by a certain spiritual instinct everything which endangers chastity. In addition let all, especially superiors, remember that chastity is guarded more securely when true brotherly love flourishes in the common life of the community.

Since the observance of perfect continence touches intimately the deepest instincts of human nature, candidates should neither present themselves for nor be admitted to the vow of chastity, unless they have been previously tested sufficiently and have been shown to possess the required psychological and emotional maturity. They should not only be warned about the dangers to chastity which they may meet but they should be so instructed as to be able to undertake the celibacy which binds them to God in a way which will benefit their entire personality.

Decree on the Adaptation and Renewal of Religious Life, n. 12

THE CHRISTIAN VIRGIN

Pope John XXIII

Dearly beloved Daughters in Jesus Christ. It is you who are the fragrant garden, the precious and hidden pearl, the providential reserve of the supernatural energies of Rome, which, in every age, has been made brilliant with the spectacle of holy and virginal souls consecrated to God. You offer the sacerdotal ministry a precious and disinterested assistance, above all by prayer, and also in the varied forms of your works approved by the Church.

It is for this reason that We insist on making to you, in all simplicity, Our recommendations, so that you may always lead a life worthy of the calling in which you have been called. Our words would wish to translate the delicate concern with which the Church follows you, with a gaze at once anxious and happy, as a mother does for her dearest children.

THE ADORNMENT OF THE CHURCH

In fact, the Holy Church of the Lord glories in and adorns herself with the noble crown of virgins consecrated to the life of prayer and sacrifice and to the practice of the fourteen works of mercy. . . .

From this Church, it is Our pleasure first of all to send a particularly fatherly greeting to Our dear Daughters whom cloister keeps in the different monasteries of Rome and of the world. In fact, it is to the cloistered Sisters that the palm of God's service is given: that is to say, incessant prayer, absolute detachment from all things and from everybody, love of sacrifice, expiation for the sins of the world.

It is to them, who We feel are present with you, in the consoling truth of the Communion of Saints, that Our thought and Our cordial benediction go in the first place.

But since We must address you, you Sisters who represent the numerous army of feminine Institutes in direct contact with souls, We love to take a thought from the *Imitation of Christ*, a book which is, surely, familiar to you, and to apply it to your life and to the exercise of the apostolate to which you are dedicated. At the end of Chapter 48 of the third Book, which invites us to love the things of heaven and there to fix our hearts, We find these words: *"Beatus ille homo, qui propter te, Domine, omnibus creaturis licentiam abeundi tribuit...."* Listen, listen to the sweet voice of this heavenly teaching: "Happy the soul, O Lord, who for love of you says farewell to every creature, who does violence to nature and through fervor of soul crucifies the concupiscences of the flesh, so as to offer to you, from the depths of a peaceful conscience a pure prayer, so that detached within and without from all that is earthly she can mingle with the choirs of the Angels!"

From this splendid passage We are going to highlight four points, which are like four invisible jewels on your religious habit, namely, detachment from creatures, strength of character, incessant prayer, heavenly life.

DETACHMENT FROM CREATURES

I. The *Imitation of Christ* speaks in the first place of an absolute detachment from creatures. It uses vigorous and penetrating words: *Beatus ille qui . . . omnibus creaturis licentiam abeundi tribuit*: "Happy the man who—to use a modern expression— is able to get rid of creatures, says good-bye to them forever." This is the first distinctive note of the religious vocation: an eager and joyous farewell to the world, so as to consecrate oneself to God in perfect virginity of heart. . . .

THE PRICE AND GLORY OF VIRGINITY

Virginity is the virtue which opens your heart wide to love which is the truest, the most immense, the most universal which can be found on this earth: the service of Christ in souls. It is not a human love which you have pursued, nor a home of your own, nor the accomplishment of duties which are strictly individual: all these things are in order and are legitimate, but they are insufficient to satisfy the aspirations of your heart. You have chosen the heavenly Spouse and the vast field of Holy Mother Church.

It is from this unreserved consecration that flow the different vocations of each religious family, which are realized in the service of God and of your brothers, making up that immense tapestry which is the adornment of the House of the Lord and where are the figures—We love to repeat this frequently—of the fourteen works of mercy.

Holy Virginity, willed, generous, vowed to the service of the sick, the old, the poor, to orphans, widows, young people, children. Virginity which passes, like an Angel of light and goodness, through the hospital room and the shelter; full of tenderness and patience, it stoops to the children in school and to relieve the solitude of sufferers, drying tears which the world knows nothing of, calling forth smiles and grateful glances. Holy virginity which irresistibly finds the sure way to the heart, to enlighten untrained minds, to counsel the doubtful, teach the ignorant, touch sinners, console the afflicted, bring back the stragglers, rouse enthusiasm to collaborate with apostolic and missionary endeavors.

In rendering homage to this marvelously beautiful flower which the charity of Christ brings to perfection in the garden of the Church, allow Us to add that virginity cannot keep its charm and its pristine vigor without a solid moral, ascetical, and even psychological formation. *And that brings us to our second thought*:

STRENGTH OF CHARACTER

II. Strength of character. Here again the text cited from the *Imitation* is expressive and energetic: *naturae vim facere*, to do violence to nature.

Now we are here treating of a force or strength which is wholly interior, coming to the support of knowledge of one's own nature, whose potentialities and gifts must be put to the exclusive service of God and souls. This strength must at the same time help us to know our lacks so that we can remedy them by long and patient exercise of virtue fostered by confidence and abandonment to God.

This strength of character keeps the soul in humility because one is conscious of one's own limitations and insufficiency. It produces meekness, leads to obedience, the tried school of strong souls. It means, in fact, submission, the better to serve; self-mastery, to attract souls to God by meekness; victory over self, so that the power of Christ may dwell in us.

Strength of character also ensures the perfect balance of intelligence, will, and sensibility, and forges that ideal 'valiant woman' whom Scripture, in accents of astonished admiration, proposes as the treasure of great price.

SUPERNATURAL JOY

On this score, permit Us to give you a reflection which bears the mark of the experience of Our already long life. It sometimes happens that relaxation in control of self, in certain effusions in which there are traces of interior sadness, of discontent, of pessimism, creates in those who hear them an uneasy feeling, and perhaps presents an example which is somewhat disedifying or ill-placed. Certain bitter words, expressions of disillusionment, and even complaints—these ought not to arise to the lips of consecrated souls, consecrated not to a human institution, no matter how noble,—for example the family, or society,—but consecrated to God.

When the whole value and the dimensions of virginity have been well understood, when we have understood the worth of active and generous service of souls, of abnegation which does not seek the applause of men but only the interior gaze of God, oh, then this sadness does not take root in the heart consecrated to God, or, if temptation comes and tries to make us accept it, it melts away, like unsubstantial mist in the morning sun.

The magnanimous and strong soul never becomes the victim of sadness, even in the hours of greatest trial. And a sign of perfect virginity and invincible strength is joy of mind, of word, of work; it is the complete renunciation of the pretended right of ownership of the ego, so as to serve God and souls, *Quasi apis argumentosa*: *like the busy bee*, as the Church sings in honoring St. Cecilia.

CONSTANT PRAYER

III. Nevertheless, these qualities are not the matter of a few weeks, nor can they be improvised. They must be asked of the Lord with great perseverance and with great confidence. Therefore, to the preceding counsels We will add the following: Pray always.

Listen to the graceful expression of à Kempis: *Serenata conscientia puram offerre orationem*: "to offer pure prayer from the depths of a conscience at peace." Prayer is born, you understand, in a peaceful conscience; that is to say, which is not puffed up

by success, and which is not cast down by physical
or moral trials; one which regulates the time of
prayer by the precise indications of obedience; one
which finds expression in a sincere love for all, in
the purest charity, having as its model the canticle
of St. Paul in the first Epistle to the Corinthians:
Charity is patient, is kind; charity does not envy, is
not pretentious, is not puffed up, is not ambitious,
is not self-seeking, is not provoked; thinks no evil,
does not rejoice over wickedness, but rejoices with
the truth; bears with all things, believes all things,
hopes all things, endures all things (1 Cor. 13:4-7).

It is from this serene and peaceful conscience
that pure prayer springs; it consists in listening to
God, in speaking to God, in the silent grounding of
the self in God, in asking what is pleasing to Him.
A prayer more of adoration and thanksgiving than
of petition. The Lord knows what we need! How
beautiful are the words of the Curè d'Ars, St John
Mary Vianney, on the prayer of the virginal soul!
"God contemplates with love the pure soul," he
says. "He grants her every desire. How could he resist a soul who lives only for Him and in Him? She
seeks Him, and God shows Himself to her; she calls
Him, and God comes; she is but one with Him . . .
She is with God as a child is with its mother."

Therefore, We wish to invite you with paternal insistence, to reflect on this subject of prayer,
because you cannot teach others to pray (and very
often this is your mission, to second parents and
priests) if you yourselves have not first learned to
pray as you should.

On this point, too, be vigilant and have a great delicacy of conscience, not scattering your energies in little devotions when you should be learning not only to recite perfectly, but to practice perfectly, the Our Father!

A HEAVENLY LIFE

Finally, a heavenly life. The *Imitation of Christ* goes straight to the essence of your vocation: "to be worthy to associate with the choirs of angels, by detaching oneself within and without from all that is of this earth."

And so we have returned to our starting point: the virginal life is a heavenly life. In this you religious who practice the active life find yourselves in perfect agreement with your cloistered and contemplative sisters: *"oportet semper orare"* according to the teaching of Jesus (Luke 18:1). The cloistered sisters have their place near the tabernacle; and you have, too: it is from the tabernacle that you must direct your steps towards apostolic action.

This constant prayer makes your life "worthy of the heavenly choirs": it is before all else the touchstone of your perfection, which looks first to the interior and is shown exteriorly in grace and simplicity.

St. Paul, dictating to his disciple Timothy prudent counsel on the choice of deaconesses, says in explicit terms: *Mulieres similiter pudicas, non detrahentes, sobrias, fideles in omnibus*: likewise the women, modest, well-spoken, sober and faithful in all things (1 Tim. 3:11).

This is your interior habit; exteriorly it is shown in the reserve of your bearing, in measured words, in habitual recollection, in the fidelity with which you accomplish your daily duties.

THE CROSS

Beloved daughters, as We close Our paternal interview with you in this admirable church, We take pleasure in drawing your attention to this cross which stands out resplendent against the fresco of the arch, the work of the inspired artist, the holy Brother Pozzo of the Society of Jesus. With profound intuition, as he depicts the glory of St. Ignatius he wishes to celebrate at the same time the triumph of the Cross, which brought into being and explains the enterprises of the Saint.

This cross shines out in all its majesty, and, with incomparable eloquence, it recalls to all of us that it is not enough to bear it on our breast or to have it before our eyes: we must above all have it graven in our minds and hearts.

May the cross be the seal of your virginity, the source of your strength, the inspiration of your prayer, and the secret of your peace in that foretaste of the joys of heaven, which your life here below prefigures and resembles. Your love of the Cross will make the offering of yourselves to the Lord and the sacrifice of all that is dearest to you as an agreeable perfume in the Holy Church of God.

Address to Nuns of Rome, January 29, 1960

THE VALUE OF CHASTITY

Pope Paul VI

With singular care, Religious should preserve chastity as a treasured gem. Everyone knows that in the present condition of human society the practice of perfect chastity is made difficult, not only because of the prevalence of depraved morality but also on account of false teachings which glamorize excessively the merely natural condition of man, thereby pouring poison into his soul. An awareness of these facts should impel Religious to stir up their faith more energetically—that same faith by which we believe the declarations of Christ when He proclaims the supernatural value of chastity that is sought for the sake of the Kingdom of Heaven. It is this same faith which assures us beyond doubt that, with the help of divine grace, we can preserve unsullied, the flower of chastity.

To obtain this blessed objective, it is, of course, necessary to practice Christian mortification with more courageous zeal, and also to guard the senses with more diligent care. Therefore, the life of the Religious should find no place for books, periodicals or shows which are unbecoming or indecent, not even under the pretext of a desire to learn things useful to know or to broaden one's education, except possibly the case, duly ascertained by the Religious Superior, where there is proven necessity for the study of such things. In a world pervaded by so many sordid forms of vice, no one can adequately reckon the powerful effectiveness of the sacred ministry of one whose life is radiant with the light of a chastity consecrated to God and from which he draws his strength.

Address to All Religious, May 23, 1964

THE SPHERE OF CHASTITY

Bernard Häring, C.SS.R.

In its essence, virginal chastity is a way to reach greater freedom and paschal joy. If we truly live the vow which deprives us of marriage for the sake of the kingdom of heaven, we shall never become sour old maids. It is an error to think that genuine chastity makes one empty, bitter and sour. Should this happen, then the meaning of chastity has been missed.

But the vow of chastity in celibacy demands sacrifice, namely the rejection of everything which might endanger one's freedom to belong to the Lord. If one wishes to have a certain sister all for herself and is not open to others, then one is also closed to God. Friendships, too intimate, which lead to selfishness, must be sacrificed. This demands the spurning of all liberties in contact with others. We must not be prudes, surely not, but we must renounce all familiarities which might become a scandal to the weak, and deny ourselves everything which brings too much distraction. I do not believe that virginal persons ought to sit long before the TV screen. We may use means for education, for a certain understanding of the world, but we must do so with interior detachment.

But this is merely the battle on the outer range. Deep down, there must be concern to be chosen by

Christ, to exist for Him only. For this reason there must be rejection of everything which may lessen the true freedom of being for Christ alone. In our times, this freedom is hampered more often in communities of men than of women because of a desire for the sensational. News cannot be missed; a stack of big headlines and radio-news seems to be needed. It would be well to resolve: "On Fridays I will not read the news unless professional work requires it; I will not listen to the radio nor watch TV." This will cut excessive desire and preserve interior freedom. This is practice of genuine ascesis.

"Asceticism in Religious Life," *Sister Formation Bulletin* (Spring, 1966).

AN UNDIVIDED LOVE

Bernard Häring, C.SS.R.

In the last thirty years, understanding of the spirituality of the married state has been deepened. Within the Church we have seen the flowering of a married "èlite" who have realized and realize better every day that matrimony can and must be a path to sanctity. Along with this deepened understanding of matrimony, however, must come a correspondingly greater appreciation of "celibacy for the sake of the kingdom of God."

The Church teaches that celibacy, lived in full as witness to the kingdom of God already near, is "greater and more blessed than matrimony." According to the teaching of the Church, this does not signal a lessening of esteem for marriage, but rather a heightening of the grandiose prospective of virginity.

All Christians are called upon to know why we speak of the *excellence* of celibacy.

Let us direct our thoughts to at least one of the many marvelous apects of this mystery of "celibacy for the love of Christ and the service of souls." I want to express the hope that the liturgy, renewed by an in-depth Eucharistic piety, may nourish more numerous vocations to virginity. For there is a close relationship between the mystery of Faith that we celebrate in the Eucharist and the mystery of celibacy.

On the lips of the virgin-martyr Agnes, the Church places these words: "When I love Him, I am chaste; when I touch Him I am pure; when I receive Him, I am a virgin." The greater the love for the Lord in the Eucharist, the greater will be the holiness of the faithful, and more generous certainly will be the response to the vocation to live celibate for love of God's kingdom, on the part of those who have been called by His grace.

In the Eucharist the kingdom of God is present and visible, that is, the love of Christ conquering our hearts through the gift of Himself and the joy of intimate friendship with Him. This is the biblical meaning of the kingdom of God, or at least one aspect of its total meaning: God leads us by means of His infinite love, incarnate and always near us. In the Eucharist, we celebrate the kingdom of Christ, who let Himself be totally led by His Father's love and His own love for the Father. In this love He consecrated Himself for the redemption of mankind. And in His submission to the loving will of His Father He evidenced His trust that the Father would glorify Him.

In the Eucharist, Christ brings us to this same trusting, joyful submission to the loving will of God and His plan of love. When Christ in the Eucharist gives Himself to us in view of His passion and glorification, His grace enables us to acquire the same trust. We know that our human maturity and eternal happiness are guaranteed only if we give ourselves in this way to Him, in the service of our neighbor.

Celibacy presupposes a love of Christ that is full of joy.

In the Eucharist we celebrate the love of Christ that gathers together the many members of His mystical body. It is His *undivided* love for the Father which makes Him the Redeemer, which leads Him, in other words, to gather together the whole human family in brotherhood.

The Protestant author Bovet, writing on celibacy, uses the most respectful terms in its regard, pointing out that if this celibacy is—as it must be—a free renunciation of marriage, it nevertheless presupposes the realization of a *real kind of religious family,* for celibacy can only be lived by one whose heart is warm with love for his neighbor and for "all neighbors."

The real presence of Christ in the Sacrament is a sign of the eternal alliance.

It is precisely the Eucharistic celebration which teaches us the sense of the family of God. Thus celibacy joins a soul intimately to Christ, expresses this union in the form of an excellent witness, and at the same time provides new possibilities for realizing the solidarity of the People of God.

Love for Christ does not lessen our capacity to love our neighbor; indeed, it purifies and continually fortifies our fraternal love. Likewise, selfless, respectful love for our brothers prepares us for the fullest Eucharistic experience.

The man who knows Christ as his best friend and knows how to live in His presence, is safe from every kind of frustration in celibacy.

The mystery of the Eucharist sets us in front of the sacrifice of Christ on the cross. The glory in which the human nature of the Risen Christ shines forth was given Him by the Father also in view of His sacrifice.

From this mystery both the married and the virgin must derive the basic rule that the fullness of joy cannot be achieved without the spirit of sacrifice. A happy marriage presupposes a struggle against selfishness. Love is capable of sacrificing other lesser values. Celibacy presupposes renunciation of marriage, in full freedom, for love of the kingdom of God. For the sake of the Lord who sacrificed Himself for us, one can give up even something as great as matrimony. Made for the love of Christ, this renunciation is transformed into paschal joy.

JESUS CHRIST, MASTER AND
TEACHER OF CHASTITY

Very Rev. James Alberione, S.S.P., S.T.D.

One day, the apostles showed their amazement at the very grave obligations and burdens of the married state as the Savior had explained them. They said to Him: "If the case of a man with his wife is so, it is not expedient to marry." And Jesus said, "Not all can accept this teaching; but those to whom it has been given. For there are eunuchs who were born so from their mother's womb; and there are eunuchs who were made so by men; and there are eunuchs who have made themselves so for the sake of the kingdom of heaven." And He concluded: "Let him accept it who can." (Matt. 19: 10-12)

Virginity is a great virtue. It is chosen in view of heaven and in order to be able to attend more freely to the things of heaven.

"Blessed are the pure of heart, for they shall see God" (Matt. 5:8). "I say to you that anyone who so much as looks with lust at a woman has already committed adultery with her in his heart" (Matt. 5:28).

In choosing to become incarnate, the Son of God selected a virgin for His mother, working a unique miracle: virginity at its sublimest was joined to divine motherhood. And Christ's foster-father, St. Joseph, was a virgin, too, and the guardian of the Virgin.

Thus we can say that three all-pure souls are involved in the Redemption: Jesus, Mary and Joseph, each in his own condition.

Redemption will also be applied to men by pure souls consecrated to God—apostles or virgins or souls who are continent after marriage.

Mary is the Virgin of virgins. The Church has defined the virginity of Mary. In the Gospel we read: "The angel Gabriel was sent from God . . . to a virgin . . . and the virgin's name was Mary." At the invitation to divine motherhood, Mary asked, "How shall this happen since I do not know man?" And the angel answered and said to her, "The Holy Spirit shall come upon thee and the power of the Most High shall overshadow thee" (Matt. 1:26-27; 34-35).

St. Joseph had his fears allayed by an angel: "Do not be afraid, Joseph, Son of David, to take to thee Mary thy wife for that which is begotten in her is of the Holy Spirit" (Matt. 1:20).

St. Paul teaches: "He who is unmarried is concerned about the things of the Lord, how he may please God." And: "I would have you free from care. . . . Whereas he who is married is concerned about the things of the world" (1 Cor. 7:32-33). "I would that you all were as I am myself; but each one has his own gift from God" (1 Cor. 7:7). And so it was that we find a band of saints surrounding Paul and following him: St. Luke, St. Timothy, St. Titus, St. Thecla, and others.

*

From the teachings of the Popes, Pius XII in particular, we derive the following points:

1) It is erroneous to hold that perfect chastity is harmful to the body or that it is impossible. History proves that it *is* possible. Man's will and God's grace can dominate the sexual instinct and concupiscence. "In order to acquire this perfect mastery of the spirit over the senses, it is not enough to refrain from acts directly contrary to chastity, but it is necessary also generously to renounce anything that may offend this virtue nearly or remotely" (*Holy Virginity*).

2) We condemn "the opinion of those who contend that marriage is the only means of assuring the natural development and perfection of the human personality." Marriage is a sacrament and religious profession is not. But the grace of the sacrament of Matrimony is to accomplish holily the duties of the married state. It was not instituted as a means of perfection as was perfect chastity vowed in religion. It would be remembered, too, that by observing celibacy the religious, and especially the priest, is far from renouncing fatherhood; the fact is that he becomes the father of many spiritual children, thus perfecting and extending his fatherhood: "Through the Gospel did I beget you" (1 Cor. 4:15).

3) Those who are consecrated to God do not suffer from a *solitude of the heart;* on the contrary, theirs is a love immensely superior, comforted by greater contacts with God, and by a pledge of that joy described by St. John when he speaks of the

men who abstained from women: "They are virgins. These follow the Lamb wherever he goes" (Apoc. 14:4).

4) Another very false and ruinous idea is the conviction that in our day the Church has greater need of good fathers and mothers living exemplary lives in the world than of religious consecrated to God. We must therefore reprove those who are led by this erroneous idea to turn young people away from the religious and priestly life.

5) "It is altogether false to assert that those who are vowed to God are practically outside the community of men" (Holy Virginity). The truth is that they are precisely the ones who promote the good of society by prayer, sacrifice and every kind of apostolate generously undertaken.

6) If one is to embrace the life of perfection, he must do so by free choice, and by a call from God, and he must feel morally certain that if he takes the necessary means (that is, "watch and pray"), he will persevere. St. Paul says: "But if they do not contain themselves, let them marry. For it is better to marry than to be burnt" (1 Cor. 7:9). Confessors, spiritual directors and superiors have very grave responsibilities when it comes to counselling, both in exhorting someone to pursue this path and in advising or directing them to give it up.

The question may be asked: For this moral guarantee that the candidate will persevere, how long a time should we require that he have spent without failings in the matter of chastity? Spiritual writers disagree on this point. Some say three years, others a year or even less. Moreover, there is a great difference between one person and another. One young man or woman, full of life and energy, might be strongly tempted, but he or she struggles hard, prays, avoids occasions, and gives every ounce of energy to duty. Another, instead, who is sluggish, a bit negligent in almost every quarter, easy-going—what will become of him when he is twenty-five, thirty-five or forty, when he finds himself in a delicate situation? He will give up prayer, he will be unaccustomed to struggle, he will not exhaust his strength and energy in love of God and in the apostolate. And then? . . .

Another factor in the decision is the kind of life the candidate will be expected to lead in the years to come. Will he work with children? Will he spend long hours studying and writing? Will much of his time be spent in the confessional? in dangerous circumstances? or in the community?

Let the one who must make the decision give it much thought and much prayer; let him also seek advice and do some penance. In a few cases, the advice of a truly conscientious doctor might also be needed.

7) In his Encyclical on Holy Virginity, Pius XII wrote: If there are any who do not feel they have the gift of chastity even though they have vowed it, let them not declare they cannot fulfill their obligations in this matter. For God does not command the impossible, but in commanding serves notice that one do what he can, and pray for what he can-

not, and He helps us to accomplish it. This must be the answer to certain doctors, at times even Catholics, who advise those whose will has been weakened by upset nerves to get married for the betterment of their mental balance: "God is faithful and will not permit you to be tempted beyond your strength, but with the temptation will also give you a way out that you may be able to bear it" (1 Cor. 10:13). And He will give you the victor's reward.

*

MEANS OF PROTECTING CHASTITY

Watchfulness and prayer are the means our Divine Master gave us: "Watch and pray that you enter not into temptation" (Matt. 26:41).

Watchfulness regarding ourselves and regarding occasions of danger is absolutely necessary throughout life. We bear our flesh about with us at all times and St. Paul points out a fact of our daily experience: "For the flesh lusts against the spirit, and the spirit against the flesh" (Gal. 5:17). And yet flesh and spirit must journey together in life.

Crucify the flesh: "And they who belong to Christ have crucified their flesh with its passions and desires" (Gal. 5:24).

We cannot feel sure of ourselves just because we are religious or priests, superiors or subjects, young or old. Hence St. Paul, though already on in years, says of himself: "I chastise my body and bring it into subjection, lest perhaps after preaching to others I myself should be rejected" (1 Cor. 9:27).

Our Divine Master warns: "I say to you that anyone who so much as looks with lust at a woman has already committed adultery with her in his heart. So if thy right eye is an occasion of sin to thee, pluck it out and cast it from thee; for it is better for thee that one of thy members should perish than that thy whole body should be thrown into hell" (Matt. 5:28-29). How dangerous it is to start to let down the guard, even in a small way.

All the Saints and Doctors of the Church declare that occasions must be avoided. Says St. Jerome: "I flee, lest I be overcome."

It is understood that there are dangers everywhere, even in religious houses, but the world offers more, with less help to resist them.

Some erroneous currents of thought today have it that all Christians, and the clergy in particular, should not be 'separated from the world' as in the past, but should 'take the risk' and put their chastity to the test in order to show whether or not they have the strength to resist and come off unharmed. Therefore, according to this mode of thought, young clerics and even young aspirants to religious life must be allowed to read everything, see everything, hear everything—even in violation of church and natural law—so as to render themselves immune to all temptations. The argument runs like this: this is the way the world goes today and if you want to do some good to the world, you have to be in it. What a grievous mistake this is! The Holy Spirit warns: "He who loves danger shall perish in it." And St. Augustine writes: "Do not say that you have a chaste mind if your eyes are unchaste." To His heavenly

Father, Christ said: "I have sent them into the world (His disciples)," but previously He had said: "They are not of the world, even as I am not of the world." And He adds: "I do not pray that thou take them out of the world, but that thou keep them from evil" (John 17:15-17).

The Church has established wise norms which are the result of centuries of experience to see to it that vocations are not ruined while they are still young and inexperienced, that consecrated souls safeguard their own souls and bring salvation to those who must live in the world.

Candidates to religious life or to the priesthood are to be separated from the world's tumult before they are sent back out into the lists of combat. This will take place gradually, under the direction of proper authority as need arises and the candidate is strengthened. Inculcate in their minds the precepts of Christian modesty; set them on fire with the holy ideal of purity. Accustom them to an elevated tenor of thought, to a taste and a desire for the good and beautiful. Take every possible kind of preventive means, especially fervent atmosphere, plenty of instruction and preaching, and frequent reception of the Sacraments of Penance and Holy Communion.

Give them a wise and holy spiritual director. Inculcate tender, trusting devotion to Mary.

The guardian of virginity is love, and the guardian of love is humility.

After all, what is profession if not a profession of love—perfect love giving itself entirely to God? Love is the profession of a religious, his job, his field, his life. . . . The religious heart is to be wholly centered and rooted in Christ. May there be, too, a "felt" love, if it please God to grant it. The Lord is to hold the center in every aspect of life—the apostolate, personal worries, efforts at reparation, at sanctification, and so forth.

＊

With regard to vacations, it will be well for a Congregation to acquire summer houses for this purpose when possible.

Before the vacation, superiors should warn of possible dangers and indicate the means to be taken. Instead of doing harm, vacations should result in physical benefits, and spiritual ones, too, such as more vocations through personal contact.

Let superiors recall what the Apostolic Constitution, "Sedes Sapientiae" has to say on the subject of vacations for religious.

A good time of the year should be chosen for the vacation period, according to the climate in various regions. Vacations should be spent in the most suitable places. Regular studies are to be discontinued during the period, and mental and physical strength is to be renewed. However, there should be no slackening off of efforts for spiritual perfection.

Leisure time remaining after rest and relaxation should be devoted to private study of literature or science, or classes in lighter subjects—in a foreign language, or art, or in some other skill, or perhaps in some apostolic experience.

*

In every type of sin and at all times the rule holds true that to grant all that is lawful leads without doubt to the unlawful. Stealing a trifle is the beginning of a life of thefts and dishonesty. Judas set out on the path to ruin by taking for himself some of the offerings given to Jesus and the apostles. One who makes it a habit to give in to venial faults without struggling against them will end by committing mortal sins.

*

Let us keep in mind these three facts:

1) Gluttony and the thirst for sensual pleasure always go together, as both experience and Sacred Scripture teach us. However, rarely is the third sister missing, laziness.

2) Pride generally goes before a fall into sensuality. For God lets the man whose heart is swelled with pride fall into the mire. Those who exalt themselves will be humbled.

3) It is between the ages of twenty-five and forty that the attacks of the enemy are usually the most violent. Greater prayer and uninterrupted watchfulness are therefore indispensable.

*

There are practical ways of training young people to holy purity. When the sensual appetite begins to make itself felt, suggest a temporary vow of chastity, to last anywhere between eight and ninety days, depending on the young person's state.

Suggest an oft-repeated consecration to Our Lady and also frequent reading of the lives of exemplary young people.

Our young candidates must be kept very well occupied—in a rich, varied liturgical and devotional life; in well-supervised study; in an intense apostolic activity; in healthy, active recreation.

In every way we can, we have to lift young spirits to great heights with noble desires, with great ideals of perfection, with the thought of souls awaiting them, with the many possibilities in the apostolate, with the desire for heaven.

Present the rewards of virginity: a happier life, lived on a higher moral plane; a more effective apostolic influence on souls; serenity in the face of death and God's judgment; a special crown of glory in heaven; a more resplendent body at the resurrection.

It is well to meditate on the parable of the ten virgins, the five foolish and the five wise. Virginity must be attended by theological, cardinal and moral virtues. A haughty virginity, for example, would be worthless.

Let us ponder the parable given us by Christ: "Then will the kingdom of heaven be like ten virgins who took their lamps and went forth to meet the bridegroom and the bride. Five of them were foolish and five wise. But the five foolish, when they took their lamps, took no oil with them, while the wise did take oil in their vessels with the lamps. Then as the bridegroom was long in coming, they all became drowsy and slept. And at midnight a cry arose, 'Behold, the bridegroom is coming, go forth to meet him!' Then all those virgins arose and trimmed their lamps. And the foolish said to the wise, 'Give us some of your oil, for our lamps are going out.' The wise answered, saying, 'Lest there may not be enough for us and for you, go rather to those who sell it, and buy some for yourselves.'

"Now while they were gone to buy it, the bridegroom came; and those who were ready went in with him to the marriage feast, and the door was shut. Finally there came also the other virgins, who said, 'Sir, sir, open the door for us!' But he answered and said, 'Amen I say to you, I do not know you.' Watch therefore, for you know neither the day nor the hour" (Matt. 25:1-13).

CRISIS OVER THE VOWS

Very Rev. James Alberione, S.S.P., S.T.D.

In our day we are witnessing a real crisis regarding the vows, which are suffering from a ruinous lack of esteem. Profession is taken lightly, then borne like a heavy burden. For such religious, violations come easily, in small things and perhaps even in serious matters. At first they feel deep remorse, but then a certain insensibility takes over. They disregard protective measures—prayer and the avoidance of danger. Catastrophe results, bringing on personal ruin, scandal both inside and outside the Institute, and the consequent prolonged suffering of good fellow religious. Graces have been lost, but the unfortunate religious show no sorrow because they are blind. They block off every road that could lead them back to their senses, rushing ahead with bravado, as though they had won some great victory. But deep in their hearts they see themselves as losers and traitors.

And let us pray that such souls do not plunge into eternal ruin.

We cannot be indifferent spectators of such tragedies. Sometimes the downfall can be foreseen; sometimes we might even be partially responsible for it. No one is corrupted all at once. Hedges are cut down, evil is introduced subtly, and thus one approaches the edge of the precipice—through too

intimate friendships, pride, certain kinds of reading, the breaking of rules, too much freedom
allowed to the senses, laxity in piety, dangerous
encounters, or a search after inadvisable entertain-
ments. Step by step, one falls back; then he recov-
ers only to return again, to aggravate the situation
and to form the habit. Finally he welds a chain that
will never more be broken.

Yet even the natural law tells us to keep the
vows we have made. And the vows of religion are a
grave matter, made after years of prayer and reflection, requested in writing, pronounced in a moment
of great solemnity in the presence of witnesses, and
sealed with one's signature. One who leaves might
say, "But I have been dispensed." Yes, but only to
prevent worse ruin befalling both yourself and
others.

Dispensations are valid, of course, and the religious of simple vows returns to the secular state.
But in God's eyes he or she has squandered graces
and has done so willfully. Little by little he put
himself in such a spiritual condition that he continually transgressed his vows, sinning doubly each
time. At last, his life became somewhat of a scandal and injurious to the institute, and in the end,
he either asked to leave or was expelled by the institute, cut off as a diseased member.

When at the Last Supper Jesus told Judas,
"What thou dost, do quickly," (John 13:27), He
was not absolving him of his responsibility, but was
rather showing him that He knew everything.

What the
Poverty of
Religious Entails

Religious should diligently practice and if need be express also in new forms that voluntary poverty which is recognized and highly esteemed especially today as an expression of the following of Christ. By it they share in the poverty of Christ who for our sakes became poor, even though He was rich, so that by His poverty we might become rich (cf. 2 Cor. 8:9; Matt. 8:20).

With regard to religious poverty it is not enough to use goods in a way subject to the superior's will, but members must be poor both in fact and in spirit, their treasures being in heaven (cf. Matt. 6:20).

Religious should consider themselves in their own assignments to be bound by the common law of labor, and while they procure what is required for their sustenance and works, they should banish all undue solicitude and trust themselves to the provident care of their Father in heaven (cf. Matt. 6:25).

Religious congregations by their constitutions can permit their members to renounce inheritances, both those which have been acquired or may be acquired.

Due regard being had for local conditions, religious communities should readily offer a quasi-collective witness to poverty and gladly use their own goods for other needs of the Church and the support of the poor whom all religious should love after the example of Christ (cf. Matt. 19:21; 25:34-46; James 2:15-16; 1 John 3:17). *The several provinces and houses of each community should share their temporal goods with one another, so that those who have more help the others who are in need.*

Religious communities have the right to possess whatever is required for their temporal life and work, unless this is forbidden by their rules and constitutions. Nevertheless, they should avoid every appearance of luxury, excessive wealth and the accumulation of goods.

Decree on the Adaptation and Renewal of Religious Life, n. 13

ON POVERTY

Institutes especially through their general chapters should diligently and in a concrete manner promote the spirit and practice of poverty according to the intention of No. 13 of the Decree *Prefectae Caritatis* while also seeking and urging new ways in keeping with the nature of their institute to make the practice and witness of poverty more effective in modern times.

It is the right of institutes with simple vows to decree in general chapter whether the renunciation of inheritances which have been acquired and will be acquired should be incorporated into the constitutions and, if this is done, whether such renunciation should be obligatory or optional. They should also decide when this is to be done, that is, whether before perpetual profession or some years later.

Ecclesiae Sanctae, on No. 13 of the Decree Perfectae Caritatis

THE VIRTUE OF POVERTY

Pope Paul VI

There are many other questions We would like to pose, with the idea of getting the same kind of frank answer you have already given. For example, what should be the main virtue characterizing your religious life? Anyone who knows that you are Franciscans will reply: poverty, the kind of poverty that is transformed into love, that wants to imitate the poor Christ and love Him, and that looks upon God as the only treasure of a religious soul. What was it that your blessed Camilla Battista of Verano used to say: Oh, how poor a person is when he wants something other than God! How rich a person is when he possesses nothing else but God![1]

But the question implies some subordinate queries. Is poverty practical nowadays? Shouldn't it, too, move along those *planiora itinera* [2] that Giovanni Cardinal Colonna advised Brother Francis to adopt right from the beginning? Shouldn't religious poverty yield to the imperious and insidious demands of modern naturalism and of a generally accepted hedonism? As you know, the Council has some stern reminders on this point,[3] and in issuing

[1] Cf. *Instructions* in *Spiritual Works*, 216.
[2] Smoother paths.
[3] Cf. *Decree on the Adaptation and Renewal of the Religious Life,* no. 13.

them it lends new strength to authentic Franciscan tradition, with its loving and courageous tendency toward a literal observance of the words of the Gospel. In this regard, as well as in certain other instances of *aggiornamento*, it is a question of adapting practical norms to reasonable new demands, but not of relaxing the spirit of the ancient rule, nor of contradicting the letter of it.

Address to Franciscan General Chapter, July 12, 1966

LOVE FOR POVERTY

Pope Paul VI

Although human conditions have changed notably in recent years, and consequently religious life must be accommodated to these changes, yet those things which follow from the very nature of the evangelical counsels still retain all their vigor and can in no wise be diminished.

Do not fail to inculcate a *love for poverty*, concerning which there is much discussion going on in the Church today. Religious must surpass all others by their example of true evangelical poverty. Therefore, they must love that poverty to which they have spontaneously committed themselves. It is not enough for Religious to depend merely on the Superior's decision with regard to their use of material things. Let the Religious, of their own will, be content with the things that are needed for properly fulfilling their way of life, shunning those conveniences and luxuries by which the religious life is devitalized. Moreover, in addition to that poverty which should characterize the life of the individual Religious, we must not fail to take into account that poverty by which *the family or whole body of Religious* should be distinguished. Therefore let the Religious Institutes avoid a too exquisite style and ornamentation in their buildings and in carrying out their functions, as well as anything else

100

that savors of luxury, always bearing in mind the social condition of the people among whom they live. Let them also refrain from excessive concern in gathering funds; rather let them be preoccupied with using the temporal goods which Divine Providence has bestowed upon them to minister to the genuine necessities of needy brethren; whether those in need of assistance be their fellow countrymen or those who live in other parts of the world.

To All Religious, May 23, 1964

MONASTIC WORK

Pope Pius XII

Work is part of contemplative life. The law of ancient monasticism: "Ora et labora"—"Prayer and Work"—has lost nothing of its wisdom and necessity.

To work is in fact, an imperative of nature itself which gave to man the strength of his body and mind, and compels him to provide for his subsistence, incites him to better his conditions of life and to increase the means of knowledge and action.

The Lord led a life of work at Nazareth for thirty years, and His apostolic ministry was burdened with heavy toils.

St. Paul in his incisive manner, wrote to the Thessalonians: "If any man will not work, neither let him eat. For we have heard that some among you are... doing no work" (2 Thess. 3:10-11).

And he himself affirms that he has worked with his hands to earn his bread and not be dependent on the Christians (Acts 20:34; 18:3). The Apostolic Constitution, "Sponsa Christi," underlines several times the duty of nuns to work to earn their bread; it therefore results that whoever adopts the contemplative life, and embraces it without reservation, fully accepts also the law of work.

Address to Cloistered Religious, July, 1958

THE VALUE OF WORK IN CONTEMPLATIVE LIFE

Pope Pius XII

The application of the rules concerning work is very close to Our heart because it pertains to the interests of contemplative convents and to all women's contemplative Orders, as well as to the entire Church, which in many places looks to the help of all the forces at its command.

"It is unfortunately true that there are convent communities which are nearly dying of hunger, neglect and privation; and others which, because of material difficulty, lead a very painful life. There are other communities which, without living in need, often decline, because they are separated and isolated from all the others.

"Moreover, laws of the cloister, often too strict, frequently provoke great difficulties" (A.A.S. 1 c. p. 10, 11).

The labor of the nuns themselves is the most normal and immediate means of relieving this suffering.

Therefore, We invite them to dedicate themselves and, above all, without thinking of depending upon the goodness and help of others.

This appeal is made also to those who are not in need and therefore are not obliged to earn their daily bread with the work of their hands.

In this way you could also procure the necessary resources to satisfy the precepts of Christian charity toward the poor.

We invite you to develop your manual aptitudes and to perfect them; as also to adapt yourselves to the conditions of today, as spoken of in article 8, para. 3, n. 2 of the Constitution, "Sponsa Christi" (Ibid. p. 19).

This same article, furthermore, reconfirmed the norms regarding work, stating that "monastic labor, to which the nuns of the contemplative life must dedicate themselves, must be as much as possible in keeping with the rule, with the constitution and with the traditions of each Order" (Ibid. art. 8, para. 1).

Certain constitutions foresee certain determined labors, mostly of an apostolic character; others instead do not detail anything on this matter.

These labors "should be so organized that, added to other sources of income, they will insure the nuns a valid and convenient sustenance" (Ibid. para. 2).

The Ordinaries of places and Superiors are bound to see that "the nuns will never lack the indispensable, appropriate and remunerative work" (Ibid. para. 3, n. 14).

Lastly, the article underlined the obligation of conscience—that the nuns have not only to earn their bread by the sweat of their brow but, besides, to perfect themselves more each day through their various labors as circumstances require. (Ibid. p. 3, n. 2).

Do not permit Our appeal to labor to be made in vain, but employ all the means at your disposal and profit by every possibility for your greater formation; first of all for your own profit or at least, if you have no immediate need, to give assistance to the sufferings of others.

Besides, a serious occupation, adapted to your ability, is an efficacious means of keeping interior balance, or to reestablish it if it has suffered any damage.

In this way you will avoid the harmful effects which total reclusion and monotony connected with the daily life of the cloister might have on some temperaments.

Address to Cloistered Religious, July, 1958

POVERTY, DEPENDENCE AND DESTITUTION

Sister Teresa Margaret, O.C.D.

"In the last decade the problem of poverty—one of the oldest and deepest that confronts the Christian conscience—has taken on a new shape, new dimensions, new urgency," said Mr. James J. Norris, addressing the Fathers of the Vatican Council on Novmber 5, 1964. "The gap between the rich and the poor is rapidly widening—side by side the rich grow richer and the poor grow poorer, in a single world community." He went on to point out that the wealthy countries represent 16 per cent of the world's population, owning 70 per cent of the world's riches, while three-quarters of the human race exist in a condition of poverty bordering on or even below subsistence level.[1]

A month earlier, Father Arthur McCormack, M.H.M., an English economist, had stated that one person in seven literally has not enough to eat—a proportion which, in terms of individuals, comes to some 400 million hungry mouths. These people are not merely poor, they are destitute: illiterates, starvelings, homeless peoples of Asia and Latin America, women and children reduced to conditions of slave labor. We can no longer feel complacent

[1] Text by courtesy of the NCWC News Service.

about such things, or dismiss the needy as feckless or irresponsible. Yet frequently one hears glib talk of "poverty" from people with very little understanding of what that word connotes. In the midst of such a situation, Father Gauthier says that the poor and the working man do not want a Church who calls herself the Bride of Christ in theory but in practice plays the grand lady, surrounded by courtiers, dressed in purple and fine linen, living like the rich man in the parable of Dives and Lazarus.[2]

"How difficult it is for us poor bishops of the Church of Christ in the twentieth century to put across the message which at its beginning was steeped in the poverty of the incarnation, the manger, the cross," said Bishop Iriarte of Reconquisita, Argentina. "... We have for our part to deliver this message from the height of our marble altars and episcopal 'palaces' ...; our people come to call us 'Your Eminence,' and genuflecting to kiss the stone in our ring! It is not easy to struggle free of all this weight of history and tradition."[3]

No one is more aware than religious themselves of the many anomalies of their situation, and today a novice often feels it is hypocritical, in view of the conditions of the world all around us, for religious to profess poverty when seemingly many of them have little idea of what the word implies for those who are poor not by choice but through hard necessity.

[2] *Christ, the Church and the Poor,* by Paul Gauthier (London: Geoffrey Chapman, 1965).

[3] Quoted by Yves Congar, O.P., in *Power and in Poverty in the Church,* (London: Geoffrey Chapman, 1965) p. 156.

They are asked to vow absolute poverty, while recognizing all too clearly the inability to carry on their work under the conditions which framed and formed the traditional concepts of that vow. Large up-to-date schools, hospitals, novitiates, electrically fitted kitchens and laundries, do not offer to the world a picture of evangelical poverty (even though the world is usually the first to recognize the necessity for these things), nor does such a milieu fit comfortably with a long and honored tradition of almsgiving. The fact might as well be put bluntly: few religious outside the mission fields actually live lives of material poverty, and if they are to carry out their apostolate they cannot do so. Is their vow, then, simply a legal fiction? We are told sometimes that it merely means that the individual religious must renounce all ownership and administration. But surely this is not enough, since a good many of us never had any considerable property or possessions to part with in the first place, and not a few have possibly acquired a higher standard of living than they knew in the world.

The perennial problem of goods permitted for the use of the religious often means nothing more or less for that individual than real wealth, without the responsibilities that would accompany legal ownership. Are we then giving away all things merely to have the best of both worlds?

Religious must live in real poverty both communal and personal. That fact is obvious, and no individual religious should enjoy a higher standard of living than a working man on the basic wage. Still, the fact seems inescapable that a community must

own property if it is to function at all. Poverty is not
destitution, nor does the Church desire her religious
to swell the hundreds of millions who are living below subsistence level, for they would soon become
a burden upon the diocese in which they lived.
Vocations such as that of Saint Benedict Joseph
Labre, for example, are singular in every sense of
the word. Clearly communities could not follow his
exceptional mode of existence. A very small and
spiritually united group of men or women might
band together without possessions of any kind, and
no knowledge where their next meal or night's lodging was to come from; but even for Saint Francis
this absolute interpretation was possible only with a
small, intimate circle.

Again, no laboring man, or even one in a higher
income bracket, has anything like the liabilities and
expenditures of a religious house. Even in the smallest cloistered communities a chaplain (or at least
some priest to visit the convent daily for Mass)
must be maintained, as well as a chapel with its endless expenses for vestments, oil, candles, hosts and
wine, heating and lighting, furnishing, repairs.
All these heavy costs must be met before we have
even begun to think of domestic upkeep, cooking,
personal needs, food and clothing, equipment for
work and administration.

Today religious communities are and must be
wage-earners; that is to say, we should support ourselves by the labor of our hands, and our earned income must suffice to cover all expenses incurred in
doing so. As we may not go out to work in factories,
much equipment is needed for such work as print-

ing, making altar breads, photography, silk-weaving, and it is mostly delicate and expensive. Yet the commercial world is competitive, and we must "deliver the goods" in competition with the open market. It is not only impracticable and time-wasting, but simply not feasible to work efficiently with shoddy tools or second-hand materials. But on the other hand, can a community which runs a farm and owns (in common) a couple of hundred acres of land and stock, buildings, and machinery insured for several hundred thousand dollars, seriously describe themselves as "poor," however low their earned income may be? [4]

Certainly they are not poor in the sense in which a man living in a pre-fab and drawing twenty or thirty dollars a week is poor. Yet I think there is a growing awareness among religious that in professing evangelical poverty they commit themselves less to actual material need than to the absolute giving in common life, which in the sense of deprivation can be a far more dedicated form of poverty. Real poverty of spirit lies in the total sharing of all things, gifts of heart and mind no less than assets realizable in hard cash. The legal, juridical aspects of the vow can only pertain to material goods, but the absolute gift of self to the community renounces individual talents, intellectual gifts, abilities, energies; one writes a blank check on the future and all goes into the general pool to be used for the good of the community and the apostolate.

[4] The author writes from a cloistered, contemplative community in England, but her remarks are all the more impressive on that account. — *Compilers' note.*

"Poverty according to Saint Thomas Aquinas," which seems to have been an article by an unidentified author, makes the following three points:

1. Poverty is not good in itself, because it is a negation. We measure the value of this religious vow according as it frees a man from hindrances to loving God.

2. Poverty of fact is a counsel of perfection, while poverty of will is the object of a commandment. The *vow* of poverty, a thing counselled, is taken in order to attain more expeditiously the *spirit* of poverty.

3. Actual poverty pertains to evangelical perfection—detachment of the will is *not* enough for *evangelical perfection.* It therefore belongs to the perfection of the Christian life to lack earthly possessions.

"The *vow* of poverty ... is taken in order to attain more expeditiously the *spirit* of poverty." Here, I think, is the nexus of the whole problem, and it is one which needs re-examination in the light of present conditions. Religious poverty is a simple enough concept if we understand by it that we renounce voluntarily the right to own anything, and to retain for our personal use only what is permitted by superiors. But concepts have a way of falling apart in daily life. Personal needs vary and multiply as inexorably as compound interest, and after a time, use or abuse widen our field of reference considerably. The cloistered religious has fewer personal needs than one whose work and apostolate keep her out of the convent a great deal, or involve considerable travelling. In the latter case, the problem soon arises: Shall I use the cheapest mode of transportation with consequent waste of time, or travel quickly (and also comfortably, if not luxuriously) by air? Nor is it always such a simple either/or problem as it appears here.

Religious poverty is not merely a juridical question, a matter of keeping the rules, because in actual situations the use of material things is endless in its possibilities, and on the other hand, there is nothing so trifling that we do not become attached to it and cling to it with tenacity. It might even be, as in the case of one of St. Thérèse's novices, a pin; perhaps a bent pin, but because it does its job better than any other, we will heatedly defend our possession should another try to replace it. Maybe we even convince ourselves and others of the perfection of our "spirit of poverty" in this preference for an inferior article.

Then, from the juridical point of view, there is the protection of seeking permission for whatever is needed for one's own use. But this is frustrated or reduced to the dimensions of the individual's conscience, because a superior will not, except in extraordinary circumstances, refuse the permission, since she presumes that the Sister really needs this article she has requested.

Another thing religious poverty must not be confused with is any form of economy. The vow was not imposed for the purpose of keeping down living costs, and any reduction in ordinary expenses demanded by a particular financial crisis should be explained as such by the superior. The community must be told it will be necessary for a short or long period to practice certain austerities, not because of holy poverty, but simply because the books show a debit balance and a common frugality is essential.

Some time last year Bishop Fulton Sheen was reported as saying that even those who took the vow of poverty in the United States lived in luxury compared to millions throughout the world (and this could certainly be extended to many other countries, even though living standards are generally higher in the U.S. than elsewhere). "These people," said the Bishop, "are under the vow of destitution, whereas the vow of poverty in this country has been reduced to a vow of dependence."

But is that not, perhaps, the very solution to the twentieth century dilemma? Luxury, of course, must never be permitted, either actual or theoretical. But if a convent in North America should voluntarily assume the conditions and standards of living obtaining in some of the more deprived areas of Latin America, that would not be evangelical poverty but supererogation; should they be teaching Sisters, it would effect an immediate and wholesale emptying of their classrooms, and before long, also, a condemnation from the local sanitary inspectors. Emotional overtones can cloud this issue or swamp reason. Those millions of destitute throughout the world are deserving of all our sympathy and wholehearted assistance—indeed, such is our duty—but is it realistic to say they have a *vow* of destitution? Was it not simply a condition forced upon them by circumstances over which they have no control, and from which they would remove them-

selves speedily were that possible? The religious
vow is a voluntary and free undertaking to live, for
the love of God, in a state of evangelical poverty.

Again, what is dependence but absolute poverty? To be a little child is to be wholly dependent,
and unless we are this, our Lord has told us we
shall not enter heaven. Without total dependence
on the Father, fundamental detachment of spirit,
simplicity of heart and life, we are not so much as
Christians, let alone dedicated religious. There are
many communities who do, through economic necessity, literally live their vow of poverty. But it is
clear that if we are to exist decently and support
ourselves, we must own goods and property to a
degree that is no longer consonant with the traditional concepts of evangelical poverty laid down
for the original mendicants.

Would it not be more honest to change the
terms of the vow to meet existing conditions than
make of it a Procrustean bed and try to squeeze
the changed milieu into an outmoded concept?
Why, instead of vowing actual poverty, do we not
understand this as poverty of spirit and total giving of self and individual endowments to the community? This, if practiced absolutely, can be a
form of poverty both penitential and practical,
without offering obstacles to efficiency in work or
the apostolate.

This would immediately free benefactors from
their obligation of almsgiving to religious. The latter
would have the freedom to acquire whatever property and equipment is necessary to support themselves, maintain house, chapel, and chaplain, and

earn their living. But they must become totally self-supporting for this to be feasible, and the former alms supplied to them should not become a subsidy, but go *in toto* to the needy poor of the world. Those generous friends who so regularly send us checks from their own wage-packets could instead give it, through one of the recognized Church or state organizations, for relief in the underdeveloped countries. The traditional concept of almsgiving as a source of monastic income is an anachronism today, and it is nothing less than an extension of the miracle of the loaves and fishes that, from the small offerings of the wage-earning laity, such a large annual amount does go to the support of religious houses and foundations. The religious, in their turn, are so inured to the idea of alms that often they think it suffices to await such voluntary assistance, and so do not set about earning their living with the same wholehearted sense of purpose as a man providing for his family. Something will come along . . . God will provide. . . . When the work is for Him, He will see us through. Look at Saint Teresa and her two ducats, or Saint Frances Cabrini, and many another saint who trusted in God and forged ahead, piling up debts and liabilities, confident in the Providence which never failed them. Is It less efficient today? Will It fail us?

Most decidedly it will not, unless we fail in our part. But the option seems inescapable. Either we own nothing, individually or communally, not even a permanent roof (thus becoming in this age vagrants and undesirables, a drain on the charitable and religious resources of the diocese), or we are permitted to own, in common, the property and equipment to work efficiently and support ourselves by the labor of our hands, vowed to the common life, the common round, the common task, for the glory of God and the salvation of men.

It must be repeated that no religious should enjoy a higher standard of living than that of the family of the average laboring man in her district, whoever that may be—factory worker, mechanic, agricultural laborer, truck driver. I am not proposing a large capitalistic enterprize where we go into big business and acquire the status of manufacturers, or enormous assets and profits. Our lives should be, and should *be seen to be,* in line with that of the lowest income group or standard prevailing in the neighborhood. This will, of course, vary not only from country to country, but from state to state. There is no obligation for the Sisters in a Texas convent to model their lives on the conditions of the unfortunate dwellers and missionaries in a Brazilian *favela* or even of immigrant laborers in California; but there is a very real need for them not to adopt by imperceptible degrees the standards of a Texas millionaire. The conditions of a northern industrial city suburb will differ radically from those in the rural midwest or the deep south, but in all these areas, the religious should be living, and known to be living, on the level of the ordinary working man of that area. Thus and thus only will we offer a witness of our consecration to God and the world. More, it seems to me that a hard-working, self-supporting community who are obviously earning their bread by their labor, would gain enormously in respect for themselves and the habit they wear, as well as being an edifying spectacle and a more telling witness, than a group of ragged and half-starved waifs, with no fixed abode, who sit and wait patiently but helplessly for God to provide, or expect gratuitous assistance from the bounty and generosity of neighbors who have worked hard to provide for their own families and dependants.

These points are not offered with any idea of providing a simple or final solution to an involved problem, but in the hope that they might provide a launching pad for fruitful discussion. If other Sisters could also put forward ideas on this matter, perhaps the ensuing dialogue would result in constructive and practical ideas. This is a period of great flux and reorientation in the Church, and a time when such problems could well be taken out and studied in the light of existing needs, circumstances, and experience.

— from *Sisters Today* (February, 1966), 193-200.

THE WITNESS OF COLLECTIVE POVERTY

It may happen that, as individual religious Institutes develop, they need more spacious quarters. It is perfectly permissible to take care of this need, but moderation and balance must be employed. May the poverty clearly evidenced in your habitual dress not be miserably obscured by sumptuous dwellings and elaborate conveniences or luxuries! May there never be a contrast between the manner of living and the manner of speaking!

Pius XII, Address to Capuchin Friars Minor, November 25, 1948

❊

The witness of religious poverty today has been reduced almost to nothing. This calls for an examination of conscience. The lack of collective poverty can be for many pagans a cause for scandal. How can religious be considered poor when they show a preference for working in areas which are economically rich rather than in those which are poor?"

Most Rev. Andrew Sol, Coadjutor of Ambonia, Indonesia

❊

Love poverty! A tendency is notable at times to indulge in luxury that is incompatible with religious poverty. Certain rugs, certain overdone lighting fixtures, certain kinds of furniture, and too much gift-giving—such things are not in keeping with the religious spirit! We have to be more careful about poverty. Take a look at the way the convents are furnished, at the Superiors' rooms, to be sure that everything conforms to religious poverty.

The excuse that an item was donated is not a valid one. Simply because ten couches were donated, would we try to use them all? We are under no obligation to use everything given us! They could be given to poorer houses or some other good use made of them, but never should one take advantage of a donation to the detriment of religious observance. What is needed is to be kept, not what is extra.

Love poverty! All that we give up will return to us, transformed, at the threshhold of eternity. "Blessed are the poor in spirit, for theirs is the kingdom of heaven." The Lord will shower His spiritual treasures on us if we are careful to stay within the proper limits of poverty—religious poverty, not miserliness.

Very Rev. James Alberione, S.S.P., S.T.D.

JESUS CHRIST, MASTER AND TEACHER
OF POVERTY

Very Rev. James Alberione, S.S.P., S.T.D.

Poverty is the greatest wealth. Every small renunciation in food, dress, or dwelling signals a great conquest for heaven.

Religious poverty has five aspects: it entails renouncing, producing, preserving, providing and edifying. The religious renounces the right of administration and independent use of goods; he gives up conveniences, things that suit his taste, his preferences.... Everything is simply *used* by him, nothing more. By his diligent labor, he is productive; he produces for the benefit of the apostolate and of others. He takes care of all that is given him to use. He provides for the needs of his Congregation. He edifies others, drawing them away from greed for possessions.

"No man can serve two masters; for either he will hate the one and love the other, or else he will stand by the one and despise the other. You cannot serve God and mammon.

"Therefore I say to you, do not be anxious for your life, what you shall eat; nor yet for your body, what you shall put on. Is not the life a greater thing than the food, and the body than the clothing? Look at the birds of the air: they do not sow, or reap, or gather into barns; yet your heavenly Father feeds them. Are not you of much more value than they? But which of you by being anxious about it can add to his stature a single cubit?

"And as for clothing, why are you anxious? Consider how the lilies of the field grow; they neither toil nor spin, yet I say to you that not even Solomon in all his glory was arrayed like one of these. But if God so clothes the grass of the field, which flourishes today but tomorrow is thrown into the oven, how much more you, O you of little faith!

"Therefore, do not be anxious, saying, 'What shall we eat?' or, 'What shall we drink?' or 'What are we to put on?' (for after all these things the Gentiles seek); for your Father knows that you need all these things. But seek first the kingdom of God and his justice, and all these things shall be given you besides" (Matt. 6:24-33).

There is a positive side to the virtue of poverty and it consists of a constant yearning for spiritual, eternal wealth, for the Supreme Good, God! It entails the effort to attain to this treasure, to detach the heart from the things of this earth and use earthly goods as means to achieve the goal. Even food and rest are taken to maintain us in the service of God and in the exercise of the apostolate.

The vow is a means, a greater commitment to practice the virtue better.

The spirit of poverty, which is the first of the Beatitudes, is the virtue at its highest level. At this point, one has formed solid convictions, love for and delight in privation and sacrifice. He practices poverty more readily and easily, and with greater joy. Such was the case with innumerable canonized saints and the majority of the uncanonized.

*

Jesus is the Master and Teacher of poverty through example first of all. Says St. Bernard: "He was poor at birth, poorer in life and poorest of all in death." St. Paul wrote to the Corinthians: "You know the graciousness of Our Lord Jesus Christ— how, being rich he became poor for your sakes, that by his poverty you might become rich" (2 Cor. 8:9). Think of the cave in which He was born, the manger in which He was laid, the poverty of the exile in Egypt, the poor house at Nazareth, the humble carpenter work, the public life supported by alms, the humiliation of being stripped of His robes in the passion, given gall and myrrh to drink, a cross for a bed, a borrowed sepulchre for His tomb. For the great miracle of the Eucharist He chose the very ordinary food of bread and wine. And Christ ever showed His preference for the poor: "The poor have the Gospel preached to them" (Luke 7:22).

Christ is the Teacher of poverty through His doctrine also. The first beatitude He taught was poverty: "Blessed are the poor in spirit because theirs is the kingdom of heaven." Since it is the first step to sanctity, those who refuse to take it, or step back down, by that very fact give up the idea of achieving perfection.

Of Christ, they asked, "Is not this the carpenter's son" (Matt. 13:55)? "Is not this the carpenter" (Mark 6:3)?

Other Gospel passages on poverty:

"The foxes have dens, and the birds of the air have nests; but the Son of Man has nowhere to lay his head" (Matt. 18:20).

"If thou wilt be perfect, go, sell what thou hast, and give to the poor, and thou shalt have treasure in heaven; and come, follow me" (Matt. 19:21).

Peter addressed him, saying, "Behold, we have left all and followed thee; what then shall we have?" And Jesus said to them, "Amen I say to you that . . . everyone who has left house . . . or lands for my name's sake, shall receive a hundredfold, and shall possess life everlasting" (Matt. 19:27-29).

"Seek first the kingdom of God and his justice and all these things shall be given you besides" (Matt. 6:33).

"Do not keep gold, or silver, or money in your girdles" (Matt. 10:9).

"Every one of you who does not renounce all that he possesses, cannot be my disciple" (Luke 14:33).

❋

The man who strips himself of possessions becomes rich in grace, in merit, in peace, in glory. Sanctity comes easier with poverty.

Poverty is a rich source of purification, fervor, and love. Says St. Ignatius: "Poverty destroys lust and pride; it serves as preparation for a spiritual atmosphere." It is indeed the guardian of many virtues.

Poverty makes it easier to keep the flesh under control, and thus, to practice the vow of chastity.

With poverty it is easier to renounce self, too, and thus to live the vow of obedience. When we are detached from what is earthly and from ourselves, God lives and reigns in us.

At times we are too superficial when it comes to receiving Christ in Holy Communion. We have to enter into the spirit of Christ and realize the extreme poverty that He practiced. We, on the contrary, would like to live comfortable lives, with all our wants satisfied. And when a certain age is reached, there comes the longing to be able to say: "Now I can take it easy." But the time for taking it easy will be in heaven. As long as we are on this earth, we have to work. And when we can no longer work, we can offer up our sufferings. Such an offering will mean a wealth of merit for the whole congregation.

Some religious understand their vow of poverty very well, whereas it doesn't seem as though some others will understand it even when they are ninety. The reason is that it takes greater light, greater prayer life, to see our duty clearly.

Authentic sanctity is only and always Gospel sanctity. Those who have the real spirit of poverty are much more apt to have the spirit of prayer, too, and a longing for heaven, where their treasure is: "Where your treasure is, there also will you heart be" (Luke 12:34).

A Congregation's poverty is its guarantee of good spirit and good development, particularly in the number and quality of vocations. God does not send vocations where religious do not work or where they are wasteful, even if only in small matters.

If one's heart is tied to something, be it only something insignificant, he is like a bird tied by a thin string: he still cannot soar up toward the peaks of holiness.

MARY

Let us think of her as she was, a woman of the people, the wife of a carpenter. At Bethlehem, this couple could afford so little that they could find no room in the inn.

Mary was the wise and hard-working woman of the house, ever at work cooking, cleaning, washing . . . always watching out for Jesus in His childhood and youth, and caring for Him in His adult life, for Joseph as long as he was with her, for the Apostle John and the other apostles after the death of Jesus, and up until she was assumed body and soul into heaven. Mary was the personification of the ideal, strong woman described in the Book of Proverbs (31:10-31).

Very few of Mary's words are recorded in the Gospel, but those few are full of Scriptural wisdom. Listen to her speak of poverty: "He has put down the mighty from their thrones, and has exalted the lowly. He has filled the hungry with good things, and the rich he has sent away empty" (Luke 1:52-53).

Mary came to the aid of the poor, using her power with God on their behalf. At the wedding feast of Cana, the wine ran out, which means this was a poor family; to their humble celebration, Mary, Jesus and His first disciples, poor fishermen, had been invited. On realizing what had happened, Mary spoke to Jesus about it, obtained the miracle of the transformation of water into wine, and thus saved the couple from embarrassment.

We note that Mary was asking nothing for herself. Her concern was for the couple. Every religious likewise must think more of his institute than of himself, never refusing to do what he can.

There is sometimes a tendency to take from the community rather than to give to it. This must not be Everyone must practice poverty in laboring for the institute with a sense of responsibility.

Mary will obtain the necessary graces for whoever begs her to give him the virtue of poverty. She will help him to love work, serenely to put up with privations and sacrifices, to seek and obtain spiritual gifts.

Very often, religious enjoy a much more comfortable standard of living than they had at home. . . .

Let us remember that our labors should take care of the cost of daily living. Then, for unusual expenses, such as a new chapel or house, we can seek help, at least to defray part of the expenses.

From one of the superiors I heard this judgment of a religious who was very well dressed and groomed, very sophisticated in manner, extremely demanding with regard to food, and quite haughty with others: "To the degree that he is concerned with externals, he is empty interiorly—without learning or knowledge, without piety, without zeal."

ST. PAUL

To Timothy he writes: "Charge the rich of this world not to be proud, or to trust in the uncertainty of riches, but in God" (1 Tim. 6:17). He praises Philemon's charity to the Christians of Colossae: "For I had great joy and consolation in thy charity, because through thee, brother, the hearts of the saints (the faithful) have found rest" (Philemon 7).

To Timothy he writes: "Godliness with contentment is indeed great gain. For we brought nothing into the world, and certainly we can take nothing out; but having food and sufficient clothing, with these let us be content. But those who seek to become rich fall into temptation and a snare and into many useless and harmful desires, which plunge men into destruction and damnation. For covetousness is the root of all evils, and some in their eagerness to get rich have strayed from the faith and have involved themselves in many troubles" (1 Tim. 6:6-10).

To the Hebrews: "For you both have had compassion on those in prison and have joyfully accepted the plundering of your own goods, knowing that you have a better possession and a lasting one" (Heb. 10:34).

He thanks the Philippians for the offerings received and he adds: "I have learned to be self-sufficing in whatever circumstances I am. I know how to live humbly and I know how to live in abundance (I have been schooled to every place and every condition), to be filled and to be hungry, to have abundance and to suffer want" (Phil. 4:11-12).

"Poverty is to be loved as the walls of the religious house" (St. Ignatius). Did not Christ say: "Woe to you rich! for you are now having your comfort" (Luke 6:24)? *Woe!* Do we not see many monasteries, convents and institutes beginning to decline or already fallen? Let this be a warning to us.

The "rich" are not only those who have great wealth and are attached to it; the term applies to those who have little, too, but are always looking for more and will take any means to get it. Though living in actual poverty they desire wealth.

*

All Congregations must practice poverty, but not all in the same way. Cistercian poverty, for instance, is not the poverty of Jesuits. As St. Thomas wrote: "Religious poverty is of instrumental value, in accord with the twofold purpose to which it is ordained: sanctification and apostolate."

It is harder to practice poverty when necessity demands that a number of people be involved in administration, but it depends on the nature of the Institute. Vigilance is needed.

The virtue of poverty, moreover, is more for the individual members than for the Congregation as a whole. The Institute has to see to the development of its apostolate, make sure of its continuing existence and insure its progress. Still, even in all this there are limits to be observed: we must never neglect trust in God, a reigning spirit of poverty, care to avoid wasting "crumbs" of time or bread, aid to the poor as far as possible, and so forth.

All Congregations are bound to work, by the natural law itself and also as penance for sins. Profession adds new laws; it does not take any away.

Before they have recourse to appeals for funds, all Congregations are bound to work, whether they be rich or poor. The possibility of working is in itself a gift of God's providence. Pius XII, in the Constitution, "Sponsa Christi," repeated this norm very clearly.

To teach a young person to be hard-working is to do him the greatest favor; you will raise him to a higher moral level and assure him of a good future, in this life and in the next.

When a person lives a disciplined life, controlling his senses and mastering the situations that arise, both at home and in society, he will be admired and respected. He will do good to himself and to his fellow-man. He will make his contribution to humanity and to the Church.

The saints were all hard workers. When we consider the length of their lives and the extent of their accomplishments in so many fields, we are amazed! They gave the place of preference to interior spiritual work, and this in turn resulted in their marvelous activities for the benefit of humanity, which won universal admiration.

St. Paul wrote to the Thessalonians:

"Indeed when we were with you we used to charge you: If any man will not work, neither let him eat. For we have heard that some among you are living irregularly, doing no work but busy at meddling. Now such persons we charge and exhort in the Lord Jesus Christ that they work quietly and eat their own bread" (2 Thess. 3:10-12).

"We toil, working with our own hands" (1 Cor. 4:12).

Paul was a great worker. More than once he declared that by the work of his hands he had supported himself and his companions on his apostolic journeys. He even worked through the night at the trade he had learned as a boy. He says of himself: " . . . in stripes, . . . in labors, in sleepless nights . . ." (2 Cor. 6:5). St. Paul is the best interpreter and imitator of Jesus Christ, and even in the matter of work, his life is Christ's. "For me to live is Christ" (Phil. 1:21).

*

An excellent rule is "early to bed, early to rise."

When religious have worked to the best of their ability and still do not have enough for their lawful needs, let them call on Divine Providence, seek contributions in a dignified way, and rejoice to be able to share the poverty of Jesus and Mary by living in want.

Confessors, preachers, and teachers are to be considered among the best of workers.

There are some people who like to brag that they have the vow of poverty, but when it comes to keeping it, it is a different story. They make all kinds of exceptions for themselves and even demand them. In fact, it often happens that the ones who work the less demand the most.

Some there are who use a community car as if it were their own. They reserve it exclusively for themselves, make all decisions concerning it, use it freely and independently—all of which is forbidden by their vow.

*

Enemies of poverty are:

1) Concupiscence of the eyes. It has been said: "Everyone, because of the desire for money, is at heart, in greater or lesser degrees, a capitalist, an owner, a miser—though only in a dormant state. But when full adulthood is reached, all these desires are awakened." So it can even happen that a religious does some work for an outsider and then pockets the money he earned.

2) Concupiscence of the flesh. Under this heading comes laziness, a yearning for money so as to be able to satisfy passions, gluttony, curiosity, desires for independence, for amusement, for comforts. Of course, for real needs, the Institute must provide.

3) Pride of life. This means vanity. Dignity is necessary, but vanity is a passion. It is superficial judgment, the world caters to the rich, even in church.

4) The worldly spirit, the bad example of fellow-religious, the indifference of superiors, the material prosperity of the Institute.

*

The vow of poverty in a religious Congregation forbids:

1) Appropriation of something that belongs to the Community for personal use.

2) Giving, selling, exchanging, disposing of things and buying on one's own initiative, lending, wasting through neglect.

3) Accepting things for personal use without permission or making unjustified demands for care of health.

4) Refusing assignments or work.

❋

The qualities of poverty:

It is to be loved, chosen, and preferred to wealth and comfort, for the love of Jesus Christ.

It is to be practiced in regard to food, clothing, living quarters, furniture. . . . One is to prefer common life.

As set forth in the Gospel, the spirit of poverty means loving the poor, not seeking frequent contacts with high society, and preaching detachment from the things of this world as taught in the Gospel.

❋

A perpetually professed religious must provide for the support of at least three or four people, as long as his strength lasts. This is because of the expenses entailed in his own years of training, because of the need to support the postulants, and because of his mature age. Aren't similar demands made on fathers of families?

Accustom young postulants to practice poverty. Let them bring in the amount prescribed by the rule; let them get used to the food served to the community and to the work being done by all. See to it that they are orderly and clean, that they take care of things, such as furniture and clothing, that they learn to conquer themselves through the practice of mortification.

To try to form people without teaching them to deny themselves, as Christ exhorted, will not result in good Christians, much less in good religious. But if the aspirant becomes accustomed to small renunciations as a matter of course, he will be prepared for the general renunciation entailed in professing and living the Gospel spirit and the example of Christ.

In the Church, only those who loved and practiced poverty accomplished lasting good or left behind edifying example, or carried out extensive apostolic labors or achieved real holiness.

There is a clear distinction between faults against poverty and faults against justice. Let Novice Masters and Superiors explain this point well and remind subjects of the duty of restitution when one has unlawfully taken from the Community, culpably damaged something, given away without permission what belonged to the Congregation, etc.

○

The spirit of poverty presupposes the practice of justice, even in small matters; the conviction that the goods of this world are ordained both to the natural and the eternal life of man; good health; cleanliness and good use of time; reasonable thriftiness.

Our time should be utilized to the utmost, from when we rise in the morning until we retire at night. Rest is needed, of course, but let everyone fill his days as much as possible with labor and merit.

Orderly housekeeping, proper care of clothes, of furniture, of materials used for the apostolate and work, and so forth—all this is only reasonable. Wise centralized administration, which both provides and foresees the needs of the religious family, is absolutely essential. It is a good sign when vanity is avoided, when unnecessary satisfactions are not indulged in, when what is only superfluous and ornamental is shunned.

In general, it is much easier to build churches and convents than to sanctify them, fill them with merits, vocations, apostolic works, joyful religious life, and prayer, thus making them antechambers of our heavenly home. "For those who have been faithful, O Lord, life is not ended, but merely changed, and when this earthly abode dissolves, an eternal dwelling place awaits them in heaven" (Preface, Mass for the Dead).

If they are to last, convents have to be kept up carefully. True, walls, doors, and windows, as well as furnishings should be made to last, with the resistance demanded by a large community with young people in it. But all in the community must take good care of everything, respecting community property as being the property of the Church (through the Congregation). Poverty demands care and attention on all sides.

Cleanliness, order, ventilation and frequent repairs to roof and floors, new paint when needed, and like care are evidence of self-respect and re-spect for our apostolate. The phrase, "O Lord, I love the beauty of Your dwelling place" is applicable here, too.

God grant that when we are near death, the sight of our room and its furnishings, our clothes, books, and other objects of personal use, may only give rise to the memory of the holy use we made of them! Indeed, what we have is only for our *use*, as means with which to prepare our eternal crown, a wonderful reward in heaven."

One day our body will be carried out the door once and for all, but we pray that our soul may en-ter its eternal dwelling place to be crowned: "Come . . . to be crowned."

What the Obedience of Religious Entails

In professing obedience, religious offer the full surrender of their own will as a sacrifice of themselves to God and so are united permanently and securely to God's salvific will.

After the example of Jesus Christ who came to do the will of the Father (cf. John 4:34; 5:30; Heb. 10:7; Ps. 39:9) and "assuming the nature of a slave" (Phil. 2:7) learned obedience in the school of suffering (cf. Heb. 5:8), religious under the motion of the Holy Spirit, subject themselves in faith to their superiors who hold the place of God. Under their guidance they are led to serve all their brothers in Christ, just as Christ himself in obedience to the Father served His brethren and laid down His life as a ransom for many (cf. Matt. 20:28; John 10:14-18). So they are closely bound to the service of the Church and strive to attain the measure of the full manhood of Christ (Eph. 4:13).

Religious, therefore, in the spirit of faith and love for the divine will should humbly obey their superiors according to their rules and constitutions. Realizing that they are contributing to building up the body of Christ according to God's plan, they should use both the forces of their intellect and will and the gifts of nature and grace to execute the commands and fulfill the duties entrusted to them. In this way religious obedience, far from lessening the dignity of the human person, by extending the freedom of the sons of God, leads it to maturity.

Superiors, as those who are to give an account of the souls entrusted to them (Heb. 13:17), *should fulfill their office in a way responsive to God's will. They should exercise their authority out of a spirit of service to the brethren, expressing in this way the love with which God loves their subjects. They should govern these as sons of God, respecting their human dignity. In this way they make it easier for them to subordinate their wills. They should be particularly careful to respect their subjects' liberty in the matters of sacramental confession and the direction of conscience. Subjects should be brought to the point where they will cooperate with an active and responsible obedience in undertaking new tasks and in carrying out those already undertaken. And so superiors should gladly listen to their subjects and foster harmony among them for the good of the community and the Church, provided that thereby their own authority to decide and command what has to be done is not harmed.*

Chapters and deliberative bodies should faithfully discharge the part in ruling entrusted to them and each should in its own way express that concern for the good of the entire community which all its members share.

Decree on the Adaptation and Renewal of Religious Life, n. 14

OBEDIENCE AND THE COUNCIL

Pope Paul VI

Beloved sons and daughters, what is the greatest need of the Church at the present time?

We ask this of you who are led here by love for the Church, for the Church in her unity, authenticity and authority, of you who have some knowledge of the state of fervor and renewal in which the Church finds itself after the council and who surely take part with good will in the post-conciliar process of renewal, of reform, of innovation, of development which places both the clergy and the faithful in ferment and movement of thought, activity, customs and institutions; of you who feel the stimulation of the Holy Spirit to arise from conformism, inertia, lukewarmness and to do something good and useful for the Church.

We shall give today a most simple answer which you can understand and accept because you are good, faithful and fervent: the Church is in need of obedience.

Yes, you sons and daughters who love the Church: the Church needs obedience. And more than a passive and enforced external obedience, she needs an inner and spontaneous spirit of obedience.

We seem to be hearing some benevolent reaction, if not from you, from hypothetical commentators on this familiar theme.

141

The first is: has there not already been mention of this subject more than once? Yes, true, we have spoken of it at other times, and together with us, bishops and superiors have spoken of it—in other words, those who hold responsibility in the communities to which obedience has particular reference. Nevertheless, the need to speak of it again and in a clear manner remains.

It remains, due to a certain intolerance, a certain spirit of indiscipline and of emancipation, which appears here and there in some sectors of God's people up to now completely exemplary in their observance of obedience, in fact proud and honored to give to this Gospel virtue their shining testimonial.

It remains, due to the necessity which has arisen, in this post-conciliar period, for internal cohesion to the ecclesiastical framework.

How can there be a renewal of spirit, of works and structures in the Church, unless the Church is solidly united within herself?

How can we approach the separated brethren if the separation, even if purely in the realm of intention or of discipline, lessens the harmony which is and must be characteristic of the ecclesial society, cools charity and attenuates the capacity for example and for explanation (of the faith) in those who address themselves to them?

And how can we speak to a world which we would want to evangelize, if wisdom and authority to do so is wanting among us through absence of that apostolic authenticity which only obedience renders identifiable and operative?

At this point a second reaction might perhaps be expressed. Does not obedience interpret the spirit of the council? Has not the council spoken on the rights of personality, of conscience and of liberty?

Yes, it did speak of these subjects but it did not indeed remain silent on that of obedience.

At this moment we do not intend to speak on these same, beautiful, though complex and delicate themes in reference to the freedom of God's children, in reference to the sacred nature of conscience and in reference to the fullness which Christian life confers upon human personality.

We wish instead to simply remind how these prerogatives of the Christian soul are not being offended, but rather safeguarded and moderated by an obedience which is at work in the communitarian texture of the Church, when we think that order, or in other words, the perfection and fullness which is the aim of the economy of Christian salvation, are not, properly speaking, anthropocentric (as the modern mentality has a tendency to believe), but theocentric.

"In Deo salutari meo" (In God is my salvation—Luke 1:47), we will say with Our Lady. And with the council we will add that we must seek not so much the satisfaction of our own desires, but the fulfillment of the divine will (cf. Decree on Priestly Ministry and Life, n. 15).

It is wonderful, Father Wenger wrote recently in "La Croix" (Sept. 15, 1966), for the council to fulfill this function of motive power in the thought and life of persons and institutions; it is likewise true that some willingly ascribe to the council their own opinions and too facilely identify the council's decisions with their own desires, and thus try to free themselves from the established norm.

Well then, perhaps our commentators will persist, has nothing changed in terms of obedience with the council? Oh no! We believe that not only the spirit, but also the forms of obedience receive a regeneration from the council. It would take too long to speak of it.

But if we have understood something of the central doctrine of the council regarding the mystery of the Church, we shall easily arrive at the persuasion that obedience, even before being a purely formal and juridical homage to ecclesiastical laws and submission to ecclesiastical authority, is first of all a penetration and acceptance of the mystery of Christ, who saved us by means of obedience. It is a continuation and imitation of this fundamental act of His: His acceptance of the will of the Father. It is an understanding of the principle which dominates the entire plan of incarnation and redemption (cf. *Lumen Gentium*, Dogmatic Constitution on the Church—no. 3).

Thus obedience becomes assimilation into Christ, who is the Divine Obedient One. It becomes the basic norm for our pedagogy of Christian formation; it becomes the indispensable coefficient of the interior unity of the Church, the source and sign of its peace.

It becomes an effective cooperation in Christ's evangelizing mission. It becomes the ascetic practice of humility and the spiritual practice of charity (cf. Phil. 2:5-12).

It becomes communion with Christ and with him who for us is the apostle and representative of Christ.

This is more beautiful when we think that the relationship between him who commands and him who obeys, or in other words between him who in the Church is vested with authority and him who is subject to such authority, becomes in the council reaffirmed, purified, determined and perfected: by the doctrines on the organic and hierarchical constitution of the Church and on the congenial operative virtues of the Church (cf. *Lumen Gentium,* Dogmatic Constitution on the Church—no. 27, 37) and also by the aims of service and by the pastoral disposition of the ecclesiastical authority, as well as by the exaltation which the council has made of God's people, of the priesthood of the faithful, of the participation of priests in the priesthood of the bishops and of the function of the laity in the Church of God.

There are those who wished to read in this a radical change in the relationship between authority and obedience, almost as though it changed into a dialogue which bound authority and freed obedience.

However, more than a dialogue which would take away its specific merit and which is suited rather to collaboration and counsel, we may note how the concept of such a relationship, without excluding that of responsibility and decision which is reserved to the authority, is enriched by elements not unknown to Catholic custom, and which are now more greatly made valuable, such as respect, trust, unity, collaboration, co-responsibility, goodness, friendship, charity . . . which carry it back to its Gospel contents and to its truly Christian and ecclesial style; there where, in other words, obedience becomes filial, active and joyful.

The Church, we were saying, has need of such obedience, so that the fruit of the council may not be rendered ineffectual, and so that the Church may truly be the Kingdom of God and the light of peoples.

We thus recommend it to you, beloved children, with our apostolic blessing.

"Obedience in the Church," address to a general
audience. October 5, 1966

THE ECCLESIASTICAL MAGISTERIUM

Pope Paul VI

We will do well to give to this feast (of the Chair of St. Peter) the veneration which pertains to it, and to recall the irreplaceable and providential function of the ecclesiastical teaching authority which in the pontifical teaching authority has its most authoritative expression.

We know, unfortunately, that nowadays certain trends of thought, which still are described as Catholic, attempt to attribute a priority in the normative formulation of the truths of the faith to the community of the faithful above the teaching function of the episcopacy and of the Roman pontificate, contrary to the Scriptural teachings and to the doctrine of the Church, which was openly confirmed in the recent council. This constitutes a grave danger for the genuine concept of the Church itself, for its inner security and for its evangelizing mission in the world.

Our only teacher is Christ, who many times laid claim to this title (Matt. 23:8; John 13:14); from Him alone comes to us the revealing word of the Father (Matt. 11:27); from Him alone comes the liberating truth (John 8:32) that opens to us the ways of salvation; from Him alone comes the Paraclete Spirit (John 15:26), that nourishes faith and love in His Church.

But it is He also who wished to establish an instrument to transmit and to guarantee His teachings, thus investing Peter and the Apostles with the mandate to transmit with authority and assurance His thought and His will.

Therefore, by honoring the hierarchical magisterium of the Church, we honor Christ the teacher and recognize the admirable balance of functions which He established so that the Church might enjoy forever the certainty of revealed truth, of the unity of the same faith, of the awareness of its true vocation, the humility of knowing that it is always the disciple of the Divine Master, of the charity which unites it in a single organized Mystical Body and enables it to give a secure testimony of the Gospel.

May the Lord preserve and increase, for the needs of our times, this loving, trusting and filial veneration for the ecclesiastical magisterium established by Christ, and may we be aided by the Apostle Peter, who was first given this mandate and who from this, his Roman chair, and by our hand, still blesses you all.

Address to a general audience, February 22, 1967

THE SUPERIOR-SERVANT

Pope Paul VI

The theme of these brief words is intended to
connect the audience, the moment it is over, to a
train of thought deserving to be remembered and
pondered. This time it is also a theme concerning
one of the more common impressions which is
usually formed in the minds of the visitor, particularly if he is a foreigner or is taking part for the
first time at such a meeting as we are now enjoying
together.

What is that impression? It is the impression
of entering a sphere that is extremely disciplined,
very demanding, and dominated by a complex and
intangible system of authority. Just as when a casual
visitor enters a great modern factory and feels
astonished, intimidated and almost overcome by
the structures and the most orderly fervor of activity
which surround him, so, very often, the visitor
here, whether he is a pilgrim or a tourist, realizes
that he has entered a kind of magnetic field trav-
ersed by powerful invisible currents which without
depriving him of his personal autonomy and without smothering his liberty—but indeed urging and
stimulating it toward conscious and spontaneous
agreement—places him in a higher order entirely
permeated by very clear laws, some of which—the

divine laws—are indisputable, inflexible and governed by an authority which it is a duty to obey.

This impression of authority is made more vivid here at the center of the Catholic Church, where all hierarchical powers are linked and where the degree of ecclesiastical authority is greater. This can give rise to two further impressions which are in contrast to one another. One is an impression of the contentment and security typical of those who have the good fortune of being a part of and of appreciating the communion in which they live, that is to say of belonging as living and organic members to the Mystical Body of Christ, the Church. Here one realizes better its united and universal structure. Here one recognizes its functionality, established by Christ, whereby the chosen brother is made the instrument and channel of divine gifts for the brother.

The other impression, however, is one of fear and diffidence, as if this hierarchical and authoritarian order worked toward abasing the personality of the follower, as if it were a human invention contrary to the brotherly equality which is to be found in the teaching of the Gospel.

Today everyone knows how widespread is this state of mind hostile to the principle of authority. It manifests itself not only in temporal society but also in various sectors of Catholic life itself. Obedience, that is to say, the welcoming and practical recognition of authority, is continually questioned as being contrary to the development of the human person, as being unworthy of free, mature and adult human beings. It is continually misunderstood as if it created weak and passive spirits, and perpetuated in modern times outworn principles of social relations. There are those who think it worthwhile to run the risk of a liberating disobedience and that it is a praiseworthy trick to confront authority with an accomplished fact.

And there is no lack of able people who delude themselves, maybe without saying it openly, that they can be excellent or at least sufficiently good Catholics while reserving for themselves an absolute autonomy of thought and action, avoiding any positive relationship, not only of subordination but also of respect and of connection, with whoever has the offices of responsibility and direction.

How vast today, unfortunately, could be the field of similar remarks! But we do not intend now to speak bitter and polemic words, just as we do not intend to make a defense of authority. You, on the other hand, well know the evidence of the Gospel from which it stems. And you know that authority seeks to be at the service of charity and salvation and nothing else.

Restricting ourself to analyzing the above-mentioned impression of having arrived in the realm of authority, we will reply synthetically to some questions which seem to spring from that impression itself.

Is this impression exact? Yes, it is exact. Here the authority of the Church has its fullest and most authentic expression. But remember that it is difficult to form an exact concept of authority and particularly of ecclesiastical authority.

Experience and history offer us images of this which are not always faithful and are not always happy ones. It is necessary to deepen the idea of the authority of the Church, to purify it of forms which are not essential to it (even if in given circumstances they were legitimate, such as, for example, temporal power) and to return it to its original and Christian principle.

We are asked: Is not the authority of the Church a service? Certainly, we have already said so. Jesus has said: "Let him who is greatest among you become ... the servant" (Luke 22:26). But here too it is necessary to understand fully the thought of the Master. What service is asked of whoever has the task of guiding and directing? Is it a service which must be subordinated to those being served, and must it be responsible before them? No, it is a service to which Christ entrusted the keys, not a servile instrument but the sign of ruling that is the power of the kingdom of God.

It is a service responsible only before God, as St. Paul says of himself: "He alone who can judge me is the Lord" (1 Cor. 4:4).

But then what is the image represented by the superior-servant who is not merely the mediator between the plurality of the opinions of the community, not merely the administrator of its immediate interests, not only the witness of the word of God, or even less the despotic leader insensitive to the dignity, needs and capacities of the faithful, whether considered as individuals or collectively? You remember the image which is full of authority and dignity and at the same time full of goodness and the spirit of sacrifice. It is the image of the shepherd which Christ attributed to Himself (John 10:11) and which in Peter, with the triple command (John 20:21 ff), He wished to be fulfilled. The authority of the Church is pastoral.

Again you will ask us: Must, then, an authority so qualified and destined to make of mankind one single flock (John 10:16) level everyone and make everything the same according to one single concrete type of religious faithfulness?

We will reply with the words of St. Gregory the Great: "When the faith is one, diversity of customs does not harm the Church" (Letters, Vol. 1, 43; Pl 77, 497).

Let this suffice for a theme of such magnitude and gravity! But not without us, to whom Providence has entrusted supreme authority in the Church, first confiding to you fleetingly how heavy are these keys which came from the hands of Peter to our weak hands. How serious it is to carry them and how still more serious it is to use them.

Therefore, most beloved sons and daughters, have compassion and understanding for all those who have the office of priest, of teacher and of shepherd in the Church of God (Cf. Heb. 13-17). Do not let obedience and cooperation be a burden to you. But let them make you proud and happy to assist the growth of the Kingdom of God and let them make you sharers in His gifts and His merits, of which our apostolic blessing is now intended to be a pledge.

Address, July 14, 1965

THE TWOFOLD PROBLEM
OF AUTHORITY AND OBEDIENCE

Pope Paul VI

One point which, in the spirit of the Council, deserves special mention on our part is the exercise of authority and consequently the practice of obedience, in the orders and instructions of your institutes. Would we say that authority has lost its prestige, its reason for being, its responsibility within the framework of a religious family which is generated, directed, inspired, educated and sanctified precisely by authority?

And would we say that obedience has melted into a democratic dialogue and the will of a numerical majority, or of an enterprising minority, when we know that this virtue is essential for the religious life and for the religious community and that, in fact, as St. Thomas teaches, "among all vows of the religious the greatest is that of obedience, maximum est"? (Summa Theol. II-II, 186,8).

No, indeed. On the contrary, we will confirm the necessity of a wise exercise of authority as well as of a sincere practice of obedience. The unity and the spirit of religious life would be fatally undermined if authority and obedience were to fail.

But, as you know, both demand new forms, better ones, forms more worthy of ecclesiastical society, more virtuous and more in conformity with the spirit of Jesus Christ.

This twofold problem—of authority and obedience—must be one of the themes more closely studied in the reframing of your rules and in the evolution of your religious mentality, and will demand attention, prudence and trust to attain the solutions prompted by the times and demanded by the council.

To you, superiors, we will now only mention a renowned and ever wise word of St. Augustine in regard to the responsible attitude of one who leads a community of nuns. The holy teacher referred to above, in his famous letter to the disturbed nuns of his times, said (a 423) that a superior must not hold herself to be a ruler by authority, but rather be happy to serve by charity: "Ipso vero non se existimet potestate dominante, sed caritate serviente" (Ep. 211; P.L. 33,964). He had also said shortly before: "The superior must be obeyed as a mother, with due honor, so as not to offend God in her."

Address to Major Superiors of Women's Religious Institutes,
January 12, 1967

A HOLOCAUST OF THE WILL

Pope Paul VI

Therefore, it is supremely important to cherish diligently *religious obedience* in your lives.

Religious obedience is and must remain a holocaust of one's own will which is offered to God. A Religious makes this sacrifice of self with a view to humbly obeying lawful Superiors (whose authority, of course, should always be exercised within the confines of charity and with due regard for the human person), even though our times summon Religious to the performance of many and heavy burdens, and to carrying out these duties more cheerfully and more promptly.

Address to All Religious, May 23, 1964

SUPERIORS CANNOT SHED RESPONSIBILITY

Pope Pius XII

It is with a real joy that We salute you in the Lord, all of you, Beloved Sons here present, whom a design of divine Providence has placed at the head of societies tending towards evangelical perfection and has thus associated you with no small part of Our own apostolic charge. In fact, as We stated in addressing the members of the First Congress on the States of Perfection a few years ago, an Institute of religious life "draws its existence and its worth from the fact that it is closely bound to the proper end of the Church, namely, to lead men to sanctity." [1] For the Church, His Spouse, would not respond fully to the desires of Christ our Lord, and men's eyes would not turn towards her full of hope as to "a standard unto the nations," [2] if she did not possess men who, by the example of their lives even more than by their words, reflect with special splendor the beauty of the Gospel.

We have, therefore, associated you, most Beloved Sons, to that part of our office, either directly by delegating to you through Canon Law something of Our supreme jurisdiction, or by establishing the bases, in your rules and constitutions approved by

[1] Dec. 8, 1950.   [2] Isa. 11:12.

Us, of your power "to command." Therefore, it is particularly important to Us that you exercise this authority of yours according to Our mind and that of the Church.

In Our exhortation of the Holy Year 1950 mentioned above, We have given a full exposition of the point which your subjects must above all preserve in our epoch and of those where there is room to innovate and adapt. Today We wish to define for you in a few words in what precise fashion you should work with Us for the end We envision.

THE SURE ROAD OF THE TRUTH

We said to you then that for those who are following the states of perfection no concession should be made, to the detriment of eternal truth, for the tendencies which are summed up in the word *existentialism*. It belongs to the one who has the first place, in a word, to lead, as surely as he can, his subjects to the goal of eternal life, with an enlightened mind, by the sure road of truth, without deviating either to the right or the left, with firm direction, and, if need arise, an energetic direction. As the patriarch of those who, in the West, are tending towards evangelical perfection has said: "The Abbot must teach nothing, institute nothing, ordain nothing that is contrary to the Lord's precepts; let his government and his teaching spread in souls like the leaven of divine justice." [3]

[3] Rule of St. Benedict, c.2.

Let religious superiors ever draw the principles which inspire them not from what the majority say, or from what is being propagated—rejecting the most ancient commentaries of the Fathers—as being the only thing which must be taught and commanded now, because it is the most recent, or from what most pleases those living in the world; rather let them draw their principles from the pure source of revealed truth and the discipline of the ecclesiastical magisterium. With real courage superiors must go against the preferences of many; if they cannot bear to appear at times old-fashioned in the eyes of certain ones of their subjects, how will they keep intact Christ's truth, always new, it is true, but at the same time always old?

In the principles which regulate the doctrine of the asceticism and of the kind of life of the states of perfection—as We have warned with regard to a more serious subject in the encyclical letter *Humani generis*—there are to be met with today minds "unduly attached to novelty . . . which are striving to withdraw themselves from the direction of the teaching authority, and, for this reason, are in danger of straying imperceptibly from revealed truth and of dragging other souls, too, into error." [4] Certainly, it is less serious to err in moral discipline than to do so in matters of faith; but each of these two errors, in its own way, leads of itself to the ruin of nature and without any doubt retards and impedes us from reaching as we should the Supreme Good.

[4] A.A.S., 42, 564.

Moreover, let superiors be firmly anchored in the solid and balanced ascetical teaching which was given to them by the first founders and has for long been approved by the custom of the Church, and let them not depart from it by novelties. The reason for adhering to the truth does not, in fact, stem from the circumstance that it has the general approval of men, but from the fact that it is the truth, placed by God in nature or revealed to men by His goodness. Let certain men denigrate it; does this make it cease to be the truth and the way which leads to God? He who would be a prudent superior will be wise to seek and to listen willingly to much advice; he will meditate and weigh within himself the opinion of prudent men and of teachers; he will never trust overmuch in himself, as if the danger of error did not threaten every man on this earth. But then, after having heard first of all those whom the Rule gives him for councillors, after having at length invoked the Spirit of Counsel, and maturely weighed every aspect, let him reach a precise and definite decision. Let him impose it, as he should with paternal and humble firmness on his subjects, and direct in accordance with it their activity and their lives: "Just as disciples should obey their master, so is it fitting that the master should dispose all things with foresight and equity." [5]

Whatever may be held by some men, for whom the yoke of religious obedience seems too heavy to be imposed on modern man, you can never lose sight of the fact that the office of superior consists

[5] Rule of St. Benedict, c.3.

in directing, with—of course—all the humility and charity of Christ, but with firmness, the souls who are subject to you. The Divine Judge will demand an accounting of souls not only from each one personally, but also from those to whom He has entrusted them: "Whatever be the number of brethren confided to his care, let him hold for certain that on the day of judgment he will have to render an account to the Lord of all their souls." [6]

SEPARATION FROM THE WORLD

With the passage of time and the appearance of new needs on the part of souls, the Church has seen the rise, under the guidance—we are permitted to hope—of the Holy Spirit, of other forms of life which tend to perfection. Each one of them asks something different from its members: requirements are not the same for monks and for clerks regular, for religious and for the members of the recently founded Secular Institutes. One thing is, however, common to all and will remain so: whoever tends towards evangelical perfection must necessarily withdraw from and separate himself from the world. This will mean, as far as the organization of his life is concerned, a separation according to the needs of the particular vocation given by God, but it will always be a total separation of the affections. We say "from the world," the world of which Our Lord and Master gave this warning to His disciples: "You are not of the world;" [7] and the Beloved Disciple: "The whole world is seated in

[6] Rule of St. Benedict, c.2.   [7] John 15:19.

wickedness;" [8] and also the Apostle of the Gentiles: "The world is crucified to me, and I to the world." [9]

It is necessary for him who wishes to live for the Lord and serve Him perfectly, to be, in his affections, a total stranger to the world. The Lord cannot be perfectly served if He is not the only one served. In fact, what created good could be in any way compared—We do not say put on the same footing—to the divine perfection? How can one who has not purified his mind and does not keep it free from pride of the world and its many concupiscences, mount up towards God, as by the wings of a free love, and live in union with Him? United, in all truth, not only by the vital bond of sanctifying grace, but also by that ardent love which is proper to him who tends towards perfection?

Unless he be among the number of perfect souls prevented by an uncommon grace, what man, morally weakened as he is by the consequences of original sin, can free himself completely from all attachment to the things of this world, if he does not separate himself from them in reality up to a certain point, having even the courage to abstain from them completely? Outside the case of an office assumed in the Church out of obedience, no one can enjoy all the commodities with which our age abounds, grant himself the diversions and joys of the senses so widely offered in our day to our contemporaries, without losing something of his spirit of faith, of his love for God. Even more, the man who has for a long time tolerated laxity in his way of life,

[8] 1 John 5:19.   [9] Gal. 6:14.

will little by little abandon his efforts for sanctity
and will expose himself to the danger of seeing the
fervor of his charity and the very light of his faith
diminish, to the point where he will fall away
lamentably from the noble state towards which he
was tending.

THE SUPERNATURAL NORMS OF ACTION

On points of doctrine and opinion as well as on
the subject of acts to be accomplished, it must be
that your norms of judgment will be different from
those of the world; your rule of conduct must be
different; and different also must be the principle
by which you will seek to have an influence over
other men. Let your norms of judgment and appreciation be drawn from the Gospel of the Lord and
the teaching of His Church: "It pleased God, by the
foolishness of our preaching, to save them that believe;" [10] "for the wisdom of this world is foolishness
with God;" [11] and truly "we preach Christ crucified." [12] If a man is not careful, instead of poisoning
his mind by the habitual occupation with the affairs
of this world, to nourish it assiduously by reading
and meditation on the things of God and by familiarity with the writings of ancient and recent authors who are distinguished for the solidity of their
faith and their piety, how can he have a relish for
the good?

But these are the same rules of action which
must be followed by your subjects. They should not
desire what is pleasing, what is agreeable, what is

[10] 1 Cor. 1:21.   [11] *Ibid.*, 3:19.   [12] *Ibid.*, 1:23.

convenient, but God alone; and they will not find him except by unceasingly curbing their senses and their wills: their wills by humility and submissive obedience; their senses by austerity of life and mortification of the body freely accepted. Without these means, recommended by the Old and New Testaments and the whole tradition of the Church, a Christian soul flatters itself in vain that it can arrive at the love of God and the love of neighbor for the love of God.

Moreover, the ways by which you can bring men to God, their last end, are they any different from those which the intelligence, left to itself, would have thought to be effective? The apostolate of which We are speaking rests in every way on the necessity of prevenient grace, which opens the hearts and the ears of those who listen; on actual grace without which no man can perform a work which leads to salvation and none can persevere in the good. The Lord's ways are not our ways. It is not always in "the persuasive words of human wisdom" [13] that is to be found the strength capable of attracting minds to the faith and the good works which lead to salvation, but in "the demonstration of the Spirit and of power," [14] in that manifestation full of mystery by which, from the simple sincerity, the charity, the strength of the believer there springs a marvelous possibility of persuading minds and leading them to God. It is not by totally new ideas which the human mind is constantly producing that men are influenced for good, but by the

[13] 1 Cor. 2:4.   [14] *Ibid.*

invisible force of grace and the sacraments, above all of Penance and the Eucharist. And again, unless one separates oneself from the world for a time, and recollects oneself in private almost every day, calmly to meditate in peace on these truths in a heart-to-heart colloquy with the Spirit of Wisdom, do we not fall into that restless and often sterile fever of 'action,' more brilliant than effective?

PERMANENT VALUE OF THE RULE

So that your sons may live in that peace and tranquillity of soul so conducive to a just appreciation of divine things, your Founders gave them, according to the ancient tradition of the Church born of the Fathers of the Desert according to the true wisdom of the Gospel, what is called a Rule or a Constitution. Although it differs from one Institute to the next according to their various ends, it is nonetheless obligatory in all. Its necessity for the end which you propose to yourselves is born of the weakness of human nature wounded by original sin. Its effectiveness for the perfection of Christian life is proved by long experience, both ancient and modern. Its holiness is ceaselessly proclaimed by the Church, as much in her declarations as in her actions.

Human nature is attracted by ease and it has always found disagreeable the discipline comprised in life in religion stemming from the Rule; and this is naturally more disagreeable to men of our day, accustomed as they have been to a freer life before embracing the religious state. Even if, on some unessential points, you have rightly adapted the Rule and are adapting it to the possibilities of those who present themselves to you, it would be inadmissible for you to demean it and still less to abandon it. The word of Proverbs is as true today as in the past: "Take hold on instruction, leave it not: keep it, because it is thy life." [15] What the divinely inspired author states on the subject of discipline which each one willingly imposes upon himself, can we not say also, with every reason, of that particular discipline to which, by the profession of a more perfect life, one obliges oneself and which one promises to observe? "Those whom love urges on the road to eternal life, for the same motive enter straightway on the narrow path; ... no longer guided by their own judgment, not obeying their desires and their satisfactions, but walking according to the judgment and command of another, they wish nothing else, in entering the monastery, than to be subject to the Abbot." [16]

It comes within the duties of your office—acting in this with paternal firmness by exhortations, warnings, reprimands, and even, if necessary, punishments—to help your subjects to walk in the right road and to keep them there according to the Rules of your own Institutes. And if a subject be negligent or at fault, no superior has the right to shed his responsibility by saying, "He is of age, it is his own affair." It is not in this way that the Lord will judge the matter when he will ask you for an accounting of the souls committed to your care: "Behold I my-

[15] Prov. 4:13.   [16] Rule of St. Benedict, c.5.

self come upon the shepherds, I will require my flock at their hand." [17] The man who by connivance has allowed his sheep to stray and has left them without counsel and has not, with a firm hand, kept them out of tortuous bypaths, the Lord will require of him the blood of his sheep! True paternal love is shown not only by caresses, but also by commands and corrections. This firmness should never be harsh, never bear the mark of anger, never lack circumspection; it must always be righteous and serene; it must be gentle and merciful, quick to pardon and to hold out a father's hand to a son who is striving to reject error or to renounce his fault; but let the superior persist in his vigilance and never grow weary.

And in your case government and vigilance must extend not only to life which is generally called 'regular,' lived inside the religious house, but to all the activities of your subjects in the Lord's vineyard. According to the norms established for you by the ecclesiastical hierarchy competent in this matter, it is your duty to supervise the activity of your inferiors so that it will admit nothing which might harm their souls or cause the Church or the faithful dishonor or harm, but rather have them show zeal to promote their own good and their neighbor's.

THE POPE COUNTS ON RELIGIOUS

It follows that zealous deference towards the Chair of Peter and the Vicar of Christ—common to

[17] Ezech. 34:10.

all the faithful—must be cultivated with special care by you who are tending towards perfection. This Apostolic See knows that you will be more docile than others to its commands; it counts on you, most faithful heralds of the doctrine of truth taught by this Chair; it hopes firmly that, more than others, you will be models and defenders of ecclesiastical discipline. And if sometimes—such is the condition of the Kingdom of God on earth where the good and the bad are side by side, the wheat growing with the cockle—if sometimes in one or another place there should be some wavering, a collapse, a straying from the right path, a separation, you at least, Beloved Sons, closely united to Us, with unshakable determination spread the "Kingdom of justice, of love, and of peace."[18] You will be able to proclaim this kingdom, not with the immoderate confidence in self under whose action Peter—not yet strengthened by the Holy Spirit—cried out, "Although all . . . yet not I,"[19] but with the same love, with humble confidence, and strong in the grace of your vocation to the state of perfection. And if it should happen that others, forgetful of the spirit of true sons, should cause concern to this Apostolic See, We at least, with God's help, We will keep in faithful memory these words of the Lord: "Thou art Peter; and upon this rock I will build my Church;" "thou . . . confirm thy brethren."[20]

God grant that the light and zeal of the Holy Spirit may descend abundantly on this chosen flock

[18] Roman Missal, Preface for the Feast of Christ the King.
[19] Mark 14:29.   [20] Matt. 16:18; Luke 22:32.

of His servants, dearest to the Lord and to Us among the other soldiers in the same army. And at the moment when We are commemorating with gratitude the sweet and miraculous apparitions of the Immaculate Virgin Mary in the grotto of Lourdes, We beg that the intercession of the Mother of Divine Grace may obtain this eminent gift, for you, her devoted servants. In pledge of this divine good will and in witness of Our love, to you, Beloved Sons, to your assistants in the government of your Institutes, to all your subjects laboring throughout the entire world, to those above all who are being harassed by the enemy of the Divine Name, We affectionately grant the Apostolic Benediction.

Address to Major Superiors of Religious Institutes,
February 11, 1958

THE EXERCISE OF AUTHORITY

Hildebrand Cardinal Antoniutti

To assist you in the orientation you have to give your institutes so as to renew them according to the views expressed by the Council Fathers in the decree, *Perfectae Caritatis,* I shall speak to you on a subject that seems to me to be of capital importance: "The Exercise of Authority."

Are our ideas about obedience exact ones? The question does not refer to the duty of submission as much as it does to the art of exercising authority —commanding, ruling, and governing.

Sometimes those in directive positions exaggerate the importance of the concept of authority and go so far as to deceive themselves by attributing to themselves more powers than they actually possess. In fact, at times it happens that these powers are looked upon as extraordinary gifts and indispensable means for exercising authority, and those who hold them assume a position of detachment, disdaining any trace of that human understanding which the religious spirit strengthens and sublimates.

On the other hand, we find some in positions of authority who do not dare exercise it in its fullness, either because of cowardice, weakness of

170

character, lack of qualities for governing, or because they are afraid of upsetting their subjects.

In both cases, there is evidently a fundamental ignorance of the true and proper concept of authority which must always be a *service*. This truth is taught us by the Pope, in whom all powers are accented and who yet gives himself such a highly significant title: "The Servant of the Servants of God."

All the teachings of Jesus emphasize this truth: "He who desires to be great among you must become as a servant," "...whoever wishes to be first must become the servant of all," "...for this has the Son of Man come, not to be served, but to serve and give His life for the salvation of the world."

In Christ's Church, from the Pope to the lowest Superior in the hierarchical order, no command must be given for the pleasure of imposing one's own will on others. The privileges are part of the responsibility, and, therefore, the exercise of authority is an apostolate which must be wholly permeated with goodness, understanding and love. It is an effective way of serving the community by coordinating the personal efforts of each for the common good. Each subject, thus, places her abilities and her work at the service of the community.

In some institutes the rule obliges Superiors to set aside a certain period of time each day to reflect upon their duties and the manner in which they are carrying them out. This is an excellent means to aid one in exercising authority well and insuring discipline in religious families.

THE CHARACTERISTICS OF AUTHORITY

Much is being said about authority, and in discussions it is considered under various aspects, with reference to the diversity of its roles.

Authority is organic when it provides for the orderly distribution of daily tasks; it is coercive when it urges the performance of actions under the influence of force; it is preventive when it strives to prevent a fall by a prompt intervention "from above;" it is punitive when it is obliged to impose a sanction—be it of the internal or external order; it is medicinal when it corrects failings or prescribes a remedy for failings; it is formative when it leads one along the right path.

These categories of authority take on a distinctive aspect when they are applied to the religious life. In fact, this state implies the free, willing, and spontaneous acceptance of a rule which is to be observed out of love, which aims at character formation, at the ideal of perfection, and at the acceptance of the responsibilities of life.

The exercise of authority would be incomplete in your institutes if it aimed merely at teaching rules and did not strive to communicate the spirit which must animate them, for it would be neglecting to give that true formation which should penetrate everyone who consecrates himself to God.

It is true that each field—spiritual, intellectual, physical, and social—requires adequate formation, but this formation must be well-balanced and integral to assure coordination, harmony, and vigilance and all those elements which direct, protect, and guide the formative aspects of those called to the religious state.

We may say, therefore, that the disciplinary aspect embraces the formation of each religious in its totality—the way she acts in chapel, in the refectory, at study or recreation, and in general, in the most varied actions of community life.

THE MISSION OF THOSE WHO GOVERN

These general points on the characteristics of authority and the exercise of discipline lead us to a consideration of the mission of those entrusted with the direction and government of religious families.

In your institutes everything must serve as a means of formation; nothing is indifferent, because everything either forms or deforms. The characteristic qualities of the religious vows must be clearly and convincingly evident in the atmosphere of your religious houses. It is difficult to preserve purity and candor in an environment that is tainted, disorderly, or lax. The spirit of poverty does not shine forth from surroundings that are luxurious and ostentatious. The practice of obedience is difficult when subjects are permitted a liberty that goes beyond the limits of good order.

It is necessary that Mothers General and Provincials understand that the discipline which they have to establish in their religious families must embrace every aspect of life, including the personal, communitarian, spiritual, educational and human. They should entrust the implementation of this responsibility to those who are duly prepared, intelligent, practical, and understanding, who are endowed with those moral and pedagogical qualities which enable them to understand their subjects, make intuition easier and regulate their actions.

Two Contemporary Currents

There are at present two methods of exercising authority: the so-called conservative one and the one defined as progressive. There has been much talk on this lately, both relevant and irrelevant. Some publications are full of it.

Traditional methods have been discussed in terms that were not always the most correct, with an evident disregard for the excellent results obtained in the formation of religious in the ascetic and disciplinary traditions which have guided our communities through centuries of indisputable mystical fervor and zealous pastoral activity.

At the same time, we hear extolled in some quarters the modern tendency which, under the pretext of highlighting personality, would like to abolish whatever is organized, collective, orderly, or controlled.

What must we think of all this? The mind of the Church is clear and precise, and the conciliar decree admits of no doubts. Renewal does not mean abandonment of the traditional observance of the rule, but rather a vigorous return to the pure sources of the authentic religious spirit as it was proposed, taught, and inculcated by the founders.

Those entrusted with authority must revive the best traditions in a renewal which will give their institutes a limpid freshness again.

It does not suffice to reduce the yardage of the habit so as to give it that simplicity, modesty, and austerity which gives witness to a life of poverty and renunciation. A more internal change in depth is needed.

We must distinguish, then, between internal and external discipline. Internal discipline must preserve its character and admits of no discussions. Religious life is essentially formative. But since the person who consecrates herself to God offers herself in complete sacrifice, with all of her qualities, she must follow the way traced out by her holy rules which she agrees to observe in their entirety.

Vatican II insists upon the need of personal study and effort to conform oneself to Christ and not upon the cult of personality or the search for liberty.

Religious discipline is based on the obedience taught by Christ, and the Gospel has today the same vigor which it had in the past and obliges in the same way.

There may be, however, a real need for a practical redimensioning in the adaptation of external discipline, with reference to vigilance, to methods, to sanctions, to customs, to the times in which we live. Superiors must know how to interpret the mind of Holy Mother Church and diffuse in their institutes a sense of reciprocal trust, of encouraging confidence, and of mutual understanding.

Do not forget, however, dear Superiors, that the formation of your daughters, while marked by serenity and orientation toward the convinced fulfillment of their specific duties, must be serious, firm, energetic, and accompanied by a certain austerity.

Discipline, St. Thomas tells us, is nothing else but order. Obedience is necessary if order is to prevail, but we must add: to secure order, one must know how to command, that is, exercise authority with goodness, moderation, without harsh or capricious demands, as a service for the well being of subjects.

Unfortunately, abuse of authority has given rise, in some communities, to the suspicion that religious life foments hypocrisy and destroys all that generous initiative which would assure the effectiveness of activities and the progress of individuals.

Religious discipline must be achieved not by coercion, but by love, which creates a family atmosphere to replace and make up for the one which religious have left in order to consecrate themselves to God.

By your manner, you must convince the religious of your Congregations that you desire to help them to correct their faults, overcome their weaknesses, and surmount difficulties. But you must also convince them that the work of formation cannot bring positive results without a determined and willing correspondence on their part.

It is not permissible to be easygoing Superiors, tolerant and weak, who spare their daughters whatever might upset or disturb them, without realizing that what you fail to correct or punish, life itself will correct with merciless blows.

Grave responsibility for so many religious who have failed weighs upon you and you must never permit that the lives and actions of your daughters be filled with tears, with failings, with self-reproach, when you can prevent them in time with a maternal correction and a gesture of generous kindness.

BE MOTHERS

Therefore, careful vigilance is necessary, but one free of repression and suspicion. Even the appearance of secret control must be avoided—all spying, which is certainly not very edifying, and any police-like methods. The good people who come to you are daughters of love, not of fear and are called "to adoption as children of God."

If a Superior possesses a spirit of faith, ardent love of God, and ordinary discernment, she will not be without the resources necessary to govern her Congregation with moderation and good results.

You must avoid authoritarian control which tries to decide everything with forceful moves. You must avoid punitive supervision which threatens, makes use of punishments and inflicts pain. Let your government be instead what love should be: kind, patient, humble, understanding, intelligent, generous, spiritually constructive and edifying.

BE FORMERS

Form your religious so as to develop in them a sense of responsibility for their actions and promote the realization of their good aspirations. Do not stifle their praiseworthy initiative, do not restrain their good impulses, do not hinder their generous activity.

Failure in this regard will fill your communities with inert and useless religious, lacking initiative and energy, who simply enlarge an amorphous and indifferent mass.

That childishness sometimes found in religious communities of women must be abolished. It is entirely unsuited to souls consecrated to God. Each aspirant, each novice, each professed sister must be convinced that she has talents which have to be made to bear fruit for the good of the community, for the service of the Church. Each has the right to be cheered on in her endeavors by the maternal encouragement of her Superiors, who must know how to interpret, excuse, encourage, and correct the inevitable failings of their daughters.

NEW THRUSTS

I could touch upon other topics, but what I have already said seems sufficient to indicate the way you must follow in order to correspond to the clear directives of the Church.

What is needed is not a break with the past, not a rejection of venerable practices, no receding from traditional teachings, but rather a generous acceptance of the obligations of the religious state which must be lived with intensity of faith, seriousness of purpose, supernatural spirit, ardent enthusiasm and complete dedication.

This is a matter of the cause of Christ, to Whom you are consecrated; it is a matter of the cause of the Church, which your Congregations must serve with faithfulness and love.

May the most holy Virgin, Mother of the Church and your Mother, help you with her benign assistance that you may gather abundant fruits of perfection and salvation in a renewal of grace, virtue and sanctity.

Address to the Major Women Religious of Italy,
May 15, 1966

OBEDIENCE, DIALOGUE, AND
THE SUPERIOR'S ROLE

Very Rev. James Alberione, S.S.P., S.T.D.

Let a superior not presume to act on his own, for the Congregation is a society, and in it there are members who are able to speak. Let us then ask for advice, as well as for information on how matters are proceeding in a convent or province or in the Congregation as a whole.

The government of a Congregation is a democratic government, not an absolutist regime. It does not simply impose itself or hand out orders. It gathers up thoughts and suggestions, reflects on them, prays on them, and then comes to decisions. It is thus much easier to conform to God's plans. At the same time, if each member feels bound to make a contribution to the Congregation, he takes responsibility, works more willingly, and accepts whatever decision is handed down because he knows the matter has been well weighed. It is necessary, then, to give great importance to the members of the Congregation. The Holy Spirit is at work in the community.

(from *The Superior Follows the Master,* St. Paul Editions, p. 176)

Thus we recall the words of the Decree on Renewal in Religious Life (n. 14): "Superiors should gladly listen to their subjects and foster harmony among them for the good of the community and the Church, provided that thereby their own authority to decide and command what has to be done is not harmed."

This closing word of warning must not be overlooked, of course. In *Ecclesiam Suam,* our Holy Father wrote:

"By obedience, in the context of dialogue, we mean the exercise of authority in the full awareness of its being a service and ministry of truth and charity and we mean the observance of canonical regulations and respect for the government of legitimate superiors in the spirit of untroubled readiness as becomes free and loving children.

"The spirit of independence, of criticism, of rebellion ill accords with the charity which gives life to the Church's solidarity, concord and peace, and easily transforms the dialogue into argument, dispute and disagreement. This most regrettable attitude, so easy, alas, to produce, is condemned by the Apostle Paul in his warning words: 'Let there be no divisions among you' (1 Cor. 1:10)."

When the members of a community get together to discuss—'to dialogue'—let each one state his thoughts with simplicity, and let the others give them due consideration. No one should impose his views on the rest. Then let the superior summarize what has been said and make the decisions. Afterwards, there should reign in the community union of thought and generous, joyful collaboration of effort, backed always by prayer.

THE REWARD OF OBEDIENCE

Very Rev. James Alberione, S.S.P., S.T.D.

The most basic of the vows is obedience, both because of its intrinsic value and because when there is obedience in the observance of the Constitutions, poverty and chastity are also practiced.

Obedience is a noble virtue and becomes more so under vow. Indeed, it gives the soul a great freedom in submitting the soul to God alone and to His representatives. Thus one is not swayed by selfishness or fleeting impressions, but by God alone, Who is our Creator and our Father.

Now let us reflect on the following points:

First we must consider that we have to follow Jesus Christ. It is He Who has given us the example. Notice that from the moment the Son of God became incarnate through the will of the Father, until the moment of "death, even death on a cross" (Phil. 2:8), He exemplified the most perfect obedience. In the Gospel we read: "He was subject to them" (Luke 2:51). He was subject to two creatures. He, the incarnate Son of God and infinite wisdom itself, submitted Himself to the will of Mary and Joseph—"subject to them." Thus He fulfilled everything His Father willed. In His private life, in His public life, and along His way of sorrows, and when He accepted the bitter chalice in Gethsemane, He declared, "Not My will but Thine be done" (Luke

22:42). Therefore He accepted the Passion, since He had to accomplish the mission His Father had given Him—the redemption of mankind.

There is no sanctification other than imitation of Jesus Christ: "obedient to death, even to death on a cross." He submitted to the will of His Father. In Heaven we will enjoy a degree of glory proportionate to our degree of submission here on earth. Blessed is he who is consecrated to God and does His will in all things; he is sure to receive special glory. We must not obey ourselves. No, we must submit ourselves to the will of God, that is, to authority—for every authority comes from God.

Let us recall that everyone must submit to authority, that one who resists authority resists God Himself, and that those who resist authority are heading for ruin.

This is a very serious matter, which brings consequences even on this earth. In fact, in his hymn to God, Tobias said, "We have not obeyed Thy commandments, therefore are we delivered to spoil and to captivity and death, and are made a fable and a reproach to all nations, amongst which Thou hast scattered us" (Tob. 3:4). St. Paul teaches, "Children, obey your parents in all things, for that is pleasing to the Lord" (Col. 3:20). Obey your parents. In entering a Religious Congregation, one places himself under the guidance and authority of its Superiors. Elsewhere St. Paul says, "Slaves, obey in all things your masters" (Col. 3:22). Jesus, at the command of His executioners, stretched out His hands to be crucified. Let us listen to all who have authority over us on earth.

Therefore we will have to give an account of how we have obeyed. One who boasts of not obeying will have a great deal for which to answer.

St. Paul clearly states that just as humanity ruined itself when it lost grace by disobedience, so was it saved by obedience, the obedience of Jesus Christ Who said, "May the Father's will be done." All evil comes through disobedience, and all good through obedience, that is, through conformity to the will of God. In the petitions of the Our Father we say, "Thy will be done on earth as it is in heaven." As the angels in heaven obey, so should we on earth obey.

In his first letter, St. Peter says to obey those who represent authority, even if they should be evil. And Jesus Christ obeyed Pilate. One who obeys gains merit, whereas one who commands, if he does not command well, burdens himself with responsibility.

Obedience is the best condition for gaining merit. The vow of obedience extends to all the articles of the Constitutions, and therefore merits are gained with the observance of all these articles. This is the immeasurable source of merits for eternal life. God be blessed for having called us to the religious life where everything is marked out for us and meritorious. We shall not go into detail, but suffice it to say that all the articles of the Constitutions are binding on us. Let us thank the Lord for having placed us where we can earn the greatest merit on earth, to be followed by the greatest glory, because the more we humble ourselves in obedience, the more we will be, exalted.

Let us endeavor to do everything we can to achieve a high place in eternity. The present life would be brief even if it were to last a hundred years, for eternity will last not just for millions of centuries—eternity is eternity.

If we truly love ourselves and desire eternal bliss, let us observe the vow of obedience. If ordinary obedience, as aspirants practice it, is still obedience, how much more so is obedience under vow! The vow doubles the merit.

Let us be alert to earn great wealth in Heaven. This is the only kind of real prudence. Prudence, as we well know, is the virtue which places us on guard against evil and points out to us what we must do in the present life with the next life in view. We entered religious life precisely because we wanted to do more and win a greater reward.

Let us pray to Mary and imitate her: "May it be done unto me according to Thy word."

OBEDIENCE—A SCRIPTURAL VIEW

Sister Mary Ruth Barrett, S.N.D.

If ever a virtue be inundated with a plethora of words, it is obedience. Scarcely a religious periodical has appeared within the past several months that has not analyzed this fundamental virtue in some fashion or other. There even seems to be an attempt on the part of "conservatives" and "liberals" to seize obedience for themselves, each side endeavoring to champion its cause with more and more philosophical and psychological arguments.

Those who are all out for the "new look" of not only the 20th but the 21st century have as their rallying cry "rational personality." At times it seems a sort of fancy dress-up nomenclature for the goddess of reason enthroned by the liberals of the French Revolution. But that applies only to the extremists. At least we may be thankful that as yet no one has suggested doing away with obedience altogether, although in some cases, to do so might be a more honest measure than stifling it under the pretext of perfecting it.

Father Willis, S.J., in an article in *Sisters Today,* assures us in the words of Karl Rahner that

there does not exist in this world a control-center of action from whose uninfluenced motion all else in existence originates.

We agree whole-heartedly. Father continues:

> A human being cannot relinquish his personality to a representative, not even in religious life. That is in no way the purpose of obedience. [1]

Again we are in total acquiesce.. A perusal of Father's entire article, however, gives the impression that obedience is to be determined by the subject. In fact, Father specifically states that "the final judgment, indeed, must rest with the subject himself."

Now, let us go back a moment to that abovementioned control-center. Father need not have confined himself to this world. Even God Himself respected Adam's free will and did not force his obedience, with what drastic results we are all too familiar. No doubt Adam's rational personality assured him that this particular "fruit" was no different from any other; if he could have that, why not this? It just did not seem reasonable to him, so he disobeyed and "by the disobedience of the one man the many were constituted sinners." By the mercy of God the story did not end there for "also by the obedience of the one the many will be constituted just" (Rom. 5:19).

Later, a son of Adam, Saul, also found his rationality opposed to the Lord's commands. In defiance of orders he spared Agag and the best of his flocks. Saul's rational personality insisted that it was a shame to destroy all those fine animals; what

---

[1] Robert J. Willis, S.J., "Obedience According to the Spirit," *Sisters Today*, v. 37, no. 1 (September, 1965), p. 9.

splendid sacrifices they would make. Besides, Agag had shown some kindness to the children of Israel so he ought to be spared. It all made marvelous sense to Saul but in chiding him for his disobedience God said, "Obedience is better than sacrifice" (1 Sam. 15:1-23).

Indeed, in the Old Testament God more than once showed Himself inexorable towards those who were not obedient to His constituted authority. "Any man who has the insolence to refuse to listen to the priest who officiates there in the ministry of the Lord, your God, or to judge, shall die" (Deut. 17:12). In the wake of such a threat we find God's chosen people asserting: "Whether it is pleasant or difficult, we will obey ... so that it will go well with us" (Jer. 42:6). Saint Paul echoes this thought in his epistle: "Let everyone be subject to the higher authorities, for there exists no authority except from God, and those who exist have been appointed by God. Therefore he who resists the authority resists the ordinance of God: and they that resist bring on themselves condemnation" (Rom. 13:1-7).

Independence is in the air we breathe. It has ever been an American trait, but today more than ever freedom and liberty are key words. I cannot *give* my free will to another, even to a representative of God, for it is an inalienable gift; but I can give the *use* of it to another as to God. That is what makes obedience such a holocaust; it is surrendering the use of a faculty which is very near and dear to me. Holy Writ has coupled holiness with obedience in the words: "As obedient children

. . . be you also holy in all your behavior" (1 Pet. 2:14-15).

What do we mean by obedient? Does it mean to obey another under whom I have placed myself in voluntary subjection for the love of that God who "became obedient unto death, even to the death of a cross" for me (Phil. 2:8)? Or am I to obey only when a command (harsh word to our twentieth century ears!) or suggestion or wish of my superior accords with my own reasoning, inclination or desire? Where is there room for obedience of faith if such be the concept of obedience? "Shall I not drink the cup that the Father has given me" (John 18:11)? Did not Christ Himself say, "The Scribes and Pharisees have sat on the chair of Moses; all things therefore that they command you, observe and do" (Matt. 23:1-5)? And again, "He who hears you, hears me; and he who rejects you, rejects me; and he who rejects me, rejects him who sent me" (Luke 10:16).

Granted that superiors may give unreasonable (to me) directives; granted that undesirable results may accrue from my obedience; granted that humanly speaking, my insights or foresight, my grasp of the situation and the best means of coping with it, are clearer than that of the superior; must I still obey, shall we say *blindly,* to use a dreadfully archaic expression so distasteful to our modern ears? No; decidedly not, if we are obeying a person subject to mistakes like ourselves. Yes; most certainly, if we are obeying God, to whom we have vowed obedience and who alone can write straight with crooked lines. "Guard your step when you go to the

house of God. Let your approach be obedience"
(Eccl. 4:17). "Obey your superiors and be subject
to them, for they keep watch as having to render
an account of your souls" (Heb. 13:17).

From his earliest days as a youth Christ gave
us an example of obedience to superiors less gifted
in intelligence and wisdom than Himself, for "he
was subject to them" (Luke 3:51), His own creatures. He thus practiced what was preached by the
Holy Spirit: "It is good for a man to bear the yoke
from his youth" (Lam. 3:27).

Does that mean that we obey the directives of
a superior regardless? Not at all. Some fail seriously
against obedience while flattering themselves that
they are obedient to the letter, but "the letter kills;
the spirit gives life" (2 Cor. 3:6). It is not obedience and not a virtue at all to obey blindly if we
interpret blind obedience to mean that we obey, no
matter what the circumstances or consequences,
and say nothing. That is foolish; it is immature; it
is not common sense. We must represent *fully* and
clearly what we know from experience to be undesirable in the command. But we must be careful
that we are not fooling ourselves; that our repre-
sentations are not born of self-love—and with all
due respect to Father Willis, our rational person-
alities are so infected by self-love that no man is
a fit judge in his own regard. "You see a man wise
in his own eyes? There is more hope for a fool than
for him" (Prov. 26:12).

We have embraced religious life in response to
Christ's invitation: "You have not chosen me, but
I have chosen you" (John 15:16). With Christ we

should be able to say, "I have come... not to do my own will but the will of him who sent me" (John 6:38). "And he, Son though he was, learned obedience from the things that he suffered; and when perfected, he became to all who obey him the cause of eternal salvation" (Heb. 5:8). It is essentially through the vow of obedience "that the world may know that I love the Father, and that I do as the Father has commanded me" (John 14:31).

How significant that Saint Paul, although converted personally by Christ, when asking what he should do, was bidden: "Go into the city and it will be told thee what thou must do" (Acts 9:6), for it is God's way to use man for His purposes.

Every bit of renewal sanctioned by the Church is profitable for our salvation, just as is every bit of Scripture (2 Tim. 3:16), but no Church authority, whether of Pope, Council or Bishop, has presumed to alter the words of God; and in the Sacred Scriptures the Holy Spirit Himself has deigned to express forcefully and frequently His concept of obedience. Dare we oppose ours to His?

from *Sisters Today*, April, 1966

Religious Vows

and

Personality

All men should take note that the profession of the evangelical counsels, though entailing the renunciation of certain values which are to be undoubtedly esteemed, does not detract from a genuine development of the human person, but rather by its very nature is most beneficial to that development. Indeed the counsels, voluntarily undertaken according to each one's personal vocation, contribute a great deal to the purification of heart and spiritual liberty. They continually stir up the fervor of charity. But especially they are able to more fully mold the Christian man to that type of chaste and detached life, which Christ the Lord chose for Himself and which His Mother also embraced. This is clearly proven by the example of so many holy founders.

Dogmatic Constitution on the Church, n. 46

PERSONALITY

Very Rev. James Alberione, S.S.P., S.T.D.

True human personality is achieved when one thinks rightly and acts rightly in line with his eternal end. This goes for every reasonable and honest man in working for his end.

Instead, true Christian personality is achieved when one thinks, seeks and acts in Jesus Christ. It is a *complete* personality when one lives completely in Jesus Christ, the Way and the Truth and the Life: for Paradise.

For souls consecrated to God, personality is perfect ("if you want to be perfect") when one thinks, seeks, and lives in Jesus Christ completely, in an absolute manner; according to the doctrine and the life of perfection as lived by Jesus Christ. This perfection is attained if one detaches himself from all that which constitutes an impediment, with regard to the vows of poverty, chastity and obedience.

It means living perfectly in Jesus Christ, the Way and the Truth and the Life, as He lived perfectly.

In every religious institute this religious personality takes on its own particular hue, as well as ends and activities proper to it.

AN EXCHANGE—NOT A GIVING UP

Most Rev. Fulton J. Sheen

... Self-discipline never means *giving up* anything—for giving up is a loss. Our Lord did not ask
us to give up the things of earth, but to exchange
them for better things. "For a man's soul, what
price can be high enough" (Mark 8:23)? All exchange involves a decision as to which things we
can get along without and which we cannot get
along without. Some souls find that they can get
along without possessions, but they cannot get along
without the joy of being free from material cares
in order to possess God alone—so they exchange one
for the other, and this is done through the Vow of
Poverty. Others find they can get along without
their own will, but they cannot get along without
union with the Will of God—so they exchange one
for the other, and this is accomplished by the Vow
of Obedience. Others find they can get along without the thrill of the flesh, but not without the ec-
stasy of the spirit—so they exchange one for the
other, and this passionless passion, this inner tranquillity, results from the vow of Chastity. If asceticism were a genuine giving up, it would be a loss, a
reduction of our natures, a narrowing of our lives.
But since it is an exchange, it is a realization—a lib-
eration of the true essence of personality from the
false attachments to which the ego is prone. Some

197

men are not willing to make even the smallest exchange; they are like the rich young man in the Gospel who "went away sad because he had many possessions." A cowardly patient can refuse to have the operation needed to cure himself of his illness, because he dreads the pain that is the price of health. Knowing of our timidity in undertaking a war against the ego, Our Lord affirmed that the peace He would give would be quite different from the false complacency we dread surrendering: "Peace is my bequest to you, and the peace which I give you is mine to give; I do not give peace as the world gives it. Do not let your heart be distressed, or play the coward" (John 14:27).

THE TENSIONS OF THE MIDDLE-AGED SISTER AND THE ROLE OF THE SUPERIOR

Sister Mary Emil, I.H.M.

The woods seem to be full of prophets these days—so much so that I am greatly tempted to palm myself off as one too. The kind of knowledge you get from a real prophet, like that you get from a real mystic, is both the best and the worst kind. It is the best, because if the prophet or the mystic has a genuine pipe-line to truth, there is no better way to get truth, directly. It is the worst because prophetic and mystical deliverances are seldom accompanied by a color-photograph, enlarged, of the pipe-line. So you should always ask the prophet, or the mystic, for his ID card. I will admit right away, that I don't have any, and if I slip into any predictions of where religious life in the United States is going, they are hunches—only that. Please evaluate them accordingly.

Besides prophets, the woods harbor experts. It is a little easier to check on them, but we don't do that as carefully as we should. The method here is to find out what they are experts *in*, and then say to yourself, "What can this kind of expertise tell me about what I need to know?"

I have been asked to talk to you about tensions —the tensions of the middle-aged sister, to be specific. Now there are all kinds of expertise from which we can draw conclusions about the tensions of middle-aged ladies. There is the expertise of the psychologist, of the psychiatrist, of the general medical practitioner, of the sociologist, of the anthropologist, of the political scientist (these are coming into their own in sisterdom), of the poet, playwright or novelist with his special insight into the human condition. I do not have any of those kinds of expertness, as your program committee knew, and I am going to talk to you as though you already knew what these wise men and women have to tell you. If you don't know, then you will have to go back and do your homework. What I would insist upon however, is that these specialized knowledges cannot of themselves say the last word about the tensions of religious, because as soon as you say the word "religious" you are in a different intellectual universe, the one we used to call "supernatural" until the new theologians got us nervous.

Symptomatic of our being nervous is that we don't quote St. Thomas any more, except when we really need him. One of the "in" quotes, however, is still the one about how "grace builds upon nature but does not destroy it." That has been an "in" quote for a long time now, but I wonder whether we have not focused too much on the "nature," and on the very true fact that nature is not to be destroyed. I wonder whether we have concentrated enough on the transcendent character of how grace builds, and the fact that although it does not de-

stroy, it may go off in a completely contrary direction than nature would by itself. Grace is not just
an elongation of nature, in other words. All of this
could be amply proven from the Gospel.

I am belaboring this point because I think it is
very important for us to remind ourselves that a
theology of the spiritual life, and above all a theology of the religious life, cannot be deduced from the
premises of psychology, sociology, anthropology,
or political science. It cannot even be pulled out of
my discipline, which is philosophy. All of these dis-
ciplines must be considered. They can tell us much
about the nature which grace builds on, but they
can tell us simply nothing about grace, or how or
why or in what direction it builds, or what we
should think of the tensions which occur in individual or group life when grace tries to build upon nature. For this we need the Gospel. We need the
theory of how the Gospel principles are to be realized in the state called religious life, and we need
the practical showing forth of these principles in the
history of religious life, the history of religious orders and the lives of the canonized religious—all of
which manifest the workings of the Holy Spirit in
men and women, and which are a very precious
kind of salvation history for us.

So what I have to say today will be on the
plane of spiritual theology and salvation history—
not proposed to you by an expert, but by someone
who has read a little and observed a little, and who
can illustrate the tensions as well as talk about them.

Let me define tension for our purposes very
simply. What we will mean by the word is "being

pulled in two directions at once." Sometimes it is
good to be pulled in two directions at once, because
these pulls are like the ropes on tent-stakes, they
keep the structure balanced. Sometimes these con-
flicting pulls are bad, because they threaten to pull
us apart.

Our question is—what can the local superior do
when the sisters are being pulled in two directions
at once? Particularly, what can she do, when she is
being pulled, too? The poor local superior is expected by general government to preserve the spirit
of the order; by the school superintendent, the public and the parents to run a first class institution; by
the sisters to make a home. She has to meld persons
of different training, outlook, and perhaps even
theology, into something called a community. We
say, she has to do it—but she certainly cannot command it. In general, if the opposite pulls are making
wholesome tensions, she should rejoice, try to implant the idea that the tension is wholesome, and
above all do nothing to disturb the source of balance. If the tensions are bad, as so many are, she
should try to change what she, as local superior, can
change, and help the sister live with what cannot be
changed. The age for preachments is gone forever.
She can speak—but as *prima inter pares*. She can
lead, but best by giving example. She should beware
of even the suspicion that she is *using* the sisters to
further her own ambitions and covering up the
whole thing by pious moralizing.

All of this can be best illustrated if we take a
few examples from the many, many tensions which
challenge or bedevil sisters today.

Let me start with some ugly ones (like the day on sin in a retreat, which is such a relief to get past). There are the pulls between bad things.

The first set involves the pull between sloth and ambition. We don't need to be fussy about words, here, just honest. Instead of sloth you can say "the desire for comfort," "the wish for an easy schedule," "the determination not to work too hard or too long or to be held to any accountability." Instead of ambition say "the desire to get ahead," "to be somebody," "to be looked up to," "to dominate in some way," "to make a mark"—and so on. Now the tension between comfort-seeking and getting-ahead-seeking is a very useful one for those of us who have responsibility for running any kind of educational or other enterprise. At least getting-ahead-seeking is useful in keeping down sloth. It keeps people on the job, and is in a way the equivalent of promotion and the pay check for the lay worker. But what of the middle-aged religious? Well, her physical energy isn't what it used to be. The pull of the easier and shorter schedule is stronger. She doesn't languish after ski togs or surf board any more, if she ever did—but a quilted robe and slippers, a rocking chair and an electric heater for her room look much better now than they did when she was generating her own steam. And into the lives of most of us middle-aged ones there comes the realization that in a worldly way, we aren't going to get much of anywhere, any more. The sister in the ranks discovers that "they" are now picking superiors from classes younger than hers; the sixth grade teacher realizes that twenty years hence she will

probably still be a sixth grade teacher doing business at the same stand. The college professor realizes that she is not going to be a renowned scholar,
or a department head, or one of the people who get
selected to go on junkets to Afghanistan.

There is a contrary development which could
take place in middle age. By this time we can be
accustomed to the deprivation of comfort, and
sleep, and a "reasonable" schedule, and the drive to
get ahead can take over. What I am saying is that
sometimes one vice holds down another. Remove
ambition, and sloth may come back full force. Kill
sloth and you may get a cruel, hard, driving personality who burns up everything and everybody in her
path. What does a local superior do when she notices this tension—or more dangerously, when she
notices a slackening of the tension so that the vices
don't cancel one another out any more? Administer
a little contrary vice? Awaken some ambition to
combat sloth? Suggest a little comfort-seeking to the
sister who is trying to get ahead? It can be done,
but this is to administer poison.

The local superior should know that what
needs changing here is a whole motivational pattern, which requires to be lifted from the merely
secular to the religious level. It needed that all
along, of course, but the balance between vices kept
the fact hidden, so that you seemed to have quite
a good sister. The middle-age disequilibrium is actually an opportunity. If the sister can be induced
to take another look at what she really wants out of
life and make a new choice—she is on the way to
holiness. The task for the local superior is to

attempt, ever so gently, without condescension, or homiletics, in a spirit of frankness and friendship— and with some degree of admission that this particu- lar ugly tension and its middle-aged slackening have been experienced by us all—the task of the local superior is to get the sister to face *why* she has been doing things, and to make a reappraisal. If the local superior herself has never faced her own motiva- tional pattern, she had better stay out of this com- pletely. The odor of hypocrisy sometimes carries even further than the odor of sanctity. But a new motivational pattern isn't enough, however. If the middle-aged sister is to get in on an apostolate for the first time, there had better be an apostolate go- ing on in her house. Here the local superior should learn everything there is to learn from the psycholo- gist, the sociologist, the anthropologist, the political scientist, about building community and engender- ing enthusiasm for the common task; she should foster exchange and dialog, but she should know that the common apostolate into which our middle- aged sister will be asked to fit as a member of the team is made into an apostolate only because of an orientation which at least some of the members have toward *God*. It is such an obvious question, but the local superior cannot ask it of herself too often. Is God the object of what we all are doing here together?

Another pair of pulls which may keep itself in uneasy equilibrium is that between coldness and selfishness in personal relations versus a sentimen- tal, or *bon vivant* attitude which is just the conven- tual equivalent of the conviviality of the bridge table or the supermarket or the eternal telephone. This is perhaps more a problem of the young than it is for us, but for the young at least, religious discipline and public opinion operate to keep the tendencies somewhat equilibrated. The superior's eye can perhaps pull you out of your room during a community get-together, or dampen the hilarity of just food-and-noise parties, or discourage languishing exclusivities. By middle-age, this tension slackens too, and there could be a temptation on the part of the superiors to try to interest the recluse in Sprite and Fanny Farmer, or to convince the sister who is writing verses to a companion or killing hours in confidential self-revelations that she could use her time in a manner which we describe as more "profitable." But, as it was with the first set of pulls, so it is here. You do not administer a contrary poison. The whole motivational pattern must be transcended.

In a religious house there can be good interpersonal relations—neither cold nor sentimental, neither harsh nor hail-fellow-well-met, neither selfish nor irresponsible—only if there is understanding of what our life is, and of how our relationships fit into it. This will not come about unless there is a spirit of prayer in the house, and a spirit of true friendship based at least in part on many strong individual friendships. What can the superior do here? Well—not preach, in any event. It will help if she prays. It will help if she does what a superior can to create an atmosphere conducive to prayer. It will be good if she is secure enough not to measure the "success" of her management of the house with a noise-meter.

It will be very good if she has enough deep and true friendships of her own not to be threatened by other friendships around her, and it will help very much if she has learned from her own friendships that the good kind tend to multiply and to widen circles.

To put this in another way: if it be true, as it is, that the virgin is a sign to the whole Church that Christ and Christ alone, fulfills—then it is a scandal when we seem to see a virgin who is not fulfilled—whether the sign of her non-fulfillment be a drying up like a persimmon, a coldness and a self-seeking that everyone knows instinctively will lead to nothing but disillusionment, or a seeking of self in a set of relations with others who bring her some kind of escape from her emptiness. The local superior, more than any one else in the house, should know precisely where the scandal is. The scandal consists not in a sister's acting in a certain way; it consists in the fact that she is someone who has made a promise and to whom a promise has been made, and neither promise seems to have been carried out. If Christ does not fulfill her, it cannot be because Christ is not ready or because God is unfaithful. It is because our vows are not magic. Within the religious state, we are still free. Perhaps in a simpler age we thought of our vows as magic and our state as something which operated automatically. If this is an age in which we are called to confront our own freedom, we must perhaps face with new courage and new honesty what we did not quite face before, that even within our state, we can miss a turn. When we miss a turn on the highway we swing around and retrace our way. In our life we cannot do that, but we can do something easier. We can turn to prayer, and Christ will always be waiting at the end of that road, which might be quite short. The superior would do well to know this, by experience.

Let us consider now a tension between a good pull and a bad one. If I would contrast faith and hope with a constellation of attitudes like cynicism, sadness and discouragement and call one good and one bad, you would surely think I was wasting your time laboring the obvious. We are living in times, however, which keep tempting us to be cynical, or sad, or discouraged, for good reasons. We hear of priests and religious leaving the Church, or abandoning their vows; we peruse one issue of the *National Catholic Reporter* and feel suicidal: we read that our orders are going to decline, that we have few postulants and will have fewer. And it seems legitimate to be sad and discouraged. So someone (and who better than the local superior) must remind us that it is faith and hope which are good. They *are* good. We *are* living in the age of the Resurrection, even though it looks to us like the hour after our Lord's crucifixion, in which the veil of the temple was rent.

We middle-aged, perhaps more than the young, feel this tension between a faith and hope which have to be rather blind these days, and a cynicism and sadness which seem to have so much reason. The young are more ebullient; they can possibly ride it out; they perhaps see this as a period in which they will rectify *our* errors. Then there is the fact that we middle-aged are now a kind of skipped

generation. It was always true in religious life that
the middle-aged period wasn't very long. You were
young a long time, which meant that you weren't
to be listened to, and when you were finally sea-
soned, they would listen to you, and they would call
you "senior," not "old." So although you felt impa-
tient about it, you knew your turn would come. But
now—it is all turned around. Youth is listened to,
and there still isn't much middle age, because now
senility seems to start rather early. In any event it is
our age group which before the Council was too
young to listen to, which now is too old to listen to.
What comes through to us is that we are on the
shelf. Well, even on the shelf, we can have faith and
hope. Our whole atomic arsenal is on the shelf, isn't
it, and it is a force to be reckoned with. I think it is
the local superior who must convince us middle-
aged sisters that we are still quite a credible deter-
rent to the forces of Personified Evil, and that in
any event, these are times in which we can perhaps
be thankful that we weren't listened to! For the
petulant, peevish, cantankerous spirit which stalks
the land, at least they can't blame us, because we
were the not-yet-responsible young ones. And whatever we are now, and more seriously, we know in
Whom we have believed and we can hope in Him.

A third class of tension results from the pull between two good things. Here the resolution must
come not by denying one or the other, or by moving
to another plane, but by recognizing that we have a
creative polarity and living with it joyfully. One
such is certainly the tension between prayer and action in the lives of active religious. I do not mean

now the action which is prayer, and which we have all discussed many times, but the prayer which is done on the knees, which takes remote and immediate preparation, and to which we give complete and unadulterated time. I cannot imagine a period in the foreseeable future when the wisest of major superiors' conferences, or mothers general, to say nothing of harrassed superiors, will be able to arrange for us the kind of schedule in which the time for action and the time for prayer will not be making some kind of opposing demands on us that will create a tension. The only situation in which I could foresee even a diminution of the tension would be one in which our lives would be structured so completely and with such monastic finality that we had no decisions to make at all. As you know every trend in modern religious life seems to be in the opposite direction—with fewer structures, fewer rules, fewer bells, more scope for responsibility. It is conceivable, but not likely, that the new freedoms will be used to cut down on action and to increase the amount of time devoted to prayer. It is obviously much more likely that we will find good reasons, excellent reasons, pious and praiseworthy reasons to leave God for God day after day and to cut down on the amount of time devoted to formal prayer until we end with not only an anemic spiritual life, but also the hollow shell of an apostolate. The tension between the demands of religious life and of action will always be with us. A few years ago there was a real need to hammer at superiors and sisters and all in any way concerned with the life of sisters, including the superintendents and pastors who should be hiring housekeepers for them, that the sisters had to have time for study and time for the personal contacts which were as much a part of the apostolate as actual teaching or nursing. Now we are in a different situation, where the tension is still with us, but the more urgent need perhaps is to insist on the inviolability of some assured prayer time. What can the local superior do?

A number of things. First of all, she can see to it that every sister really feels free and comfortable about *taking* the time she needs for prayer. None of us *have* the time any more, we *take* it, for what we feel is important. How do we make the sister feel free and comfortable in this way? Well, we may not succeed entirely, but we should do what we can. Obviously, the superior should take the time herself, and the sisters should know it. Then she should give some indication of what she thinks are the priorities. You know, in a situation in which all of us have much more to do than we possibly can do, it is very tempting, in fact, it is necessary, to have recourse to the principle that we are not obliged to the impossible. Therefore if someone does not indicate the priorities, we can make our own choice of what the possible things are—and leave in or leave out of our list just about anything we want. This means the practical eclipse of the practice of obedience. The superior has this kind of cynicism coming if she tries to pretend that all the things she exhorts the sisters to are simultaneously possible although she knows they are not. She may think, for instance, that she can wring out the last ounce of effort by assigning too many things and not designating which ones should be done first. She may end by just frustrating the sister, who will let them all go—or worse, who will make the tragic choice of cheating on her prayer life.

Secondly, the superior has to believe herself, and then to make it somehow clear to the sisters that the religious community *owes* us an opportunity to *be* good. It does not owe us an opportunity to *look* good. If all we want and expect from the community is an opportunity to be good, then we know that we cannot be expected to do more than one thing at a time, and when we have used up all our time and strength according to the priorities obedience has indicated, then we can say of our daily sacrifice that it is indeed consummated, and there should be no frustration, no self-reproach. But if we expect that the community will somehow make itself responsible for us to look good on the job to which we are assigned (some of us will look good some of the time; all of us will look bad some of the time) there is limitless scope for frustration, self-pity, outrage, and feeling that we have been unjustly treated. Now either a sister can understand what I am saying or she cannot. If she does understand it, it must be on a more-than-natural level. This is where grace departs from nature. It does not destroy it, because it takes a naturally well-balanced person to have the interior calm to be able to understand this doctrine. Someone who does understand it and live with it will be a naturally better and more mature kind of person. But we are in the area of the tenth station of the Cross.

Another kind of creative tension terribly needed in our day, and terribly in need of being maintained as a tension, is that between detachment and involvement. To use the language of Teilhard de Chardin, we must combine a passionate involvement in the things of the world, with an absolute detachment. In our religious congregations today we are rapidly breaking down the old structures which prevented a passionate involvement in the needs and cares of our fellow-men—and this is good. It is not so clear to me what structures we are building to safeguard the detachment which will enable us to bring to the needs and problems of men the strength of our religious dedication. Some of this is going to be determined at the level of general chapters and general government, but many of these determinations will merely reflect what has been previously decided on the missions. And here the leadership, the intellectual leadership and spiritual leadership of the local superior, is invaluable. Of course the problem is difficult—exasperatingly so. Admittedly there are no books which contain all the answers. But the books actually do contain *more* answers than we get when we read them selectively. I think often of how Teilhard, who is certainly the prophet of involvement-spirituality, is also the author of some of the most moving passages written in our time on the diminishments which must occur if we are to move toward our own omega point. Certainly in his life, characterized by what Father de Lubac calls a fastidious attention to the least detail of his religious rule, and a detachment from his own will and his own success which are heroic by any standards, there are answers for his disciples who have learned only part of the lesson. Nor do we have to strike a fine balance between evaluating of the exemplary life of Teilhard and assessing his controversial teaching, in order to get our answers on involvement and detachment. The Gospels are there; the section of salvation history which is the history of religious life is there; the conciliar documents which urge us to take to ourselves the problems of our fellows and to be faithful to the spirit and tradition of our orders, are there. We need to ponder them together, and no one is better able than the religious superior to see that we do.

So we have talked about the tension caused by the pull of opposing bad things—which must be transcended entirely; the tension caused by the opposition of good and bad, which we must resolve in favor of the good; the tension caused by the apparent, and only apparent, opposition of goods, which we must learn to make into a strengthening and purifying force rather than a weakening and debilitating one.

Finally, let me talk about the generalized tension brought about in us by our being caught between forces which we cannot identify as good or bad but which now seem inseparable from living in the Church of 1967, a Church whose boundaries we do not even know, a pilgrim Church whose destination is often dark to us. As the people of God go swirling around—apparently in all directions at once it is hard for us to stay up on top of our mountain, giving them the splendid witness the Council called for, when we are confused ourselves. I have been somewhat intimately connected with the affairs of sisterdom for a few years now, as you may know, and I must say that as I look out on what is happening in some of the religious orders I am tempted to despair. But I know equally well that there are many good sisters, more generous and more highminded than I, who think that it is only the fears of such as I which are cause for despair. Who is right? Only God knows. Perhaps both are right, in the sense that both positions are permitted in order to balance out the other. Think of what Rahner says about the Three Days' Loss, where there was a real conflict between Jesus' duty to obey his parents, and his duty to obey the Father. Rahner observes that in life we may often have real conflicts with both sides right, and only the unappealable Freedom of God to decide. Think of what Guardini says about St. Francis, working all his life for the establishment of a way of life and a religious rule which the Church refused to establish then and which has never been established. Today perhaps we are seeing a comparable effort to cut down on legalism and live the pure Gospel. Perhaps we can resolve these difficulties in our day. Perhaps we cannot.

Our problem today is to discuss how we can live with the tensions which these uncertainties bring about, and how the local superior is to assist us. First of all, we have to accept our times. These are the ones God chose for us. He could have chosen any other. But we do not have the actual graces to live in any other. We do have the grace, one day at a time, one hour at a time, one minute at a time—as it is needed, not before, and not after, but as it is needed—to meet the problem of the moment. A religious priest—a scholar and a leader of our times, a man of the world in the good sense, wrote me at Christmas in commenting on the changes going on in some religious communities and their loss of sisters from the formation period, "Now we know what it was like to have lived at the time of the Protestant Reformation or the Fall of Rome." That sentence startled and appalled me—coming from a non-traditionalist source as it did—but whether the parallel be accurate or not, there were people who had to live out the Protestant revolt. We are going to have to live out more revolts in the Church, and our question is how can we avoid taking scandal, how can we strengthen our brethren?

Obviously we should not retreat to some familiar holes like so many frightened ostriches. We should think the problems out as they occur, one at a time. We should take stands. We should take leadership if we are called on for leadership, and local superiors are always called on for leadership. We should be involved. On the other hand, we should be willing to be pushed around; we should be content to be in darkness if light is temporarily withdrawn from us; we will have to find strength to watch good institutions break up around us if necessary.

All of this makes us feel tired, and very old. So this is just the time when we should return to the Gosepl and remember that even in the post-conciliar age it is more true than ever that unless we become as little children we shall not enter the kingdom of Heaven. There are perhaps few groups who have as much cause to resent the advice to become as children, as we sisters, because often it has been real infantilism which was expected of us, but I think that in this crisis the spirit of the child as Father Voillaume holds it out to his followers in *Brothers of Men* is what we need.

The child is eager—ready to learn new things—willing to go to new places—to do things in new ways—to embark on new adventures. And with this he is willing to learn, willing to ask for and to receive direction. He is not mistrustful, not cynical. He relies upon his father. Our Father can take care of us in any period of history, even our own.

When I wrote this paper—several weeks ago, this was its end—an ending which fits our times, I guess.

But before I had it typed up I went back, for curiosity's sake, to another paper which I wrote on the same subject—Tensions in Religious Life—in 1958. 1958 now seems an eternity ago. So much has happened. We have changed in so many ways. Most of that paper would have to be radically altered today. But it struck me that one part would not, and that I should end with you where I ended before, because as we bear witness to change we should also bear witness to the unchanging, and I would like to close with a reference to what is for us the most timeless verity of all.

In closing with an audience of superiors at the College of St. Catherine, we had worked up to the idea of a hopeful, eager buoyant spirit which should be brought to every aspect of our apostolate. "We can dream," we said, "and work toward multiplying our hospitals, our schools, our institutions, toward making the works of mercy more effective, toward forming our sisters, toward taking the leadership in social action." That is still true today—with vastly greater hopes and vastly greater hazards. But we went on, with something which is true today in exactly the same way, and I shall just quote it now.

"Somewhere, in all of this mighty effort which sisters will make in the Church of our day, there is a task for me, large or small, but mine. And here is the last tension.

"I give myself to this task. But I know that whatever I do for God I do in the mysterious framework of our Christian destiny. If I recapitulate the life of Christ, then I will indeed accomplish little or much for a while. God will cooperate. and the Palm Sundays you and I will have will be various. But the pattern of Christ's life will have to be repeated. God will seem not to cooperate all the way. Evil will seem to triumph. We will seem to be abandoned, and our work will go into eclipse. How this will come, when it will come, we do not know. But we do know that we must be ready, for the disciple is not above his Master. As a matter of fact, we have never deserved to accomplish at all, and it is abundantly clear what a limitation upon our usefulness as instruments is set by our imperfections. This Christian pattern is a hard one to accept—the symbol of it is on our persons and on our walls, and we make the sign upon us a hundred times a day. But we still hope that it will not have to be—or at least there is a tension in waiting. This revulsion from the cross all the time that we know we are walking toward it, and all the time that, please God, we try to will to walk toward it, this is the supreme tension. Our Lord bought for us the strength to endure it with a sweat of blood."

Address to New England Sister-Formation Conference,
Annhurst College, February 3, 1967

Common Life

Common life, fashioned on the model of the early Church where the body of believers was united in heart and soul (cf. Acts 4:32), and given new force by the teaching of the Gospel, the sacred liturgy and especially the Eucharist, should continue to be lived in prayer and the communion of the same spirit. As members of Christ living together as brothers, religious should give pride of place in esteem to each other (cf. Rom 12:10) and bear each other's burdens (cf. Gal. 6:2). For the community, a true family gathered together in the name of the Lord by God's love which has flooded the hearts of its members through the Holy Spirit (cf. Rom. 5:5), rejoices because He is present among them (cf. Matt. 18:20). Moreover love sums up the whole law (cf. Rom. 13:10), binds all together in perfect unity (cf. Col. 3:14) and by it we know that we have crossed over from death to life (cf. 1 John 3:14). Furthermore, the unity of the brethren is a visible pledge that Christ will return (cf. John 13:35; 17:21) and a source of great apostolic energy.

That all the members be more closely knit by the bond of brotherly love, those who are called lay-brothers, assistants, or some similar name should be drawn closely into the life and work of the community. Unless conditions really suggest something else, care should be taken that there be only one class of Sisters in communities of women. Only that distinction of persons should be retained which corresponds to the diversity of works for which the Sisters are destined, either by special vocation fom God or by reason of special aptitude.

However, monasteries of men and communities which are not exclusively lay can, according to their nature and constitutions, admit clerics and lay persons on an equal footing and with equal rights and obligations, excepting those which flow from sacred orders.

Decree on the Adaptation and Renewal of Religious Life, n. 15

LIVING THE COMMON LIFE

In institutes devoted to works of the apostolate the common life, which is so important for Religious as a family united in Christ to renew fraternal co-operation, should be promoted by every means possible in a manner suitable to the vocation of the institute.

In institutes of this kind the order of the day cannot always be the same in all their houses, nor at times in the same house for all the members. The order, however, is always to be so arranged that the Religious, aside from the time given to spiritual things and to works, should also have some periods to themselves and be able to enjoy suitable recreation. [1]

General chapters and synaxes should explore ways in which members who are called "conversi,"

[1] Commenting on this point in a volume put out by the Study Center of the Union of Major Superiors of Women in Italy (*Commento Teologico-Giuridico alle Norme per L'Attuazione del Decreto Perfectae Caritatis*), Rev. Gerard Escudero, C.M.F., points out that the time which the Instruction asks be given to religious, in addition to recreation, is obviously not given to be wasted. Time is too precious for anyone to waste it! Religious have to be educated to profit by free time for their personal perfection. This time is to be devoted to perfecting the culture "they have received in matters spiritual and in arts and sciences," which effort should continue "during the whole course of their lives" (n. 18).

"cooperatores," or by any other such name, may gradually obtain an active vote in specified community actions and elections and also a passive vote in the case of certain offices. Thus indeed it will come about that they are closely joined with the life and works of the community and the priests will be freer to devote themselves to their own ministry.

In monasteries where the stage of having one class of nun has been achieved, choir obligations should be defined in the constitutions, taking into consideration the diversity of persons which the distinction of activities and special vocations requires.

Sisters devoted to the external service of the monasteries, whether called oblates or some other name, should be governed by special statutes in which consideration should be given to the needs of their vocation which is not contemplative only and also to the needs of the vocation of the nuns with whom their lives are joined, even though they themselves are not nuns.

The superioress of the monastery has a grave obligation to have solicitous care for these Sisters, to provide them with a fitting religious training, to treat them with a true sense of charity and to promote a bond of sisterliness between them and the community of nuns.

Ecclesiae Sanctae, on no. 15 of the
Decree Perfectae Caritatis

COMMUNITY LIFE
IN THEORY AND PRACTICE

Very Rev. James Alberione, S.S.P., S.T.D.

"Congregavit nos in unum Christi amor." One and the same love has gathered us, heart and soul, around the Heart of Christ. This is true of every religious congregation, which will not dissolve even with death. A Congregation may have members on earth, in purgatory and in heaven—bound together in the bond of love.

Hence our brothers of the Church in heaven offer help to the brothers of the Church being purified and those of the Church on earth. Brothers in purgatory, on the other hand give glory to those in heaven, while also, it is believed, praying for their brothers on earth and looking to both of them for help. And finally, the brothers on earth offer suffrages for those in purgatory and ask the help of those in heaven and in purgatory. What a marvelous exchange of gifts! This wondrous exchange takes place through the communion of saints in the Mystical Body which is one and the same Church.

"We, the many, are one body in Christ" (Rom. 12:5). We are members of one another, and all together, of the Mystical Body of Christ.

With death, every Congregation is consolidated and perfected. We are all brothers or sisters, in different situations, yes, but united in one goal: the glory of God and peace to men.

*

This community life is prepared for especially in novitiate.

Even though people live together in hotels, colleges, homes for the aged, etc., this is not real community life, for there is no unity in thought, in aims, in affection. Each is in that community for different reasons—some because of need, some only temporarily, some for other personal reasons. They are not united by any common duty of obedience deriving from the vows.

In the religious meaning, on the other hand, community life springs from the very nature of the community, be it called society, institute, Congregation, or religious family. It is always an association of people who want to help each other attain to sanctity.

Thus, it is a supernatural end that is being pursued through mutual help under the guidance of an authority, in the manner prescribed by the Constitutions, following the schedule, task assignments, and offices as determined by the Superior.

In this way, union of thought, love, activity and prayer is achieved. It demands, of course, both effort and emulation in spiritual progress.

This community life is particularly evident in the care given in old age, in sickness, in death, and in suffrages offered after death.

The religious community is an organism, not a mechanism. The individual serves the community and the community serves the individual.

*

In community life, personality is not repressed. Indeed, it is developed and bettered due to the new social and supernatural factors entering in. Community life is a constitutive element of the state of perfection. By making it such, the Church publicly indicates its importance for Christian sanctity.

In its formal meaning, community life entails the incorporation and enrollment of a person into a society or organism, to live its spirit. In its material sense, instead, it is the life lived under the same roof with the same group of people, following the same practices, the same regulations, etc.

In secular institutes, members are incorporated into a society and therefore, what is required for the essence of community life is there. What is missing is community life in the material sense, that is, living under the same roof, eating together, doing the same things together, etc.

However, secular institutes have to own one or two central houses, by reason of which they do have in part the material type of community life, too. This is actually sufficient for a state of perfection. The rest depends upon the particular ideal pursued by each institute.

Finally, in every form of community life, there is a material, economical aspect, for an efficient organization of the assets of the society; there is specialization in work to be done; energy is opportunely freed for activity that is directly apostolic; order is introduced into such matters as meals and leisure, for the edification of all.

*

Common life should be a check on deviation and on the almost inevitable imperfections.

There are general and common dangers involved in community life, however. We could summarize them thus: rigid conservatism, because of which details are blown up out of all proportion; incapacity for collaboration with fellow-religious; stubborn narrow-mindedness in one's approach to achieving the ideal; lack of understanding for the ideals and apostolate of others, and so forth.

In addition, there are partial failures in community life which hurt the life of sanctification. An environment barren of enthusiasm, for example; a community life lacking in generosity; constant and at times ill-willed misunderstandings between diverse, shallow characters—such things can discourage even the most courageous souls and impede, at least apparently, the full radiance of authentic sanctity.

Life becomes depressing under such circumstances; members are discontented, and they live on memories or pessimism or inconclusive criticism of one another or of another house of the Congregation.

Defects of a worse nature, perhaps, are those which may be said to be transferrals to a collective level of non-virtuous tendencies which one has avoided on the personal, individual level. Thus, one

may be humble personally yet full of pride or
ambition for his community. One may be poor and
detached from possessions personally yet stop at
nothing to enrich his institute. Again, one may show
no self-interest at all, but resort to exaggerated
propaganda to achieve community goals. Or finally,
one might be preoccupied about promoting community obedience while striving to increase every
form of personal exemptions.

*

There are innumerable advantages in community life. It is a source of great merit, due to
the continual renunciation it requires, since food,
clothing, dwelling and schedule are common to all.

It promotes constant faithfulness to prayer, to
maintain fervor and to promote progress; in addition, it provides for spiritual reading, for preaching,
for correction.

The assistance of Superiors helps to avoid many
dangers which are faced in a free, independent life.

Community life brings happy, serene companionship with good brothers or sisters who are united
in the pursuit of the same ideal.

The eucharistic presence of Christ in a religious
family, through the common sacrifice and the eucharistic agape, is the source of unity, nourishing
and assuring it. Jesus is living therein as a member
and as head of the members of the community, and
by reason of His real and always active presence.
He is the Way, the Truth and the Life.

In community life, study becomes easier because of the silence and recollection, good teachers, good libraries, etc.

The apostolate benefits, due to the collaboration of members, just as any artistic endeavor benefits from the collaboration of specialists. On the other hand, how many times individual efforts, lacking organization, fade out in empty desires, unsuccessful attempts, and final disillusionment— and this despite energetic effort. What is needed is collaboration to prepare the bread of spirit and truth.

*

Common life has certain requirements. It demands sociability. The human person is a social being by nature. . . . With the exception of special and very rare vocations, man tends spontaneously to congregate, to share views, to live with others, at every age. Isolation is generally feared.

But the ideal is not a sheep-like following of others to the point of absorbing everything from one's surroundings and fellow religious; not blind compliance to the point of losing one's personality. One must know how to be sociable and still keep apart somewhat to avoid being wholly influenced by such things as empty reading, films, television, and radio. Otherwise, a kind of stupidity of slavish possessiveness can develop, a lack of reflection and consequently a lack of guiding ideas and principles.

Community life requires obedience. In taking the vow, religious assume the obligation of living a life of observance. If later on they begin to quibble about the Superior's authority, about directives given, about opportunities to do things, and so forth, what will happen? Little by little, what was given to God will be taken back, which is injustice. When he professes his vow, the new religious signs a blank check, in a real sense, and the Superior will fill it out. The religious will be required to pay, no matter what desires he may have.

And is injustice also involved if he does not? Yes. As a member of society, each must contribute to the common good, just as he shares in the common benefits.

✻

Common life requires charity. Selfishness militates against it. For self-centeredness gradually prods a religious to formulate his own *modus vivendi*, a very personal thing. And then his one thought is to get all he can from the Congregation while giving as little as he can.

What pitiable situations thus develop! You see some generous brethren overloaded with work, while others play the role of critical, fault-finding spectators.

Burdens have to be distributed in a community, just as offices and benefits are. At times Superiors make the mistake of piling work on a few, who always respond generously. At other times they receive unjustified refusals from subjects who find ways and excuses to avoid shouldering the burdens of the community. And these very people are often just the ones who are the most demanding when it comes to food and dress, to vacations and conveniences, to rest and exaggerated care of health.

"Let us consider how to arouse one another to charity and good works" (Heb. 10:24).

"May the Lord direct your hearts into the love of God and the patience of Christ" (2 Thess. 3:5).

"God is love, and he who abides in love abides in God, and God in him" (1 John 4:16).

"Bear one another's burdens and so you will fulfill the law of Christ" (Gal. 6:2).

"Owe no man anything except to love one another; for he who loves his neighbor has fulfilled the Law" (Rom. 13:8).

✽

In communities, there are individuals who try to dominate others and become ringleaders, so to speak; they find followers to applaud them on without looking into the matter and exercising self-control. Thus, it takes just one such person to lower the moral level of the whole community.

Let Superiors teach subjects the art of reflecting, of acting on principle. Let them form religious who are docile; but let them keep their subjects from being infantile. How many religious let themselves be entirely ruled by the influence of the group, beyond all proportion, to the point of becoming de-personalized! If one is to make wholesome spiritual progress, he has to learn how to withdraw into himself at times, make decisions, live as an adult, in other words. Decisiveness, energy, resoluteness, sureness of principle—these are the qualities which give us excellent religious, excellent educators, excellent guides of souls.

The ability to make living together warm, joyous and serene is a great gift. In such an atmosphere, there will be fun and jokes, but nothing undignified; seriousness, but at the right time; a readiness to give in but not weakness; order, but not to the point where it becomes a mania; the habit of yielding to others, but not from motives of too intimate friendship; respect for a variety of ideas and customs, but not renunciation of one's own ideas if they are upright and sure.

*

Let there be love in obedience and obedience in love. The party spirit in an institute brings grave consequences: discord in thought, in aims, in character, in principles, in apostolic activity, and so forth. The Congregation's spirit is destroyed in its foundation and in its life. Unity is so important that for its sake all individual interests and views must be sacrificed.

May the Holy Spirit let us see our superiors as having been given us by God for our sanctification and our fellow religious as co-travellers toward eternity. May He help us to live in supernatural love, showing goodness to all, praying for all, giving edifying example to all. May our religious houses be filled with the warmth of this love of God in neighbor, which makes His presence so strongly felt.

Discord among major superiors, general councillors and provincials is the worst thing possible. Warm understanding between them, on the other hand, is of immense inspiration to all.

Discord among provincial councillors is serious, too, whereas fraternal unity strengthens and consolidates the whole of religious and apostolic life.

Less serious, but still the cause of much suffering, is discord among local councillors. Here again, harmonious relationships, on the contrary, lighten the daily load and make for happy living.

In council meetings, every councillor is free to express his view humbly and clearly—indeed, it is his duty. But once a decision is reached, only one opinion must remain. Nor is it permissible to reveal afterwards which councillor held this or that opinion in the meeting.

*

Let us take a lesson from the fact that our Divine Master repeated the petition, "that they may be one," four times in His priestly prayer.

In His priestly prayer, Jesus prayed for His apostles thus: "Holy Father, keep in thy name those whom thou hast given me, that they may be one even as we are" (John 17:11).

"Yet not for these only do I pray, but for those also who through their word are to believe in me. That all may be one, even as thou, Father, in me and I in thee; that they also may be one in us, that the world may believe that thou hast sent me. And the glory that thou hast given me, I have given to them, that they may be one, even as we are one: I in them and thou in me; that they may be perfected in unity, and that the world may know that thou hast sent me, and that thou hast loved them even as thou hast loved me.

"Father, I will that where I am they also whom thou hast given me may be with me; in order that they may behold my glory, which thou hast given me, because thou hast loved me before the creation of the world. Just Father, the world has not known thee, but I have known thee, and these have known that thou hast sent me. And I have made known to them thy name, and will make it known, in order that the love with which thou hast loved me may be in them, and I in them" (John 17:20-26).

We are all servants. No one is a lord. We are all striving for perfection. No one is already perfect.

FAMILY SPIRIT

Very Rev. James Alberione, S.S.P., S.T.D.

The second greatest commandment, according to our Divine Master, is "You shall love your neighbor as yourself." We have to love our brethren in God, but love has to be orderly: in other words, greater love must be had for those who are closer to God and for those who are closer to us as members of our family.

Religious families resemble natural families and have the same basic foundations as these natural societies. But religious families are immensely superior.

The members of a family are united by a blood tie. The family is founded on a contract-sacrament. God is its author. Indissoluble obligations unite the members, and there is deep solidarity there.

A religious family, which is of its nature spiritual, surpasses this natural family. You join it through a divine call, which takes the place of the call of blood ties. "He who loves father or mother more than me is not worthy of me," said our Divine Master. And again: "Everyone who has left house, or brothers, or sisters, or father or mother or wife or children, or lands, for my name's sake, shall receive a hundredfold and shall possess life everlasting" (Matt. 19:29).

Religious families are much larger than human families.

It is the Heavenly Father who sends members to the religious family, and He is the Father of this family. Jesus Christ is our older Brother. The Holy Spirit is the soul of the family. The ideals shared by the members are sanctity and the apostolate. The fraternal help they give one another consists in prayer, example and active collaboration.

THE IMPORTANCE OF THE PRACTICE OF FRATERNAL LOVE IN GENERAL

All that refers to charity is to be applied to the religious community, but with greater urgency, for the family spirit which should reign in a community of religious is an especially tender charity, wholeheartedly dedicated, and very necessary.

Social reasons: The very close, uninterrupted relationships that life imposes on the members of a religious community result in a social spirit of an absolute nature. A religious community that enjoys a family spirit is a heaven on earth, whereas one in which this spirit is missing runs the risk of being a little hell.

Demands of the Congregation's particular spirit: Every Congregation has its own spirit, its "own gift." It is this spirit which is its soul and the source of its productiveness—as well as its reason for existence, as approved by the Holy See. If in studying the spirit, the members of the Congregation become enthusiastic over this gift of God, they will experience the family spirit much more intensely.

Moreover, because of their family spirit, they will take a personal interest in the Congregation's particular spirit and defend it. Only true religious living in accord with the very soul of their Institute assure its fervor and vitality.

Means of apostolic fruitfulness: "United we stand. . . ." The family spirit achieves union, as if all the members possessed but one soul. Right here we see a guarantee of success, but from the supernatural point of view, even more so. For where God is, His blessing is, and God is love. Where two or three are gathered together in the name of Jesus Christ, He is in their midst. So, then, what great things will He not do when a community and above all an entire Congregation are gathered together in the love of Christ?

Condition for Development: The family spirit urges every member instinctively to work for the community's growth in number and in the quality of its works. Furthermore, a supernatural factor enters in: fervor and the family spirit in an institute arouse in others the desire to join, to enter into it. And they will find happiness and the means of sanctifying themselves and others.

Every Congregation and every religious community is a family of God. Superiors must be fathers or mothers, not the heads of a firm; subjects are not employees, they are sons or daughters. These principles will determine the reciprocal relationships.

On the part of Superiors, there should be: A *father's or mother's love,* which is a sharing in the

love of the Father for His favorite children—generous children who have left everything behind to
consecrate themselves to the love of God and the
service of their fellow man. It is essential, therefore,
especially in delicate situations, for Superiors to remember that they are at the head of the Congregation or community not in their own name, but in
God's, and that their subjects are sons or daughters
of God, brethren of Jesus Christ. So their duties
toward them are those of a supernatural fatherhood
or motherhood. This consideration will inspire the
Superior's manner of thinking and speaking, and his
directives. Subjects must feel themselves to be sons
and daughters loved with a supernatural love, for
God and themselves, and not for services they might
render the Superior.

There should be trust. The whole Congregation or community is striving for the same goals.
Let the Superiors, then, on certain occasions, share
with the members whatever discretion permits, concerning successes achieved, difficulties encountered,
and plans for the future. They will find that their
subjects show far greater interest and readiness even
for sacrifice, happy to see their efforts appreciated.
The results will be a community achievement and
much surer.

Discretion is required. Superiors have to remain silent on all that is to be kept secret, particularly on the conduct of members or on what their
sons or daughters have told them in confidence,
even when silence is not strictly obligatory.

There must be understanding. There are times when one must interpret the rule in view of a greater good to be attained or an evil to be prevented. Let the Superior always be a father or mother, not an official applying a rigid regulation with unyielding uniformity. Souls can find themselves in unusual circumstances; life's moments are never all the same. Even Congregations themselves are subject to crises—unfavorable circumstances and needs not all can understand.

There must be responsibility. Superiors are obliged to see to it that the rule is kept, and they are guilty if they neglect this duty; they must prevent the community from becoming lax. Naturally some situations need careful handling. Before giving orders or making some correction, it pays at times to think about the matter at length, to pray and seek advice, so that everything will be done in the best way possible and at the best time. Always try to foresee whether a given procedure will arouse good will and not irritation.

On the part of the subjects there should be:

Guiding principles and goals that are supernatural.

Love. Let them see and love the Lord in those who have the duty of guiding them to sanctity.

Respect. Let them neither consider nor rest their obedience on the natural qualities of their Superiors. Rather should they see them as the representatives of God.

Trust. Let subjects not accept the authority of their Superiors from personal reasons or advantages.

Rather, they should always keep before their eyes the goal to be achieved, which is spiritual and apostolic progress. Superiors may well be especially competent at governing, but what is more important is the fact that they are enlightened by God in ways that others are not. Moreover, they are sustained by special graces in carrying out their office.

Submission. "He who hears you, hears me; and he who rejects you, rejects me; and he who rejects me, rejects him who sent me" (Luke 10:16). Obedience is a required condition for achievement of the Congregation's goal, both general and particular.

Dedication. In other words, there should be a cheerful readiness so that the Superior will not be confronted with protests or a wave of ill humor.

*

Relationships between religious should draw their inspiration from fraternal love, though in a higher degree than is found in natural families. Always there should be "one heart and one soul," as was said of the early Christians.

For this reason, whatever could cause division and rancor is to be eliminated. Let there be no detraction, no unjustified denunciation, no reciprocal criticism. The Book of Proverbs hurls a terrible curse at those who create divisions: "There are six things the Lord hates, yes, seven are an abomination to him: . . . he who sows discord among brothers" (Prov. 6:16-19).

St. Basil, St. Bernard and St. Ignatius wanted to see sowers of discord dismissed from the Congregation if possible or at least separated from the rest of the community.

If character differences, certain failings or some particular act has chilled the atmosphere somewhat, union, peace and love should be re-established by having recourse to the thought that each religious is a brother or sister to the others and all are children of our Heavenly Father.

Union of mind. Charity does not demand that religious entertain no personal views or that they be obliged always to accept the ideas of others. Yet it produces a visible widespread agreement of opinion, of feeling and of aims. Shared principles, shared goals, shared means to the end, and the same formation received in religion all contribute to drawing viewpoints close together. Still there will be cases of difference of opinion, and St. Augustine's rule can then be applied: "When things are certain, let there be unity; if there is doubt, let there be freedom; in all things, let there be charity."

Union of heart. This will not come hard if the supernatural spirit is the guiding principle. Indeed, such union will run deep.

Union in speech and manner. What is required here is careful avoidance of biting words and harsh mannerisms. Let religious treat one another with the thoughtfulness that faith and courtesy inspire. The habit should be formed of taking a humble approach in our dealings with others, of being inclined to receive the worthwhile ideas of our brethren.

Union in activity. This unity is necessary for the success of all undertakings to promote God's glory, peace for men, and personal sanctification. True, in any institute, there are a variety of duties and tasks, but let each member do his part in the achievement of the mission as a whole.

Union of prayer. It has been said that in addition to the communion of saints in general, which unites all members of the Church on earth, in purgatory and in heaven, there is another special communion of saints: the sharing of merits, prayers and good works of all the members, living and deceased, of every Congregation. Members of the same religious family should willingly pray for one another, call on deceased brethren, and offer suffrages for those who may still be in purgatory. Their prayers ought also to be offered for those outside the community to whom its apostolate is addressed: students, readers, patients, cooperators, etc.

The spirit of faith is of course indispensable here. Let every member of the religious family remember always that this family is an image of the Heavenly Family, and that its members will one day be reunited in heaven.

The Holy Family of Nazareth gave us the best example on this earth of a religious family. What exquisite thoughtfulness was shown there! What mutual respect! What concern for one another! They shared everything—joys, sorrows, trials, and consolations. Their common aim was to carry out God's plans for the redemption of mankind.

✽

To achieve what can and must be achieved, that is, a "religious life that is heaven on earth," two conditions must be fulfilled:

Faith, by which we shall always see Christ in our brethren. In trying moments, it will be well to remember the Gospel words of Jesus foretelling the general judgment: "I was hungry and you gave me to eat; I was thirsty and you gave me to drink, I was a stranger and you took me in; naked and you covered me; sick, and you visited me; I was in prison and you came to me.... As long as you did it for one of these, the least of my brethren, you did it for me" (Matt. 25:35-36, 40). "And the just [will go] into everlasting life" (Matt. 25:46).

Renunciation, which is indispensable in community life, since the latter is life in society. Differences in temperament, in age, in habits, in thinking, in experience, in occupations and tendencies—all this is bound to result in suffering for all. For this reason, we must always be ready to put up with things, to renounce our own views, to admit our faults, to show kindness, etc. And all this entails renunciations of every kind.

Nor is this renunciation concerned only with our duties toward our brethren. It is more extensive than that. Very often renunciation is needed to accept tasks or offices, and to offer one's help to the Congregation and the community in its many needs.

✽

One heart and one soul!

COMMUNITY LIFE
IN THE LIGHT OF THE
COUNCIL OF LOVE

Rev. Mother Ignatius, D.S.P.

In the past few years we lived through the Church's *historic hour*. We followed the developments of the Council, perhaps not in its particulars, which are not of prime importance, but in its basic outlines, its character and purpose, and therefore in its decrees, constitutions, and declarations.

Much prayer was offered for the Council. All over the world, in diverse languages, people prayed, "O dear Guest of souls, confirm our minds in the truth and dispose our hearts to obedience, so that the deliberations of the Council may find in us wholehearted assent and prompt fulfillment."

Much has been said about the Church in these last few years. The lives and accomplishments of the Popes, especially the recent ones, have exalted it and made it known to the world in a truer and clearer light. Paul VI, continuing the work of his predecessors, especially of John XXIII, has invited the Church to *study* itself, in order to present itself to the world in its true light—without spot or wrinkle, to speak to everyone, whether Catholic, Christian or Non-Christian, the words of peace and love which flow from the Heart of Christ, Master and Savior of mankind.

We have witnessed this tremendous spectacle; we were moved by it and rejoiced over it. We felt happy to be children of this Church, to have, in a sense, placed our lives at its service for the glory of God and good of souls. The progress of our Mother, the Church, is also our progress. Her accomplishments stir and gladden us; we feel that her concerns and desires are also ours. Let us thank God for this awareness of being in the Church, for this "feeling with the Church," for laboring in the Church, with the Church, and for the Church.

However, this favored position of ours, of such special importance and so delicate, makes us aware of a proportionate responsibility. We must think of this and face up to it with humility and faith. In other words, now more than ever before, we must have an ardent desire and firm intention *to live our vocation* in its fullness, without compromises or half measures—and this with ever-growing, ever-deepening serenity and trust. For extensive and deep indeed are the reasons for serenity and trust in one who lives with God and for Him every minute of her life.

Our collaboration in spreading the light and fire of the Council must embrace our whole lives, extending to each moment, because our lives,—our personal lives, our community life, and our life in contact with externs for reasons of apostolate—must be illumined by this supernatural light, enkindled and inflamed by this fire of love of God.

Let us not forget that we must cooperate actively for the realization of the aims of the Council, that Council which has been so aptly called the Council of love. And this collaboration is to be carried out in the practice of genuine love. of Christian charity. This charity, as we well know, is ordered; it must first be directed toward ourselves, in the right sense, and then toward our fellow religious, who share our lives. Yes, to actualize the aims of the Council of love we must first of all consider, practice, and bring to perfection our interior life and *fraternal charity*. Unless we take this as our point of departure, we run the risk of deceiving ourselves as to our share in the historic hour in which the Church is living. We would show that we did not grasp the spirit and significance of the Council of love. Thus our external activity, our apostolic collaboration would be likely to be very superficial, devoid of soul, deprived of God's blessings and, therefore, of effectiveness.

Let us not think that we can somehow reach and help distant brethren if we are unable to put up with and indeed sincerely love the companions of our daily life—love them just as they are, with their less pleasing qualities, and love them supernaturally, for love of God, seeking to see His image in them even if the image has been obscured by the defects inherent in our nature. Let us render our charity always more supernatural; it will thus be more perfect, more pleasing to God and more meritorious. And it will be easier to practice. Let us all love one another, have compassion for one another, put up with one another, forgiving and helping each other. In a word, let us *love* one another with the Love which Jesus gave us and taught us.

Thus we will effectively collaborate in the actualization of the Council of love, in a concrete way devoid of illusion. This ought to be the endeavor of all, but especially of Superiors. These fraternal words I address to them; to them I entrust the task inherent in their office of reflecting, in the light shed by the tabernacle and the Gospel, on how to put this into practice in their own communities, each with its own members, on how to accomplish this duty which pertains to all but especially to those who hold positions of responsibility.

Pray, reflect, and ask objectively: *Here and now, in the circumstances in which I find myself, what must I do, what can I do, to collaborate with the Council of love?*

The response will be clear, convincing and enthusiastic, especially if one ponders the examples of the Divine Master, Who "taught first with example and then with word."

The Religious

State as

Witness

By their state in life, religious give splendid and striking testimony that the world cannot be transformed and offered to God without the spirit of the beatitudes.

Dogmatic Constitution on the Church, n. 31

Religious should carefully keep before their minds the fact that the Church presents Christ to believers and non-believers alike in a striking manner daily through them. The Church thus portrays Christ in contemplation on the mountain, in His proclamation of the kingdom of God to the multitudes, in His healing of the sick and maimed, in His work of converting sinners to a better life, in His solicitude for youth and His goodness to all men, always obedient to the will of the Father who sent Him.

Ibid. n. 46

YOUR LIFE MEANS
CHRIST LIVED AND WITNESSED

Pope Paul VI

Beloved daughters, we welcome you with fatherly feelings. And in greeting you our thoughts turn to the immense ranks of your fellow Sisters who are surely spiritually present with you here at this meeting with the humble successor of St. Peter.

Our greeting, filled with respect, gratitude, and reverence, is extended to them; to all those who happily and actively, *quasi apes argumentosae* (as busy bees), pray and work in your religious families of different names and places, toward the interests of God's kingdom, toward helping the Church, and for the good of souls.

Our greeting also extends to all the Sisters in Italy, humble and reserved, generous and sacrificing, who spend their lives in cloistered convents, or in contact with the poor, with children, the sick, with those who are forsaken by society; or in asylums and schools, in hospitals and orphanages, in the seminaries and in the parishes, in a teaching post or behind a printing press, in humble daily services, as well as in delicate commitments for the apostolate.

We express our thanks and our open and moving encouragement to all of them. And to all of them we wish to say: the Church loves you, for what you are and for what you do for the Church, for what you say and for what you give, for your prayer, for your renunciation, for the gift of yourselves.

Do you perhaps hold doubts as to this love of the Church for you? No, indeed not. The words of our predecessors are there to give evidence to you of the feelings of the Chair of Peter toward you; the council documents in the beautiful passages devoted to sanctity and religious perfection, as well as to a renewal of the religious life, are also there to show you how much the Church of our times holds you dear and how much she expects of you.

The Church loves you above all for the religious state you have chosen, because you have desired the better part, that which will not be taken from you (cf. Luke 10:42).

Your life means, in fact, a search for Christ; Christ put at the peak of all thought, Christ lived and witnessed in the world, Christ seen and served in your brethren.

Your life is the imitation of Christ, bringing to the fullness of development the consecration received in holy Baptism. As the council said in the Dogmatic Constitution on the Church, "the religious state more faithfully imitates and continually represents in the Church the form of life which Christ, as the Son of God, accepted in entering this world to do the will of the Father, and which He proposed to His disciples who followed Him" (n. 44).

And then again, through you the Church presents "Christ to the believers and nonbelievers, or as He is contemplating on the mountain, or announcing God's kingdom to the multitude, or healing the sick and the maimed, turning sinners to wholesome fruit, or blessing children, doing good to all and always obeying the will of the Father who sent Him" (*ibid.*, n. 46).

In this light of the imitation of Christ, we may understand the meaning of perfection, either already achieved or to be achieved, which is a continuous extending of oneself toward Him, in accordance with the Pauline thought: "For his sake I have suffered the loss of all things, and I count them as dung that I may gain Christ and be found in him . . . so that I may know him and the power of his resurrection and the fellowship of his sufferings: become like to him in death. . . . Not that I have already obtained this, or already have been made perfect, but I press on hoping that I may lay hold of that for which Christ Jesus has laid hold of me" (Phil. 3:8-12).

Still in this light, your life presents needs worthy of consideration, which the Church will not fail to keep always present in order that the state of a life consecrated, under all of its human and supernatural aspects, be more and more strengthened and may respond more and more clearly to the ideal of which it is the mirror and example.

The Church, again, loves you for what you give to her, through the contemplative and active life:

—She loves you for the faithfulness which you profess to Christ and to the Gospel spirit of the

Beatitudes, of which you are in the world the living testimonial;

—She loves you for the vivid and leading example which, in spite of everything, in spite of criticism and aversions, makes you extremely precious, because, if there is still so much good in the world, it is also because there are those who look to you, though they may not let you know, and who draw from your example the strength to remain faithful, though amidst difficulties and temptations.

The Church loves you for the services that you lend to her, in the variety of your vocation, for the effectiveness with which you support her prayer, her apostolate, her struggles, through the continuous contribution of a life spent for her.

No, you have not become strangers to the world, or useless to the earthly city. This the council also wished to say in pointing out that the Religious "though in some instances do not directly mingle with their contemporaries, yet in a more profound sense are united with them in the heart of Christ and cooperate with them spiritually. In this way the work of building up the earthly city can always have its foundation in the Lord and can tend toward Him. Otherwise those who build the city will perhaps have labored in vain" (Dogmatic Constitution on the Church, n. 46).

The Church loves you for all of these reasons. . . .

Address to the 14th General Conference of the Union of
Major Women Superiors of Italy, May 16, 1966

WITNESS TO OFFSET MATERIALISM

We should show how authentic living of the religious life, in the spirit of faith, through the practice of the vows and the common life, can give the world the witness it needs to offset materialism, lust for riches and that deification of liberty or reckless individualism which is so common.

Father Germaine-Marie Lalande,
Superior General of the Congregation of the Holy Cross

The Religious Vocation:

Exceptional Choice

of Service to God

and the Church

Members of each institute should recall first of all that by professing the evangelical counsels they responded to a divine call so that by being not only dead to sin (cf. Rom. 6:11) but also renouncing the world they may live for God alone. They have dedicated their entire lives to His service. This constitutes a special consecration, which is deeply rooted in that of baptism and expresses it more fully.

Since the Church has accepted their surrender of self they should realize they are also dedicated to its service.

This service of God ought to inspire and foster in them the exercise of the virtues, especially humility, obedience, fortitude and chastity. In such a way they share in Christ's emptying of Himself (cf. Phil. 2:7) and His life in the spirit (cf. Rom. 8:1-13).

Faithful to their profession then, and leaving all things for the sake of Christ (cf. Mark 10:28), religious are to follow Him (cf. Matt. 19:21) as the one thing necessary (cf. Luke 10:42) listening to His words (cf. Luke 10:39) and solicitous for the things that are His (cf. 1 Cor. 7:32).

It is necessary therefore that the members of every community, seeking God solely and before everything else, should join contemplation, by which they fix their minds and hearts on Him, with apostolic love, by which they strive to be associated with the work of redemption and to spread the kingdom of God.

Let those who make profession of the evangelical counsels seek and love above all else God who has first loved us (cf. 1 John 4:10) and let them strive to foster in all circumstances a life hidden with Christ in God (cf. Col. 3:3). This love of God both excites and energizes that love of one's neighbor which contributes to the salvation of the world and the building up of the Church. This love, in addition, quickens and directs the actual practice of the evangelical counsels.

Drawing therefore upon the authentic sources of Christian spirituality, members of religious communities should resolutely cultivate both the spirit and practice of prayer. In the first place they should have recourse daily to the Holy Scriptures in order that, by reading and meditating on Holy Writ, they may learn "the surpassing worth of knowing Jesus Christ" (Phil. 3:8). They should celebrate the sacred liturgy, especially the holy sacrifice of the Mass, with both lips and heart as the Church desires and so nourish their spiritual life from this richest of sources.

So refreshed at the table of divine law and the sacred altar of God, they will love Christ's members as brothers, honor and love their pastors as sons should do, and living and thinking ever more in union with the Church, dedicate themselves wholly to its mission.

Decree on the Adaptation and Renewal
of Religious Life, n. 5 and 6

MORTIFICATION

Religious should devote themselves to works of penance and mortification more than the rest of the faithful. However, the special penitential practices of institutes should be revised insofar as it is necessary so that, taking into account traditions whether of the East or of the West, and modern circumstances, the members may in practice be able to observe them, adopting new forms also drawn from modern conditions of life.

Ecclesiae Sanctae on nos. 5 and 12
of the Decree Perfectae Caritatis

MENTAL PRAYER

In order that Religious may more intimately and fruitfully participate in the most holy mystery of the Eucharist and the public prayer of the Church, and that their whole spiritual life may be nourished more abundantly, a larger place should be given to mental prayer instead of a multitude of prayers, retaining nevertheless the pious exercises commonly accepted in the Church and giving due care that the members are instructed diligently in leading a spiritual life.

Ecclesiae Sanctae, on no. 6
of the Decree Perfectae Caritatis

WHAT *IS* RELIGIOUS LIFE?

Pope Paul VI

Beloved Sons,

We find ourselves filled with a spirit of great joy and no little hope as we gaze out upon this select gathering—an assembly of men burdened, as you are, with the government of such venerable and distinguished religious families within the Church. We take pleasure in greeting you here and in giving expression to that extraordinary esteem and gratitude which We hold in your regard.

You have come here to Rome to conduct the General Chapter for each of your various Religious Institutes. While these Chapters primarily have relevance to your own Orders and Congregations, yet they also influence the life of the Church; for the Church, to a great extent, derives her vigor, her apostolic zeal, and her fervor in seeking holiness of life, from the flourishing condition of her Religious Institutes.

Moreover, you have presented yourselves to Us, not only to offer your obedience to the Vicar of Christ as devoted and loving sons, but also to obtain the Apostolic Blessing that it might benefit you yourselves, your Institutes, and especially those matters that are being treated of in your Chapters. We have firm confidence that out of these deliberations and decisions there will come forth beneficial fruits whereby your religious life will be lived with greater earnestness and enthusiasm.

Although We would have most willingly granted separate audiences to each of your Capitular groups, and would have addressed each group in accordance with its proper character and current needs, yet We preferred to receive all of you together. By addressing the various Institutes all at once, We felt that We would thereby give greater weight to Our words, all the more since this occasion provides Us with the opportunity to set forth matters of importance to all Religious, however many they may be, throughout the world.

RELIGIOUS INSTITUTES
NECESSARY FOR THE CHURCH

In the first place, We wish to note the very great importance of your Religious Institutes, and to observe that your work is wholly necessary for the Church in these days. Admittedly, the doctrine of the universal vocation of all the Faithful to holiness of life (regardless of their position or social situation) has been advanced very much in modern times. This is as it should be, for it is based on the fact that all the Faithful are consecrated to God by their Baptism. Moreover, the very necessities of the times demand that the fervor of Christian life should inflame souls and radiate in the world itself. In other words, the needs of the times demand a *consecration of the world* and this task pertains preeminently to the laity. All these developments are unfolding under the counsel of Divine Providence and that is why We rejoice over such salutary undertakings.

THE RELIGIOUS STATE AND OTHER WAYS OF LIFE

However, we must be on guard lest, for this very reason, the true notion of religious life as it has traditionally flourished in the Church, should become obscured. We must beware lest our youth, becoming confused while thinking about their choice of a state in life, should be thereby hindered in some way from having a clear and distinct vision of the special function and immutable importance of the religious state within the Church. Therefore, it has seemed good to Us to recall here the priceless importance and necessary function of religious life; for this stable way of life, which receives its proper character from profession of the evangelical counsels, is a perfect way of living according to the example and teaching of Jesus Christ. It is a state of life which keeps in view the constant growth of charity leading to its final perfection. In other ways of life, though legitimate in themselves, the specific ends, advantages and functions are of a temporal character.

RELIGIOUS LIFE: A SOCIAL AND PUBLIC WITNESS TO THE CHURCH

On the other hand, right now it is of supreme importance for the Church to bear witness socially and publicly. Such witness is proclaimed by the way of life embraced by the Religious Institutes. And the more it is stressed that the role of the laity demands that they live and advance the Christian life in the world, so much the more is it necessary for those who have truly renounced the world to let their example radiantly shine forth. In this way it will be clearly shown that *the kingdom of Christ is not of this world* (Cf. John 18:36).

MEANING OF RELIGIOUS VOWS

Hence it follows that the profession of the evangelical vows is a super-addition to that consecration which is proper to Baptism. It is indeed a special consecration which perfects the former one, inasmuch as by it, the follower of Christ totally commits and dedicates himself to God, thereby making his entire life a service to God alone.

All these observations are connected with another point which solicitously, We wish to make with a fatherly heart. It is necessary that you hold the religious vows in highest esteem and that you attach the greatest importance to their religious function and practice. Only in this manner will you be able to lead a life that is becoming and in harmony with the state you have embraced—a state that you have freely chosen and in which, consequently, you now find yourselves caught up from day to day; only in this way will your state of life efficaciously aid you to progress toward the perfection of charity; only in this way will the Faithful thereby receive from you your witness to the Christian life and be inspired to follow it.

Address to the general chapters of religious
orders and congregations, May 23, 1964

FOR RELIGIOUS, A SPECIAL PLACE
IN THE CHURCH COMMUNITY

Pope Paul VI

You are the Church's. You belong to the Mystical Body of Christ through bonds of very special adherence, and you have a special place in the Church community. You are the Church's joy, you are her honor, you are her beauty, you are her consolation, you are her example. You, 'We could add, are her strength! Your piety, your humility, your docility, your spirit of sacrifice make you the specially loved daughters of the holy Church.

RENEWING A "FEELING FOR THE CHURCH"

This meeting ought to bring back to life in you a "feeling for the Church." Sometimes it happens that this "feeling for the Church" is given less attention or is less cultivated in certain religious families, by reason of the fact that they live apart and find all the objects of their immediate interest within the confines of their own communities and know little of what is going on beyond the limits of their own activities, to which they are completely dedicated. Sometimes it happens that their religious life has limited horizons, not only with regard to the course of events in this world, but even with regard to the life of the Church, her major occurrences, her thoughts and her teachings, her spiritual ardor, her sufferings and her good fortune.

This is not an ideal situation for a Sister; she loses sight of the great overall vision of the divine plan for our salvation and for our sanctification. It is not a privilege to remain on the fringes of the life of the Church and to build a spirituality of your own that has nothing to do with the sharing of words, of grace and of charity that is proper to the catholic community of the brethren in Christ.

FULLER PARTICIPATION IN THE LIFE OF THE CHURCH

Without depriving Sisters of the silence, the recollection, the relative autonomy, and the special manner that the type of life they are leading requires, We hope that they may get back a more direct and full participation in the life of the Church, in the liturgy in particular, in social welfare, in the modern apostolate, in the service of the brethren. A great deal is being done in this direction; and We feel that it is to the benefit of the Sister's sanctification and to the benefit of the faithful who are edified.

Now, then, this meeting will, We repeat, serve to re-enkindle love for the Church in you and, We hope, throughout the vast ranks of women Religious. It will serve to put you in ever closer communion with her. This is a great thought—remember it—and one that can open a window onto the spiritual reality to which you have dedicated your life; the Church is the work of salvation established by Christ. It is a great thought that can comfort and sustain the modest and the hidden nature of your works; the Church is the kingdom of the Lord, and whoever belongs to it and whoever serves it shares in the dignity and fate of this kingdom. Yes, the Church is something great to think about, and the thought opens up to your generosity pathways that enable it to be ever more productive of apostolic results, wise charity, immense merits.

Address to Women Religious, September 8, 1964

THE CHURCH NEEDS
YOUR SANCTITY

Pope Paul VI

We love the religious of Holy Mother Church. We hold in high esteem the state of sanctification and of apostolate chosen by them; with confidence we observe them blossoming in the midst of the people of God; with pleasure we recognize the importance, the generosity, the usefulness and the beauty which our religious represent not only for the Church but also for society and the world at large which, while it contends for their silent, valuable service, nonetheless often questions the legitimacy or fitness of their existence and their contribution. Indeed, we would like to see their ranks continue to swell, with never a lack of youthful souls, ardent and pure, still able today amid the hubbub of the thousands of voices and sounds of the modern world, to heed the secret, strong and sweet invitation to the following of Christ, to the highest love, to the purest, most heroic, most personal and happiest love—the call to the religious vocation. May God make it so!

Our greeting to you today, dear religious, whether you are described as contemplative or active, is meant to have both meaning and purpose. Its meaning is, as we have said already, a recognition of the special position, the very privileged position, neither set aside nor forgotten, which the religious life of women holds in the great and complex family of Christ, the holy Church. Yours is a distinctive position which calls for its own particular style of living, its own undertakings, its own mentality, its own relative autonomy. Nevertheless, it is a position which is a part of the unified plan of the ecclesiastical community; you constitute a member of the Mystical Body of Christ able to perform higher and more spiritual functions, but still essentially and organically a part of the whole body. You well know that this harmony between the Church, considered in its totality as one, hierarchical, and communitarian, and religious institutes, has been placed in a better light and made more effective by the Holy Spirit and the Decrees of the Ecumenical Council. It has come about, certainly under the impulse of the Holy Spirit Who vivifies the Church, that the Church herself feels a growing need to be adorned by the religious institutes, while these, in turn, feel a need to be joined more closely to the hierarchy and to the community of the faithful.

This is a phenomenon, a consoling sign full of promise for the spiritual life of our era and for the renewal of the Church. And note that this higher evaluation of the religious state and its closer ties with the whole ecclesiastical body is not coming about merely because of the practical and apostolic services which consecrated souls like yourselves can and do effectively and generously render to pastoral, charitable and scholastic undertakings. Nor is it due solely to organizational and operational efficiency (which would itself be enough to justify the encouragement of this advance). Rather it is also and especially due to your consecration to Christ the Lord. This is happening, in other words, not only because of what you religious do, and are capable of doing, for the good of the Church, but especially because of what you are—vowed to perfection, able to make your lives resplendent with the complete authenticity of baptism carried to those extreme renunciations which the baptismal mystery offers to those who live it in its fullness. The Church needs your sanctity no less than she needs your activity. You may draw your own conclusions, beloved Daughters in Christ; here it is enough to state one for all: today more than ever, the religious life must be lived in its genuine integrity, in its lofty, tremendous requirements, in its depth, always nourished by punctual and regular prayers, by its watchful interior life, in austere, normal, almost inborn, observance of the holy vows; in a word, it must be holy, and holy taking into account the greater needs of modern psychology and the moral battle made more difficult and strenuous by the modern laxity around us. Either the religious life is holy or it is not religious life.

THE JOY OF YOUR RELIGIOUS PROFESSION

And here we come to the particular purpose of this encounter with you—the purpose of redirecting your attention to the joy which should both clothe and permeate your religious profession. We are referring to a phrase of Our Lord's which is applied to Mary Most Holy and can also be applied to you. Recall that lively episode in the Gospel in which a woman of the people, enthusiastic over the words of Jesus, cried out: "Blessed is the womb that bore thee, and the breasts that nursed thee," to which Jesus answered: "Blessed are they who hear the word of God and keep it" (Luke 11:27-28). With regard to the Blessed Mother this reply certainly did not deny the very unique excellence of her divine maternity, but rather emphasized a personal and outstanding merit of Mary, who not only generated Christ the Lord, but also believed in Him, held fast to the word of God, and joined the merit of her docile obedience to the privilege of her election. Already Elizabeth had greeted her with the words: "Blessed are you who have believed" (Luke 1:45)! St. Augustine comments, "Mary was more blessed in accepting the faith of Christ than in conceiving the flesh of Christ" (De Virg. 3 PL 40, 398).

BLESSED ARE YOU!

Now then, dearest religious, you have listened to the voice of God and you have followed it. Is not this the hinge and secret of your lives? You have listened; you have followed; what then should we say other than that phrase of Christ's: "Blessed are you"? The beatitude of the vocation followed should be yours.

This is not an obvious and trite observation; no, it concerns a well-known mark of the religious life, which ought to be brimming with holy joy precisely because it is full of grace and love. If St. Paul declared and repeated to all Christians: "Rejoice in the Lord always; again I say, rejoice!" (Phil. 4:4) how much the more should this exhortation be directed to you, sisters and dearest daughters. The humility, poverty, hiddenness, mortification, spirit of sacrifice, and many trials and sufferings with which the path of this earthly life is strewn, should not sadden you and cannot take away the inner joy of the heart consecrated to charity. And it is just this that We wish to say to you, recommend to you and wish for you as a remembrance of this holy reunion: be happy! Be happy because you have chosen the better part; be happy because as St. Paul exclaimed, who or what could ever separate you from the love of Christ? (Rom. 8:35). Be happy because you have channeled your life into the unique and highest love. Be happy because you are the privileged daughters of the Church, and you share the Church's joy and sorrow, fatigue and hope. Be happy because nothing of your activity, prayer or suffering is lost; nothing is overlooked by that Father Who sees in secret and will let nothing go unrewarded. Be happy because, like Our Lady, you have listened to the word of God; you have entrusted yourselves to it and have followed it. And allow Us to confirm this wish for your holy happiness with Our apostolic blessing.

Address to the Franciscan Missionaries of Mary,
September 11, 1965

RELIGIOUS MUST ALWAYS LIVE AND FEEL WITH THE CHURCH

Augustine Cardinal Bea

Religious should draw their inspiration from the purest sources of doctrine, namely Sacred Scripure and the Liturgy. They also need to develop the missionary spirit and the ecumenical spirit. The riches of the Church are placed in evidence by the variety of religious institutes. It is essential for religious to remember that as well as being members of their institutes they are also members of the Church with the obligation to live its life and co-operate with the Church as she renews herself through the Council. It is the duty of religious to guard faithfully the gifts received from their founders. Nevertheless they must be ready to collaborate with others, unless there is to be a repetition of the discord and damage which have marked too many periods of the Church's history. They must not merely follow their own spirit mechanically, but must always live and feel with the Church.

**Religious
and Their
Fellowmen**

Let no one think that religious have become strangers to their fellowmen or useless citizens of this earthly city by their consecration. For even though it sometimes happens that religious do not directly mingle with their contemporaries, yet in a more profound sense these same religious are united with them in the heart of Christ and spiritually cooperate with them. In this way the building up of the earthly city may have its foundation in the Lord and may tend toward Him, lest perhaps those who build this city shall have labored in vain.

Dogmatic Constitution on the Church, n. 46

THE FIELD OF ACTION OF CONSECRATED VIRGINS

Pope Pius XII

We feel the deepest joy at the thought of the innumerable army of virgins and apostles who, from the first centuries of the Church up to our own day, have given up marriage to devote themselves more easily and fully to the salvation of their neighbor for the love of Christ, and have thus been enabled to undertake and carry through admirable works of religion and charity. We by no means wish to detract from the merits and apostolic fruits of the active members of Catholic Action: by their zealous efforts they can often touch souls that priests and religious cannot gain. Nevertheless, works of charity are for the most part the field of action of consecrated persons. These generous souls are to be found laboring among men of every age and condition, and when they fall, worn out or sick, they bequeath their sacred mission to others who take their place. Hence it often happens that a child, immediately after birth, is placed in the care of consecrated persons, who supply in so far as they can for a mother's love; at the age of reason he is entrusted to educators who see to his Christian instruction together with the development of his mind and the formation of his character; if he is sick, the child or adult will find nurses moved by the love of Christ who will care for him with unwearying devotion; the orphan, the person fallen into material destitution or moral abjection, the prisoner, will not be abandoned. Priests, religious, consecrated virgins will see in him a suffering member of Christ's Mystical Body, and recall the words of the Divine Redeemer: "For I was hungry, and you gave me to eat; I was thirsty, and you gave me to drink; I was a stranger, and you took me in; naked, and you covered me; sick, and you visited me; I was in prison, and you came to me.... Amen I say to you, as long as you did it to one of these my least brethren, you did it to me." [1] Who can ever praise enough the missionaries who toil for the conversion of the pagan multitudes, exiles from their native country, or the nuns who render them indispensable assistance? To each and every one We gladly apply these words of Our Apostolic Exhortation, "Menti Nostrae": "... by this law of celibacy the priest not only does not abdicate his paternity, but increases it immensely, for he begets not for an earthly and transitory life but for the heavenly and eternal one." [2]

Encyclical, Holy Virginity

[1] Matt. 25:35-36, 40
[2] A.A.S. XLII, 1950, p. 663

Renewal-
What It Entails

The adaptation and renewal of the religious life includes both the constant return to the sources of all Christian life and to the original spirit of the institutes and their adaptation to the changed conditions of our time. This renewal, under the inspiration of the Holy Spirit and the guidance of the Church, must be advanced according to the following principles.

a) Since the ultimate norm of the religious life is the following of Christ set forth in the Gospels, let this be held by all institutes as the highest rule.

b) It redounds to the good of the Church that institutes have their own particular characteristics and work. Therefore let their founders' spirit and special aims they set before them as well as their sound traditions—all of which make up the patrimony of each institute—be faithfully held in honor.

c) All institutes should share in the life of the Church, adapting as their own and implementing in accordance with their own characteristics the Church's undertakings and aims in matters biblical, liturgical, dogmatic, pastoral, ecumenical, missionary and social.

d) Institutes should promote among their members an adequate knowledge of the social conditions of the times they live in and of the needs of the Church. In such a way, judging current events wisely in the light of faith and burning with apostolic zeal, they may be able to assist men more effectively.

e) The purpose of the religious life is to help the members follow Christ and be united to God through the profession of the evangelical counsels. It should be constantly kept in mind, therefore, that even the best adjustments made in accordance with the needs of our age will be ineffectual unless they are animated by a renewal of spirit. This must take precedence over even the active ministry.

Decree on the Adaptation and Renewal
of Religious Life, n. 2

THE CRITERIA OF RENEWAL
AND ADAPTATION

The norms and spirit to which adaptation and renewal must correspond should be gathered not only from the Decree *Perfectae Caritatis* but also from other documents of the Second Vatican Council, especially from chapters 5 and 6 of the Dogmatic Constitution *Lumen Gentium.*

The institutes should take care that the principles established in No. 2 of the Decree *Perfectae Caritatis* actually pervade the renewal of their religious life; therefore:

(1) Study and meditation on the Gospels and the whole of Sacred Scripture should be more earnestly fostered by all members from the beginning of their novitiate. Likewise, care should be taken that they share in the mystery and life of the Church in more suitable ways;

(2) The various aspects (theological, historical, canonical, etc.) of the doctrine of the religious life should be investigated and explained.

(3) To achieve the good of the Church, the institutes should strive for a genuine knowledge of their original spirit, so that faithfully preserving this spirit in determining adaptations, their religious life may thus be purified of alien elements and freed from those which are obsolete.

Ecclesiae Sanctae nn. 15-16

RELIGIOUS IN THE POST-CONCILIAR ERA

Pope Paul VI

Venerable brothers and beloved sons, we welcome you to this audience which lets us embrace all and each of you with our glance and our heart and which from this first moment brings to our lips the most precious words of our scriptural storehouse of kind and cordial expressions: "My brethren, beloved and longed for, my joy and my crown" (Phil. 4:1).

Yes, venerable major superiors of the religious orders of Italy, we welcome you who, simply by the outline of your habits and the announcement of your respective titles, bring to us the remembrance of the saints whose students, heirs and successors you are, as though a concilium sanctorum (a council of saints) were gathered around us.

We welcome you who, like an inter-allied general staff, make us think of your "forces," of your respective religious families, as peaceful armies lined up behind us and spiritually drawn up in line before us.

We welcome you who, gathered in your assembly—a genial and promising innovation promoted in God's Church in recent years—give us proof by your simultaneous and compact presence, of a faithfulness which is rendered stronger and more significant by unity. Furthermore, you give us proof of a purpose made more practical and active by your revival, and of a need which similarly is apparent to us from your new methods of activity thought out and agreed upon to define your place in the Church and in the world.

We welcome you. Though lacking news, until these last days, of your assembly and of your visit, we tacitly were expecting this meeting. What news of the Religious, we are asked from different sources. What is their reaction after the Council? What is their orientation?

And what of this wave of modern life, which overthrows thought, mentality, culture, institutions of the past, a wave which reaches out to innovations, the goddess of modern life! What of this modern life, feverish and proud of its technological and scientific changes, satisfied with its stammering spiritual expressions, disconcerting and paltry and at times even puerile and painful, nevertheless its own, springing from a residual and unquenchable thirst for values, which remain its own, primitive if you like, but free, spontaneous, personal and existential! This wave, we were saying, of modern life, overwhelming and overturning, how do your ancient monasteries, your convents, your communities, your institutions, react to it?

What penetration, what welcome, what effect has been had on the framework of your institutions by the great questions of this newly matured mentality among men—questions of personality, liberty, the dignity of temporal values, progressive development in every sphere of humanity?

We know of the attention that each of you and all of you together devote to these problems in the new confederate forms proposed to you by the Church; we do not intend to enter at this point into the merits of such vast and complex questions. We limit ourselves to exhorting you to persevere in the perusal of the questions themselves. This is a historic hour, or better God's hour, to accomplish it with a deep commitment in the light of the stupendous words which the council spoke on the life of the Religious, beginning with those of the Constitution on the Church. There the definition of the religious life, which is doubted by certain trends of contemporary thinking, is magnificently re-established, not only in its elemental juridical elements which derive from the profession of the "Gospel counsels," but also in the spiritual and social relationship it bears in the great framework of the mystery of the Church, where the religious life is said to be a sign of God's Kingdom, a fullness, a perfection, which edifies God's people, and which directs "all members of the Church to an effective and prompt fulfillment of the duties of the Christian vocation" (*Lumen Gentium*—Constitution on the Church, 44).

The mystical, theological and ecclesiological concept having been vindicated and re-established, it will be logical, even if not always easy, to re-establish or confirm if already active, the complex observance of the requirements which are proper to the religious state. We mean to say, first, its ascetics strongly oriented toward the imitation of Christ, poor and free, and the participation, experienced daily, in His redeeming sacrifice (cf. Col. 1, 24).

Second, we mean to say its framework of discipline, which needs so greatly to be and to ap-

pear regular, and perhaps also needs to be re-
thought, not only as an arid and peremptory
relationship, but also, when it must assume severe
forms and a commanding practice on the one hand,
and docile on the other, as a fact of communion
and of brotherly association, a training ground for
charity, a garrison and an aid for faithfulness
toward the great duties of Christian perfection, a
permanent practice of conformity to the will of God
and to the example of Christ, which as is sought in
him who proposes and imposes it and such as is
welcomed in him who carries it out.

Lastly, we mean to say, its inner wealth, its
spiritual depth, its mystical and loving extension
toward union, dialogue and love of God.

We invite each of you and together with your
respective institutes, to consider what great need
the Church has of you today. The Church needs
your genuine search for Christian perfection; your
effective consecration to the sole and supreme love
of God; your example in the lived representation
of Christ; your apostolic, pastoral and missionary
collaboration; your vigorous adherence to the faith
and to the ecclesiastical teaching authority that preserves and proposes it; the epiphany of your characteristic virtues; your living and flaming charity;
your ability for prayer and evangelization. . . . Yes,
the Church needs your sanctity!

And as the Pope tells you this and asks you
for it, he exhorts and encourages you toward it with
his apostolic blessing.

Address to Major Superiors of the Religious Orders of Italy,
December 31, 1966

GUIDELINES FOR RENEWAL
Pope John XXIII

The greatest Church of Christendom is preparing to welcome the Fathers of the Second Vatican Ecumenical Council. On October 11 there will begin the great celebration on which is centered the prayerful expectation of all Catholics and, we might say, the expectation of all men of good will.

This is a solemn hour for the history of the Church. It involves, therefore, increasing the fervor of its efforts for spiritual renewal, which are always at work, in order to give new impetus to the works and institutions of its milennial life.

The clergy is already reciting their daily breviary in union with Us for the happy outcome of the ecumenical council. [1] The laity, invited more than once to offer prayers and sacrifices for this purpose—especially the children, the sick and the aged—are responding with generous promptness. All wish to collaborate in order that the council may become "as a new Pentecost." [2]

It is natural that, in this atmosphere of intense preparation, those who have given themselves completely to God and who have become familiar with the exercise of prayer and of most fervent charity, should distinguish themselves.

[1] Apostolic Exhortation *Sacrae Laudis,* Jan. 6, 1962, Acta Apostolicae Sedis LIV, 1962, pp. 66-75.
[2] Prayer for the Council, cf. A.A.S. LI, 1959, p. 832.

Beloved Daughters, the Church has welcomed you under its mantle, it has approved your constitutions, it has defended your rights, it has derived and still derives benefits from your works.

You deserve that the words of the Apostle Paul should be applied to you as an expression of gratitude for all that you have done until now, and as a joyful wish for the future: We remember you in our prayers "that the God of Our Lord Jesus Christ, the Father of glory, may grant you the spirit of wisdom and revelation in deep knowledge of him: the eyes of your mind being enlightened, so that you may know what is the hope of his calling, what the riches of the glory of his inheritance in the saints." [3]

Make this letter an object of consideration. Hear in the words of the humble Vicar of Christ whatever the Divine Master may suggest to each of you. The preparation for the council demands that souls consecrated to the Lord according to the forms approved by canonical legislation should reconsider with renewed fervor the commitments of their vocations.

Thus, in its time, the response to the decisions of the council, having been prepared through a more intense personal sanctification, will be prompt and generous.

In order that the life consecrated to God correspond always more perfectly to the desires of the Divine Heart, it is necessary that it should in

[3] Eph. 1:15-18.

reality be 1) a life of prayer, 2) a life of example and 3) a life of apostolate.

LIFE OF PRAYER

We turn with our thoughts especially towards the nuns and Sisters of the contemplative and penitential life.

On the feast of the Presentation of Jesus in the temple, February 2, 1961, while We were distributing the gifts of candles which We had received on that day, We said: "The first destination (of the candles) to the religious houses of more rigid mortification and penance is intended to affirm once again the pre-eminence of the duties of worship and of complete consecration of life to prayer over any other form of apostolate; and at the same time it emphasizes the greatness and the necessity of vocations for this kind of life." [4]

The Church will always encourage its daughters who, in order to conform more perfectly to the call of the Divine Master, give themselves in the contemplative life.

This corresponds to a universally valid truth, also for the women religious of a chiefly active life: that is, that the only foundation and soul of the apostolate is the interior life.

May all of you meditate on this truth, beloved daughters, who are justly called *"quasi apes argumentosae"* (like industrious bees), because you are

[4] Discourses, messages and allocutions of Pope John XXIII, vol. III, p. 143.

in constant practice of the fourteen works of mercy in sisterly community with your other fellow Sisters. You also who are consecrated to God in the secular institutes must derive all the efficacy of your undertakings from prayer.

The life offered to the Lord entails difficulties and sacrifices like any other form of coexistence. Only prayer gives the gift of happy perseverance in it. The good works to which you dedicate yourselves are not always crowned with success. You meet with disappointments, misunderstanding and ingratitude.

Without the help of prayer you could not continue along on this hard road. And do not forget that a wrongly understood dynamism could lead you to fall into that "heresy of action" which was reproved by our predecessors. Having overcome this danger, you can be confident that you are definitely cooperators in the salvation of souls, and you will add merits to your crown.

All of you, whether dedicated to a contemplative or an active life, should understand the expression "life of prayer." It entails not a mechanical repetition of formulas but is rather the irreplaceable means by which one enters into intimacy with the Lord, to better understand the dignity of being daughters of God and spouses of the Holy Spirit, the "sweet guest of the soul" Who speaks to those who know how to listen in recollection.

Your prayer draws nourishment from the sources of a deep knowledge of the Sacred Scriptures, particularly the New Testament, and from the liturgy and the teachings of the Church in all its fullness.

The Holy Mass should be the center of your day, so much so that every action converges on it as a preparation or as a thanksgiving. Let Holy Communion be the daily food which sustains, comforts and strengthens you.

Thus you will not run the risk, as happened to the foolish virgins of the parable, of leaving the lamp without oil. You will always be ready for everything: for glory or for ignominy, for health and for illness, to pursue your work and to die. "Behold the Bridegroom is coming, go forth to meet Him!" [5]

It would be fitting at this point to recall to you Three devotions which We consider fundamental also for the simple faithful of the laity: "Nothing is enlightening and encouraging the adoration of Jesus than to meditate upon Him and invoke Him in the threefold light of the Name, the Heart and the Blood." [6]

The Name, the Heart and the Blood of Jesus: this is the substantial nourishment for a sound life of piety.

The name of Jesus! In reality "nothing is sung more sweetly, nothing heard more joyfully, nothing more gently contemplated than Jesus the Son of God." [7]

[5] Matt. 25:6.
[6] Discourse at conclusion of the Roman Synod, A.A.S. LII 1960, p. 305.
[7] Hymn at Vespers of the Feast of the Holy Name of Jesus.

The Heart of Jesus! Pius XII of venerable memory, in the encyclical *Haurietis Aquas*, of May 15, 1956, which We recommend for attentive meditation, teaches thus:

"If the arguments on which the worship given to the wounded heart of Jesus are rightly weighed, it is clear to all that we are dealing here, not with an ordinary form of piety which anyone may at his discretion slight in favor of other devotions, or esteem lightly, but with a duty of religion most conducive to Christian perfection." [8]

The blood of Christ! "This is the highest mark of the redeeming sacrifice of Jesus, which is renewed mystically and really in the holy Mass, and gives sense and orientation to Christian life." [9]

HONOR POVERTY

Hear the words of Jesus: "For I have given you an example, that as I have done to you, so you should also do." [10] Here there is presented to souls who wish to follow faithfully in the footsteps of the Lord the practice of the evangelical counsels which are "the royal life of Christian sanctification." [11]

Jesus was born in a stable. During His public life He had no place to rest His head at night [12] and

[8] A.A.S. XLVIII, 1956, p. 346.
[9] Discourse to the Religious Family of the Most Precious Blood, June 2, 1962, cf. Osservatore Romano, June 3, 1962.
[10] John 13:15.
[11] Enc. Letter *Sacerdotii Nostri primordia*, A.A.S. LI, 1959, pp. 550-551.
[12] cf. Matt. 8:20.

He died naked on the cross. This is the first requirement that He makes of anyone who wishes to follow Him: "If thou wilt be perfect, go, sell what thou hast, and give to the poor, and thou shalt have treasure in heaven." [13]

You were attracted by the example of the teaching of the Divine Master and you offered Him everything: "the joyful oblation of all." [14] In the light of the imitation of Christ Who made Himself poor, the vow acquires full value.

It makes us satisfied with the day to day necessities. It makes us give to the poor and to good works the superfluous of our goods according to obedience. It leads us to entrust the unknown future, sickness and old age, to the care of Divine Providence, while not excluding prudent foresight.

Detachment from earthly goods attracts the attention of all, showing them that poverty is not pettiness nor avarice, and it makes one think more seriously of the Divine saying: "For what does it profit a man, if he gain the whole world, but suffer the loss of his own soul?" [15]

Live integrally the vow or the promise which makes you like Him Who, though being rich, became poor that we might become rich through His poverty. [16]

Temptations are not wanting in this respect, such as the search for small comforts, the satisfaction of food or the use of goods. You know that poverty

[13] Matt. 19:21.
[14] cf. II Paralipomenon 29:17.
[15] Matt. 16:26.
[16] cf. 2 Cor. 8:9.

has its thorns which must be loved in order that they may become roses in heaven.

On other occasions, the legitimate need for modernization could exceed limits in ostentation of construction and of furnishings. These things have sometimes given rise to unfavorable comments, even though such novelties may not have concerned the modest lodging of the Sisters.

Understand Us, beloved daughters: We do not mean that that which is necessary for physical health and for wise and fitting recreation is in contrast with the vow of poverty.

But We like to be confident that the eyes of the Divine Master may never be saddened by that elegance which could even have a negative influence on the interior life of persons consecrated to God when they live in an environment lacking an atmosphere of austerity. May poverty be given great honor among you.

We would like to direct a word of comfort especially to the cloistered nuns for whom "Sister poverty" often becomes "Sister destitution." Jesus the Son of God become poor will come to comfort you.

Meanwhile, in His name, We Ourself extend for you a hand to your fellow Sisters who are in more secure economic conditions and to generous benefactors. We encourage undertakings of this sort by the Federations of Cloistered Convents, affiliated with the Sacred Congregation of Religious, reminding all of the Divine promise: "Blessed are you poor, for yours is the Kingdom of God."[17]

Radiate Chastity

The Gospel tells us of all that Jesus suffered, of the insults that fell upon Him. But, from Bethlehem to Calvary, the brilliance that radiated from His divine purity spread more and more and won over the crowds, so great was the austerity and the enchantment of His conduct.

So may it be with you, beloved daughters. Blessed be the discretion, the mortifications and the renouncements with which you seek to render this virtue more brilliant.

Pius XII wrote about them in a memorable encyclical letter.[18] Live its teachings. May your conduct prove to all that chastity is not only a possible virtue but a social virtue, which must be strongly defended through prayer, vigilance and the mortification of the senses.

May your example show that the heart has not shut itself up in sterile egoism, but that it has chosen the condition which is necessary for it to open itself solicitously to its neighbor.

For this purpose We urge you to cultivate the rules of good conduct—We repeat it—cultivate and apply them, without giving ear to anyone who would wish to introduce into your life a conduct less befitting the thoughtfulness and reserve to which you are bound.

[17] Luke 6:20.
[18] Enc. Sacra Virginitas, A.A.S. XLVI, 1954, p. 161.

In the active apostolate reject the theory of those who would speak less or not at all of modesty and decency in order to introduce into the methods of education criteria and tendencies which are in contrast with the teachings of the sacred books and of Catholic tradition.

Though theoretical or simple practical materialism on the one hand or hedonism and corruption on the other threaten to break every barrier, Our mind is quieted by thought of the angelic legions who have offered their chastity to the Lord and who through prayer and sacrifice obtain prodigies of divine mercy for the errant in propitiation for the sins of individuals and nations.

SWEETEN OBEDIENCE

The Apostle St. Paul develops the concept of the humiliation of Jesus made obedient unto the death of the Cross. [19] In order to follow better the Divine Master you have joined Him with the vow and promise of obedience.

This constant sacrifice of your "ego," this annihilation of self can cost much, but it is also true that herein lies the victory, [20] for heavenly graces correspond to this spiritual crucifixion for you and for all humanity.

The teaching of the Church on the inalienable rights of the human person is clear and precise. The special gifts of every man must be free to be duly developed in order that each may correspond to the gifts received from God. All this is acquired.

[19] Phil. 2:8.   [20] cf. Prov. 21:28.

But, if one passes from the respect of the person to the exaltation of the personality and to the affirmation of personalism, the dangers become serious. May the words of Pius XII in the exhortation, *Menti Nostrae,* be of valuable direction also for you:

"In an age like ours, in which the principle of authority is grievously disturbed, it is absolutely necessary that the priest, keeping the precepts of faith in mind, should consider and duly accept this same authority, not only as the bulwark of the social and religious order, but also as the foundation of his personal sanctification." [21]

Here We address ourself to those who have duties of direction and responsibility.

Demand a most generous obedience to the rules, but also be understanding of your fellow Sisters. Favor in each of them the development of natural aptitudes. The office of superiors is to make obedience sweet and not to obtain an exterior respect, still less to impose unbearable burdens.

Beloved daughters, We exhort all of you, live according to the spirit of this virtue, which is nourished by deep humility, by absolute disinterestedness and by complete detachment. When obedience has become the program of one's whole life, one can understand the words of St. Catherine of Siena:

"How sweet and glorious is this virtue in which all the other virtues are contained! Oh, obedience, you navigate without effort or danger and reach port safely! You conform to the only-begotten Word ... you mount the ship of the most holy Cross to

[21] A.A.S. XLII, pp. 622-663.

sustain the obedience of the Word, to not transgress it or depart from its teachings. . . . You are great in unfailing perseverance, and so great is your strength from heaven to earth that you open heaven's gates." [22]

LIFE OF APOSTOLATE

St. Paul teaches that the mystery revealed to us by God is the plan ordained from all eternity in Christ which is to be realized in Him in the fullness of time, that is: "to re-establish all things in Christ, both those in the heavens and those in the earth." [23]

No soul consecrated to the Lord is dispensed from the sublime duty of continuing the saving mission of the Divine Redeemer.

The Church expects much from those who live in the silence of the cloister, and especially from there. They, like Moses, have their arms raised in prayer, conscious that in this prayerful attitude one obtains victory.

So important is the contribution of women religious of the contemplative life to the apostolate that Pius XI wished to have as co-patron of the missions —and a rival therefore of St. Francis Xavier—not a Sister of the active life, but a Carmelite, St. Theresa of the Child Jesus.

Yes, you must be spiritually present to all the needs of the Church militant. You may not be alien to any disaster, to any mourning or calamity. Let

[22] Dialogues, ch. 155.   [23] Eph. 1:10.

no scientific discovery, cultural convention, social or political assembly lead you to think: "These things do not concern us."

May the Church militant feel that you are present wherever your spiritual contribution is needed for the good of souls, as well as for real human progress and human peace. May the souls in purgatory have prayers so that they may be hastened to the beatific vision. Continue to repeat with the choirs of angels and saints the eternal alleluia to the august Trinity.

May those who are dedicated to the active life realize that not only prayers but also works can bring about a new course of society which is nourished by the Gospel, and in which all things work toward the glory of God and the salvation of souls.

Since the areas of education, charity and social service require personnel who are prepared for the increased demands imposed by the present-day order of things, you must strive in obedience to study and obtain the degrees which will allow you to surmount every difficulty.

Thus, in addition to your merited and proven capability, you may be better appreciated also for your spirit of dedication, patience and sacrifice.

There, is, moreover, the presage of further demands in the new countries which have entered the community of free nations. Without lessening one's love for his own country, the world has become more than ever before a common fatherland.

Many Sisters have already felt this call. The field is immense. It is useless to deplore the fact that the sons of this world arrive before the apostles of Christ. Lamentations solve nothing: one must act, forestall and trust.

Not even the Sisters dedicated to contemplation are exempt from this duty. The people in certain regions of Africa and the Far East feel a greater attraction to contemplative life, which is more congenial to the development of their civilization.

Certain of the more cultured social classes almost complain that the dynamic life of the missionaries can have a lesser influence on their manner of conceiving religion and of following Christianity.

You can see, beloved Sisters, how many reasons prompt the encouragement of meetings among superiors general which have been arranged by the Sacred Congregation of Religious on the national and international level. In such meetings you can bring yourselves more up to date on present-day conditions, profit by mutual experience and comfort yourselves in the thought that the Church has a host of brave souls who are capable of facing any obstacle.

The consecrated souls in the new secular institutes should know also that their work is appreciated and that they are encouraged to contribute toward making the Gospel penetrate every facet of the modern world.

It is right that those who are able to attain positions of more outstanding responsibility should make themselves appreciated for their competence, diligence, sense of responsibility and also for those virtues which are exalted by grace.

By doing so they may prevent that those who depend almost exclusively upon human cleverness and upon the power of economic, scientific and technical means should prevail. "But we call upon the name of the Lord our God." [24]

We invite all of you, souls consecrated to the Lord in the contemplative or active life, to draw close together in fraternal charity. May the spirit of Pentecost prevail over your chosen families and may it unite them in that fusion of souls which was seen in the cenacle where, together with the Mother of God and the Apostles, several pious women were to be found. [25]

PRAYER AND RENEWAL

These are Our wishes, Our prayers and Our hopes. The Church has called upon all the faithful on the eve of the Second Vatican Council, proposing to each of them an act of presence, testimony and courage.

May you, beloved daughters be among the first to cultivate holy enthusiasm. The "Imitation of Christ" has a touching word on this point: "Every day we ought to renew our purpose, and stir ourselves up to fervor, as if it were the first day of our conversion."

And to say: "Help me, O Lord God, in my good purpose, and in Thy holy service; and grant that I may this day begin indeed since what I have hitherto done is nothing." [26]

---

[24] Ps. 18:8.   [25] cf. Acts 1:14.
[26] Bk. 1. ch. 19, para. 1 (Cath. Book Pub. Co. edition).

May the Mother of Jesus and Our Mother fire you with new fervor! Trust in this heavenly Mother, and at the same time remain familiar with her Spouse, St. Joseph, who is also the patron of the Second Vatican Council.

Pray also to those sainted men and women who are held in special honor in your individual institutions, so that they may join their efficacious intercession to the purpose that the "holy Church, gathered in unanimous and intense prayer around Mary, the Mother of Jesus, and guided by Peter, may spread the Kingdom of the Divine Savior, which is the kingdom of truth, justice, love and peace."

We impart to all the religious communities and to each individual consecrated to God the most abundant apostolic benediction, which We intend to be a token of heavenly favors and an encouragement to live and act well "in the Church and in Christ Jesus." [27]

Letter of Pope John XXIII
"To Women Religious" July 2, 1962

THE FOUNDER'S SPIRIT
AND RULE OF LIFE

Pope Paul VI

It is quite evident that the proper way of living religious life requires discipline. There must be laws and suitable conditions for observing them. Therefore, the principal task of the General Chapter is, as time goes on, to keep intact those norms of the Religious family which were set up by its Founder and Lawgiver. Therefore, it is your responsibility to firmly shut the door against all those modes of conduct which gradually devitalize the strength of religious discipline, namely, practices which are dangerous to religious life, unnecessary dispensations, and privileges not properly approved. You must likewise be wholly on guard against any relaxation of discipline which is urged, not by true necessity, but which rather arises from arrogance of spirit, or aversion to obedience, or love of worldly things. Moreover, with respect to undertaking new projects or activities, you should refrain from taking in those which do not entirely correspond to the principal work of your Institute or to the mind of your Founder. For Religious Institutes will flourish and prosper so long as the integral spirit of their Founder continues to inspire their rule of life and apostolic works, as well as the actions and lives of their members.

Religious Communities, inasmuch as they resemble living bodies, rightly desire to experience
continual growth. However, this growth of the Institute must be based firmly on the more diligent
observance of your rules rather than on the number
of members or the making of new laws. Multiplicity
of laws is not always accompanied by progress in
religious life. It often happens that the more rules
there are, the less people pay attention to them.
Therefore, let the General Chapters always use their
right to make laws moderately and prudently.

NORMS FOR ACCOMMODATING THE
    RULE TO THE TIMES

The most important work of the General Chapters is the studied accommodation of the rules of
their Institute to the changed conditions of the
times. This, however, must be done in such a way
that the proper nature and discipline of the Institute is kept intact. Every Religious family has its
proper function and it must remain faithful to this
role. The fruitfulness of the Institute's life is based
on this fidelity to its specific purpose, and in this
matter an abundance of heavenly graces will never
be lacking. Therefore, no renovation of discipline
is to be introduced which is incompatible with the
nature of the Order or Congregation and which, in
any way, departs from the mind of the Founder.
Moreover, this renovation of discipline demands
that it proceed only from competent authority.
Therefore, until this accommodation of discipline
is duly processed and brought into juridic effect,

let the Religious members not introduce anything new on their own initiative, nor relax the restraints of discipline nor give way to censorious criticism. Let them act in such a way that they might rather help and more promptly effect this work of renewal by their fidelity and obedience. If the desired renovation takes place in this way, then the *letter* will have changed, but the *spirit* will have remained the same, in all its integrity.

Address to all Religious,
May 23, 1964

HOW HAVE YOU ACCEPTED RENEWAL?

Pope Paul VI

... With what spirit have you accepted the invitation to the renewal, not of course of the unchangeable structures, but of that which in the Church may make its methods appear as tired, out-dated, customary; may make its youthful freshness appear as dimmed; its situation appear as conven-ient; the regal way of the Cross appear as calm?

With what faith have you accepted her direc-tives in the faith, experienced and aware of her maternal and sweet authority, which is the genuine expression of the will of her Divine Founder? "Amen, I say to you, whatever you bind on earth shall be bound also in heaven; and whatever you loose on earth shall be loosed also in heaven" (Matt. 18:18).

We feel certain that all of these questions have already found and do find in you, as in all your fellow Sisters, the fullest and most ardent adher-ence; and we thank you for it from our heart.

We would like, however, to point out to you three particular directives with which to proceed in this manner of generous love for the Church:

—First of all, an ever greater participation in the liturgy, as the council decree indicated in refer-ence to a renewal of the religious life. The Religious, it said, "should enact the sacred liturgy, especially the most holy mystery of the Eucharist, with hearts and voices attuned to the Church; here is a most copious source of nourishment for the spiritual life" (Decree on the Adaptation and Renewal of Religious Life, no. 6).

—Furthermore, to be familiarized with the books inspired by the Old and, particularly, the New Testament, in accordance with the invitation of the Council: "they should take the Sacred Scriptures in hand each day by way of attaining 'the excelling knowledge of Jesus Christ' (Phil. 3:8), through reading these divine writings and meditating on them. . . .

"So refreshed at the table of divine law and the sacred altar of God, they will love Christ's members as brothers, honor and love their pastors as sons should do, and living and thinking ever more in union with the Church, dedicate themselves wholly to its mission." (Decree on the Adaptation and Renewal of Religious Life, no. 6).

—Lastly, we recommend the sense of community that surely cannot be wanting when these solid and strengthening foundations are applied. In fact, the liturgy, and above all the Eucharistic life, essentially nourishes the charity of the individual members of the Mystical Body preventing piety from becoming rigid in the sterility of individualistic and sentimental forms.

Furthermore, the knowledge of Scripture, with the wide vistas that it opens over history and the development of God's People, cannot but give open, solid, nourishing ideas on this community obligation. And where else could it better shine in example than in the religious families that make of their community life their characteristic form open to all eyes as a living testimonial of the presence of Christ? *Ubi caritas et amor, Deus ibi est. Congregavit nos in unum Christi amor.* (Where there is charity and love, there is God. Love of Christ brings us together as one.)

Here, beloved daughters, is what we wanted to say to you today. Take to your houses the words of our satisfaction, the expression of our hopes, the encouragement of our commitments.

May our prayer, which we lift up for you and all your fellow Sisters, be of comfort to you in reference to the above, together with our apostolic blessing.

> *Address to the Union of*
> *Major Superiors of Italy,*
> May 16, 1966

PERFECT CHARITY—
IDEAL OF RELIGIOUS LIFE

Pope Paul VI

... Have you told yourselves over and over
again what religious life really is in substance? You
know that full awareness of the state chosen as a
plan of life calls for recurring, constant questioning.
This is the vigilance which every intelligent person
exercises over himself and which every follower of
the divine Master imposes all the more on his own
spirit and conduct, in order to be faithful and con-
sistent with his own vocation.

You also know what a clamor has been raised
these last few years over the traditional notion of
religious life, as if this notion had to be "demyth-
ologized," as they say, or shaken and awakened
from a kind of drowsiness and enchantment which
has enveloped it over the centuries. This drowsiness is thought to be crystallized in a kind of arti-
ficial existence that lacks any profound dramatic
experience and instead is completely taken up with
ascetic and disciplinary forms which nowadays
seem a useless burden rather than a wise aid to the
attainment of that Christian perfection to which
the religious life is supposedly dedicated.

THE IDEAL OF PERFECT CHARITY

Finally, you know the words that the Ecumenical Council used to recall religious life to its essentials. Read back over Chapter 6 of the Dogmatic Constitution on the Church; re-read the Council Decree on the Adaptation and Renewal of the Religious Life. You will find a wealth of teaching that vindicates the ideal of religious life and locates it in a perfect charity. This charity is sought and attained through the practice of the evangelical counsels and the imitation of Christ, under a wonderful variety of forms that give evidence of the multiplicity, and hence the relative liberty, of the ways the Holy Spirit uses to lead souls to the goal of Christian perfection.

Read back over them and meditate. As each of you moves along the broad, steep path of the Franciscan school, he ought to think back over the marvelous figure of the lowly but great Little Poor Man of Assisi and see it reflected in the course of his own life. Each one, in the forum of his own inner experience, ought to answer the question just proposed: what is the religious life?

It means hearing in the depths of your own soul a singular and unmistakable voice calling: come! It means a paradoxical act of courage in which a person dares something beyond his own powers and—while practically suspended by a sustaining force from on high—answers yes. Then it means that impetuous but liberating detachment which has taken away from the obedient candidate, as it did from Francis, everything of his own, everything beautiful, everything most useful and dear as far as earthly goods are concerned, in order to make the chosen one free, light-hearted and unencumbered on the journey he has undertaken.

A LIVING ANSWER

Next, it means that interior absorption, unknown to those in secular life, which makes a person find within the cell of spiritual or choral prayer the meeting-point for the anticipated blessed conversation of heaven. And then it means the new friar's somewhat sublime and somewhat ridiculous return into the midst of his old acquaintances and the secular world, no longer to ask anything of them but simply to give everything, along with the discovery of a new communion with former brothers and with men who are curious to see the peculiar phenomenon of a "man who is a friar." This communion makes it possible to speak to them evangelically as no one would dare to do in ordinary conversation, and also allows a person to listen to secret confidences that are whispered to no one else except that lowly apprentice in the school of Christ. This is the answer—one that is lived rather than expressed in speculative terms. This is what religious life is.

Address to the 180th General Chapter
of Conventual Franciscans,
July 12, 1966

THE IMPORTANCE OF KNOWING
CHRIST THROUGH SCRIPTURE

Pope Paul VI

The first knowledge is that of the senses, that which St. Francis wished to give to himself and to others by means of setting up the manger, that of viewing in some way with physical eyes.

It is a very natural form of knowledge that Christ wished to grant to those fortunate people who were able to approach Him during His temporal life at that time, as the Gospel reading of Holy Mass instructs us.

It is a form greatly desired, which all of us would wish to enjoy and the saints more so than others.

Do you recall what the shepherds said, following the announcement by the angel: "Let us go over . . . and see" (Luke 2:15)? and the desire of the gentiles who were present at the triumphal entrance of Jesus in Jerusalem: ". . . We wish to see Jesus" (John 12:21)? Also the witnessing of the Apostles: ". . . What we have seen with our eyes, what we have looked upon and our hands have handled . . ." (1 John 1:1).

It was the desire of the Apostle Thomas: "Unless I see . . . and put my hand . . . I will not believe" (John 20:25).

However, this sensible knowledge had its initial, partial and temporary function so as to give concrete, positive and historical certainty to those who later would have the mission to proclaim the testimony concerning the human and prodigious reality of Jesus and to activate that new form of knowledge upon which the entire religious edifice established by Christ is founded: the faith.

It was He who admonished us: "Blessed are they who have not seen, and yet have believed" (John 20:29). St. Paul writes: "For we walk by faith and not by sight" (2 Cor. 5:7).

The fact remains that Christ's coming into the world generates for us the problem and duty of knowing Him. How to know Him? This is the question that each must put to himself: Do I know Jesus Christ? Do I truly know Him? Do I know Him sufficiently? How can I know Him better?

No one is able to reply satisfactorily to these questions, not only because knowledge of Christ poses problems and hides depths of such extent that only ignorance and not intelligence could call itself satisfied with any knowledge of Christ. But also because any new degree of knowledge which we acquire of Him, instead of calming the desire for knowledge of Christ, awakens it more: the experience of scholars and, more so, that of saints, tells this.

Therefore, beloved children, we must engage ourselves in a search for Jesus, in other words, in a study of what we can know in reference to Him.

Thus the image of the manger, in other words, the remembrance of the Gospel story, comes back to us.

The first knowledge we should have of Christ is that documented by the Gospels. Not having had the fortune of a direct and sensitive knowledge of the Lord, we must endeavor to have a historical knowledge, a sure remembrance of Him, giving due importance to the human form by means of which the Word of God has revealed Himself.

And here, at once, there arise great discussions, great difficulties, great sorceries of studies and interpretations, which try to lessen the historical value of the very Gospels, particularly those that refer to the birth of Jesus and to His infancy.

We make brief mention of this devaluation of the historical content of the admirable Gospel pages, so that you will know how to defend, through study and faith, the consoling certainty that those pages are not inventions of the popular fantasy, but tell the truth.

"The Apostles," writes one who understands these matters, (Augustin) Cardinal Bea, "have a genuine historical interest. It is obviously not a question of historical interest in the sense of Greco-Latin historiography, in other words, of logical and chronologically ordered history, which is an end in itself, but, on the contrary, of an interest in past events, as such, and an intention to report and to faithfully hand down facts and sayings of the past."

A confirmation of this is the very concept of "witness," "giving evidence," "witnessing" which recurs in its various forms in the New Testament more than one hundred and fifty times "The Story of the Synoptic Gospels," (*Civiltá Catt.* 1964; II, 417-436 and 526-545). Nor has the authority of the council pronounced differently: "The sacred authors wrote the four Gospels, selecting some things from the many which had been handed on by word of mouth or in writing, reducing some of them to a synthesis, explicating some things in view of the situation of their churches, and preserving the form of proclamation, but always in such fashion that they told us the honest truth about Jesus" (Dei Verbum, 19).

Thus reassured, the faithful must devote themselves above all with devout passion to the reading and study of the scriptural sources that speak to us of Jesus.

Faith must be nourished with this sacred doctrine. We must desire the "excelling knowledge of Jesus Christ" (Phil. 3:8) which St. Paul put before any other thing.

To know Jesus Christ: this today is our exhortation, beloved children, together with our apostolic blessing.

Address to a general audience,
January 31, 1967

KNOW, IMITATE AND LIVE JESUS

Pope Paul VI

To know Jesus, to imitate Jesus—is this not the highest norm, the all-inclusive norm of all our duties? He is to be followed, with that obedience which makes the lowly great, wherever He wishes, however He wishes, all the way to Gethsemane, all the way to Calvary! We are to announce Jesus— what joy, what love, what merit could surpass this? —Jesus is to be lived: "For me to live is Christ." This is everything, beloved brothers and sons!

Address at the Consecration of
Seventy Deacons for Latin America

PRINCIPAL MOTIVATOR FOR RENEWAL

Rev. Anastasio of the Holy Rosary, O.C.D.

Seven special aspects of the life of the Church in our day are singled out for particular attention on the part of consecrated souls. These are the biblical, liturgical, dogmatic, pastoral, ecumenical, missionary, and social aspects. Attention focused on them should be the principal motivator for renewal. Merely naming them is sufficient to grasp their importance.

There is deep meaning even in the order in which they are listed, as well as profound respect for the religious vocation itself, for its innermost characteristics.

Matters biblical, liturgical, and dogmatic—In listening to the word of God, in participating intimately in worship of the Lord, in gaining an in-depth knowledge of divine mysteries, we who are consecrated to God honor Him.

The pastoral aspect—Here we have a sharing in the Church's concern and anxiety for the salvation of men.

Ecumenical, missionary, and social matters—These are various types of the Church's pastoral ministry actuated in contacts with the Churches which do not enjoy perfect communion, in contacts with those who do not know our Blessed Lord, and also in purely social matters apart from religious questions; for service rendered to mankind is always preliminary to the leading of man to God.

From: *"La Vita Religiosa nella Chiesa"*

SACRED SCRIPTURE IN OUR LIVES

Very Rev. James Alberione, S.S.P., S.T.D.

The Sacred Council, Vatican II, in its "Dogmatic Constitution on Divine Revelation," states:

"The Church has always venerated the divine Scriptures just as she venerates the body of the Lord, since, especially in the sacred liturgy, she unceasingly receives and offers to the faithful the bread of life from the table both of God's word and of Christ's body.... The sacred synod earnestly and especially urges all the Christian faithful, especially Religious, to learn by frequent reading of the divine Scriptures the 'excellent knowledge of Jesus Christ' (Phil. 3:8). 'For ignorance of the Scriptures is ignorance of Christ.' Therefore, they should gladly put themselves in touch with the sacred text itself, whether it be through the liturgy, rich in the divine word, or through devotional reading, or through instructions suitable for the purpose and other aids which, in our time, with approval and active support of the shepherds of the Church, are commendably spread everywhere. And let them remember that prayer should accompany the reading of Sacred Scripture, so that God and man may talk together; for 'we speak to Him when we pray; we hear Him when we read the divine saying'" (n. 21).

The Holy Bible is the divinely inspired Word. St. Paul wrote to St. Timothy: "But do thou continue in the things that thou hast learned and that have been entrusted to thee, knowing of whom thou hast learned them. For from thy infancy thou hast known the Sacred Writings, which are able to instruct thee unto salvation by the faith which is in Christ Jesus. All Scripture is inspired by God and useful for teaching, for reproving, or correcting, for instructing in justice; that the man of God may be perfect, equipped for every good work" (2 Tim. 3:14-17).

The Divine Master often quoted Sacred Scripture, confirming both it and His own mission. For example, He declared, "You search the Scriptures . . . and it is they that bear witness to me" (John 5:39).

In addition to the reasons valid for everyone, the religious has two special reasons for venerating and reading the Bible: First, the Bible contains the message of salvation which we must give to souls: that is, truth, moral teaching and worship; it is thus the *most pastoral of books*. Second, the Bible is the model book to which the apostle must conform himself. God created man and knows well how man's heart has been fashioned; His Word, therefore, meets the innermost needs of the human heart.

"In the sacred books, the Father who is in heaven meets His children with great love and speaks with them; and the force and power in the word of God is so great that it stands as the support and energy of the Church, the strength of faith for her sons, the food of the soul, the pure and everlasting source of spiritual life" (Constitution on Divine Revelation, n. 21).

MODEL PROGRAM FOR READING THE ENTIRE BIBLE IN ABOUT FOUR YEARS, A CHAPTER A DAY

a) The New Testament: the historical books, the didactic books, and the prophetical book. The New Testament comprises 260 chapters.

b) The Old Testament: the historical books, the didactic books, and the prophetical books. The entire Old Testament comprises 1065 chapters.

The total number of chapters in the Bible is 1325. By reading a chapter a day, one may easily read the entire Bible in about four years.

Since the Bible is divine, it is the most useful of all books for prayer life. It may be used for spiritual reading, meditation and prayer—not only because it contains many prayers, such as the Psalms, but also because it serves to unite us intimately with God in mind, sentiments and will. It unites us to God in mind by presenting the truths of faith, so that we share His thoughts; in heart, by means of its sentiments of love for God and men after the example of the Sacred Heart of Jesus; in will, by rooting and grounding our lives in the will of God until we attain to the heights of perfection.

May the reading of Scripture, and especially the Gospels, be our delight! Nothing is better suited to lead us to imitation of our Divine Master, to transform us, to give us wisdom and a rich interior life. May we thus know Christ unto our own sanctification and the salvation of our brethren: ". . . so that by hearing the message of salvation, the whole world may believe, by believing it may hope, and by hoping it may love" (Dogmatic Constitution on Divine Revelation, n. 1).

CAUTION MUST BE OBSERVED
IN RENEWAL

Francis Cardinal Spellman

Caution must be observed in any discussion of renewal of religious life and activity, because renovation is not infrequently used as a pretext for the introduction of elements which could eventually lead to the weakening of religious life. Some people today want all religious without exception to be engaged in the external apostolate. They forget that the whole life of a religious is an apostolate. We cannot ask our teaching sisters and our nursing sisters, after their difficult day in their respective apostolates to go out and engage in other works. If we want religious to take over the direction of Catholic Action, to visit the sick, take the parish census, visit families and the like, then special institutes must be founded or individual religious must be provided with specialized formation. These are the worries which are of concern to many Mothers Superior today. Nothing which would ultimately tend to the weakening of religious discipline and spirit would produce any lasting good for the Church. In the United States, traditionally known for its activism, contemplative religious are making tremendous contributions to the effectiveness of the Church's apostolate.

A RETURN TO PRIMITIVE FERVOR

Rev. Anastasio of the Holy Rosary, O.C.D.

The words *renewal* and *adaptation* can generate a confusion of ideas. To prevent this it is necessary to stress that these words signify a return of individual members and of communities to their primitive fervor and an adaptation to the needs of our day. We must not lose sight of the supernatural design if we are not to risk fossilization on the one hand and the exaggerated pursuit of novelty on the other. The spirit of each founder must be preserved, otherwise there is danger of standardization which would be detrimental to the holiness and fecundity of religious life. The distinction must be maintained between different orders and congregations which have sprung from different charisms and which have different ideals to offer to young people.

KNOWLEDGE OF THE TIMES
WE LIVE IN

Rev. Anastasio of the Holy Rosary, O.C.D.

The need for religious to have a better knowledge of the times in which they live is the logical consequence of that basic factor of renewal which is adaptation to our times. If we are going to adapt to them, we must know them. Otherwise, truly ridiculous attempts will result. This is a possibility to which we religious are especially open: to think we have become modern when we start doing today what people of our day stopped doing twenty years ago. It all happens because of a lack of information —not lack of "newsy" information so much, as lack of reflection on the basic characteristics of an era, rather than on its superficial demands.

It is absolutely necessary that we make this distinction, particularly today, because it would be most unfortunate if we had to judge our times by those sensational aspects and multiform superficial realities which invade us on all sides. Our times are to be subjected to a depth judgment on their deepest characteristics, neglecting the surface foam. . . .

At this point it is clear that it would not be right for religious institutes to open their doors—as some concluded too quickly—to every paper that gives world news. Rather what is needed is a thoughtful, pondered, meditated concentration on the nature of the times in which we live. This is no simple task, for it entails a choice of the media of information, which unfortunately are not easy to handle—press, dialogue, conversation, and the audio-visual media. All these can help us to know our times, but presuppose a careful selecting if this knowledge is to be authentic and not a petty, "newsy" acquaintance that everyone has today, with the result that no one knows what age we are living in.

By "our times," let us note, we are not referring to calendar time. We are speaking of today's people, society, institutions, and human events above all. Hence, implicit in knowledge of the times is the effort to know not only the happenings of the day but more important, the men and the social institutions of our day. And among these institutions characteristic of our times we find the Church. It is clear, then, that knowledge of our times is a rich, complex reality.

Religious families will have to carry out this principle of renewal in a way consonant with the spirit proper to each. They need to find a way that is also truly useful and results in a substantial, in-depth understanding of our era, not merely a passing, conventional acquaintance.

To conclude, the principle involved here is a very wise and important one. Putting it into practice entails no little difficulty and effort.

From: *"La Vita Religiosa nella Chiesa"*

THREE DANGERS CONNECTED WITH AGGIORNAMENTO

Very Rev. James Alberione, S.S.P., S.T.D.

To the Members of the Five Religious Congregations He Founded

Let us speak of "aggiornamento," and place it under the protection of St. Paul, who always strained forward. We, too, must strive for greater love for Christ, for a more extensive apostolate, for a higher place in Heaven. The word *aggiornamento* may be interpreted in various ways, but we shall use it in the sense of progress.

The principle point on which you must update yourselves is that of your spirit.

You have progressed in the area of study; however, you must progress further. You have progressed, and are continuing to do so in the area of apostolate. You have progressed—and must still progress—in the areas of human formation and poverty.

Regarding the first area, that of your spirit, four points are concerned: faith, that is, "the spirit of faith;" the spirit of poverty; conscientiousness, especially regarding charity; and, finally, more supernatural obedience of the judgment and will.

There can be dangers connected with speaking of *aggiornamento*. The word "aggiornamento" can be wrongly interpreted.

The dangers are three:

1) To want to reform everyone except ourselves; 2) to want to reform what must not be reformed; 3) to refuse to reform what must be
reformed.

The first danger is to want to reform others,
first. There has always been this tendency in the
Church, and we find it reflected in religious Institutes, too. There are those who want to change
their Institutes in certain respects; they want the
other members to do better. We should realize,
instead, that the Institute makes good progress if
its individual members progress.

Every Congregation is a society, that is, a
moral body. What happens in a body when the
heart and lungs are sound, when the eyes and arms
are sound, when all the individual members are
physically fit? We say that the person is well. But
when the teeth and the eyes are diseased, when the
lungs do not work well, the body is sick. Sometimes
just a few individuals are enough to make a community sick.

A community may have been going along
peacefully before someone with a rather difficult
character is assigned to it. Shortly thereafter the
peace of that convent was diminished; it no longer
enjoys the serenity it once had. Some people have
the habit of contradicting everybody, for instance.
As soon as someone says white, they say black—and
if one says black, they say white. This tendency has
always been found within the Church of God. Here-
tics started by setting out to reform the Church. In-

stead, such true reformers as St. Charles Borromeo,
St. Francis of Assisi, St. Ignatius of Loyola and
St. John Bosco reformed themselves first of all.
Their powerful example and preaching came as a
result. They could say: "Do as I do." That is reform;
and that reform was successful. But when one turns
against authority, especially ecclesiastical or religious authority, his life is no longer exemplary.
Indeed, he does more harm than good.

Every religious must renew himself. Each must
strive to become a better religious. The means is
greater devotion to the Constitutions. Renewal of
the Congregation must be based on reading, meditating, applying and practicing the Constitutions in
the letter and the spirit. Be devoted to the Rule. If
one is an excellent religious, and another an excellent religious, then the moral body which is the
Congregation will also be excellent, and will be a
living and productive member of the Church.

2) There is the danger of wanting to reform
what must not be reformed. Some things are not reformable. Unfortunately there is a tendency to say,
"Today things no longer have to be thus. Education
has changed. You older ones were not trained well,"
etc. It seems to me that first we must examine
whether or not the older members are always imi-
tated by the younger. Remember the sacrifices they
made in earlier, harder times, their generous dedication and their spirit of faith.

"Things are not the same!" some say. I ask:
What is not the same? The Gospel? It is still the
same, and we must always go back to it. Do

you find anything to be reformed in the Gospel? "If anyone wishes to come after Me, let him deny himself, and take up his cross, and follow Me" (Mark 8:34). And is not this double commandment always found in the Gospel: "Thou shalt love the Lord thy God with thy whole heart, and with thy whole soul, and with thy whole strength, and with thy whole mind; and thy neighbor as thyself" (Luke 10:27)? And does not the Gospel always say, "Go and preach?" Can we perhaps tear out the page of the Gospel where the Beatitudes are proclaimed?

As an example of the unreformable, take separation from the world, the "cloister" in the sense of the Constitutions. You are not a cloistered Institute, but there must be cloister, and it has to be observed. You must not establish relationships which do not conform to your religious life. You must not, because of such relationships, hold up the schedule, or put off your duties, especially your spiritual exercises. Let men stay with men, and women with women. "But she is a benefactress; he is a benefactor." Those who respect your spirit and your Constitutions are the real benefactors. The others, even though they make donations, do harm.

Do not try to reform what must not be reformed.

3) The third danger is an attitude of opposition to renewal—not wanting to reform the reformable. Some things need to be reformed: aspects of poverty, aspects of obedience (which some mistakenly try to turn into a mere reasoning process), some matters regarding study. We must not have

the attitude of opposition that declares: "This ought not to be touched; this is fine as it is." If it is defective, it is to be retouched. If during the painting of a beautiful picture, a defect appears, it should be corrected. If the Blessed Mother is depicted in a posture which does not express virtue at its best, that must be corrected. Let the artist take his brush in hand and retouch the painting. Likewise with us.

Now we come to reform. Regarding the spirit, I have mentioned four things: spirit of faith, poverty, conscientiousness in charity, and obedience.

How important it is to believe what we are told, to have the spirit of faith. If there is faith, if one believes, he will see things come true in proportion to his faith! Blessed are those who do not see, and yet believe. Faith! Let us have faith that in performing those small, daily duties, the soul is enriched with great merit. It makes no difference whether one writes, or sews or cooks, as long as his activity is directed to heaven. In fact, if one is in a humbler office, he has less to overcome in himself. He is not so easily tempted to pride. Let us have faith that those deeds of ours, so insignificant, those hidden deeds that men would call unimportant or worthless, really do produce fruits of eternal life. "For I reckon that the sufferings of the present time are not worthy to be compared with the glory to come that will be revealed in us" (Rom. 8:18).

Next we consider poverty. A false interpretation of poverty is replacing the true one. The idea seems to be to live poorly only as long as means are lacking. As soon as there is the possibility of having more, then one begins to find reasons for getting this and that—to be "more modern," to "display better taste," "to keep up with others. . . ."

Examine yourselves to see if you have devotion to poverty. It is true that care must be taken of health. A little *aggiornamento* is needed insofar as health, being in general weaker than before, requires more attention. But the "spirit of poverty" must always be the same. What was Jesus' preference? Does not sanctity today still consist in imitation of Jesus? What did He look for? The poorest—from the manger to the cross. And then He was laid in a tomb not His own!

In general, poverty should be practiced better. Poverty means privation, poverty means production, poverty means providing, poverty means elevating oneself toward eternal treasures—ever more thirsty for eternal goods! Love true riches, those which are celestial!

Conscientiousness in charity is to be examined next. News of faults is very apt to be spread from one house to another. Such matters are spoken of and sometimes even exaggerated. What does charity teach us—that charity which is patient, which regards the others as superiors? "Charity is patient, is kind . . . thinks no evil . . ." etc. (1 Cor. 13:4 ff.)

And regarding obedience? There is an ever more marked tendency to reason things out, to pass judgment on dispositions and directives. This deprives us of many merits. Let us obey, even when at first glance we do not understand. "Be you, therefore, imitators of God, as very dear children" (Eph. 5:1). Let us change ourselves into children of God. The first thing to do when we receive a disposition, directive or schedule is to say, *yes*. Oh, how many souls are sanctified by that '*yes*'! "Behold the handmaid of the Lord." That is a great *yes* to imitate. "Not My will, but Thy will be done." May Your will be done, not mine.

In substance, *aggiornamento* should consist in this—in living the life of Jesus Christ more perfectly: "Christ lives in me" (Gal. 2:20). This is an ascent! God became man that man might become God. Live in Jesus Christ.

Practical Aspects

of Renewal

The manner of living, praying and working should be suitably adapted everywhere, but especially in mission territories, to the modern physical and psychological circumstances of the members and also, as required by the nature of each institute, to the necessities of the apostolate, the demands of culture, and social and economic circumstances.

According to the same criteria let the manner of governing the institutes also be examined.

Therefore, let constitutions, directories, custom books, books of prayers and ceremonies and such like be suitably re-edited and, obsolete laws being suppressed, be adapted to the decrees of this sacred synod.

Decree on the Adaptation and Renewal of Religious Life, n. 3

An effective renewal and adaptation demands the cooperation of all the members of the institute.

However, to establish the norms of adaptation and renewal, to embody it in legislation as well as to make allowance for adequate and prudent experimentation belongs only to the competent authorities, especially to general chapters. The approbation of the Holy See or of the local Ordinary must be obtained where necessary according to law. But superiors should take counsel in an appropriate way and hear the members of the order in those things which concern the future well being of the whole institute.

For the adaptation and renewal of convents of nuns suggestions and advice may be obtained also from the meetings of federations or from other assemblies lawfully convoked.

Nevertheless everyone should keep in mind that the hope of renewal lies more in the faithful observance of the rules and constitutions than in multiplying laws.

Decree on Adaptation and Renewal of Religious Life, n. 4

THE MANNER OF PROMOTING THE ADAPTATION AND RENEWAL

That the fruits of the Council may carefully mature, it is necessary that Religious institutes promote first of all a renewal of spirit, and then that they take care to carry out this renewal adapted to their life and discipline prudently and yet skillfully by applying themselves assiduously to the study especially of the Dogmatic Constitution *Lumen Gentium* (chapters 5 and 6) and the Decree *Perfectae Caritatis,* and by putting into effect the norms and teachings of the Council.

To speed up the implementation of the Decree *Perfectae Caritatis* the following norms which will affect all Religious, whether Latin or Oriental, with suitable adjustments, establish a procedure and give certain rules.

These norms, to be in force for Religious of the whole Church, leave untouched the general laws of the Church, both of the Latin Church and of the Eastern Churches and the special laws of Religious institutes, unless they explicitly or implicitly change them.

Concerning Those Who Are Bound To Promote Adaptation and Renewal

The most important role in the adaptation and renewal of the Religious life belongs to the institutes themselves, [1] which will accomplish it especially through general chapters or, among the Orientals through synaxes. The task of the chapters is not completed by merely making laws, but especially by promoting spiritual and apostolic vitality.

The cooperation of all superiors and members is necessary to renew Religious life in themselves, to prepare the spirit of the chapters, to carry out the works of the chapters, to observe faithfully the law and norms enacted by the chapters. [2]

A special general chapter, ordinary or extraordinary, should be convened within two or at most three years to promote the adaptation and renewal in each institute.

This chapter can be divided into two distinct periods, separated generally by not more than a year, if the chapter itself so decides by secret vote.

[1] In the previously cited commentary (p. 225) Father Escudero notes that renewal and aggiornamento are the proper concern of the institutes themselves because of the particular spirit of each—which no one knows better than they—and because of the freedom of their members. The Church wants this spirit and this freedom respected in every case. He adds that this is important to keep in mind so that there will be no intrusion in the institute's personal field by those who have no right to do so.

[2] Here Father Escudero stresses the fact that attention must be given before all else to renewal of religious life in the members themselves, for without this, any other attempt at renewal would be apt to end in a vindication of rights, in demands for conveniences and comforts, or in imposition of personal views.

The general commission in preparing this chapter should suitably provide for full and free consultation of the members and arrange the results of this consultation in time so that the work of the chapter may be helped and directed. It will be possible to accomplish this, for example, by consulting conventual and provincial chapters, by establishing commissions, by proposing series of questions, etc.

For stauropagial monasteries it shall be the duty of the patriarch to set forth the norms for pursuing this consultation.

This general chapter has the right to alter certain norms of the constitutions, or among Orientals the norms of the Typika, as an experiment, as long as the purpose, nature and character of the institute are preserved. Experiments contrary to the common law, provided they are to be undertaken prudently, will be willingly permitted by the Holy See as the occasions call for them.

These experiments can be prolonged until the next Ordinary general chapter, which will have the faculty to continue them further but not beyond the chapter immediately following.

The general council has the same faculty during the time that intervenes between chapters of this kind, in accordance with conditions to be determined by the chapters, and among the Orientals in independent monasteries the Hegumen with the minor Synaxis has this power.

The definitive approval of the constitutions is reserved to the competent authority.

As far as the revision of the constitutions of nuns is concerned, each monastery by means of a chapter, or even the individual nuns, should make known their wishes which, to safeguard the unity of the Religious family in keeping with its nature, should be collected by the highest authority of the order, if she is present, otherwise by the delegate of the Holy See; among Orientals, by the patriarch or the local hierarch. The wishes and opinions can be sought from the assemblies of the federations or from other gatherings legitimately called together. The bishops' pastoral solicitude should also lend benevolent assistance to this end.

If at times in monasteries of nuns certain experiments with respect to observances are judged opportune for an interval, these can be permitted by the superiors general or by delegates of the Holy See, and among Orientals by the patriarch or the local hierarch. Yet special consideration should be given to the special outlook and frame of mind of those who are cloistered and who have so great a need for stability and security.

It shall be the duty of those authorities mentioned above to provide for the revision of the texts of the constitutions with the help and consultation of the monasteries themselves and for their submission for the approval of the Holy See or the competent hierarch.

Revision of Constitutions and Typika

The general laws of each institute (constitutions, Typika, rules or whatever name they bear) should ordinarily include these elements:

(a) The evangelical and theological principles of the religious life and of its union with the Church and suitable and clear words in which "the spirit of the founders and their specific aims and healthy traditions all of which constitute the patrimony of each institute, are acknowledged and preserved" (No. 2b of the Decree *Perfectae Caritatis*);

(b) the necessary juridical norms for defining clearly the character, purpose and means of the institute, which norms should not be excessively multiplied but should always be presented in an adequate manner.

The union of both elements, spiritual and juridical, is necessary so that the principal codes of the institutes have a stable foundation and that the true spirit and life-giving norm pervade them; care must therefore be taken that a merely juridical or purely exhortatory text is not composed.

Those matters which are now obsolete, or subject to change according to a particular era, or which correspond with merely local usages, should be excluded from the fundamental code of the institutes.

Those norms however which correspond with the needs of the present time, the physical and psychological conditions of the members and particular circumstances should be set down in supplementary codes called "directories," books of customs, or in books bearing other titles.

Those elements are to be considered obsolete which do not constitute the nature and purpose of the institute and which, having lost their meaning and power, are no longer a real help to religious life.

Nevertheless, consideration must be given to the witness which the religious state has as its role the obligation of giving.

The form of government should be such that "the chapters and councils ... each in its own way express the participation and concern of all the members for the welfare of the whole community," (No. 14 of the Decree *Perfectae Caritatis*). This will be realized especially if the members have a really effective part in selecting the members of these chapters and councils. Similarly the form of government should be such that the exercise of authority is made more effective and unhindered according to modern needs. Therefore, superiors on every level should be given sufficient powers so that useless and too frequent recourse to higher authorities is not multiplied.

Nevertheless, suitable renewal cannot be made once and for all but should be encouraged in a continuing way, with the help of the zeal of the members and the solicitude of the chapters and superiors.

Ecclesiae Sanctae, nn. 1-14, 17-19

TRUE RENEWAL

Pope Pius XII

This complete renewal of ourselves and of all that touches us is not in any sense an abdication or an unreflecting contempt of all that our forebears have laboriously established, and which should be regarded by each one as the glory and the honor of his Institute. Rather it consists in not growing numb with inertia, in translating into life the great examples of the Founders, in an intense nourishing of the flame of piety, in putting everything to work so that the holy laws of each Institute will not degenerate into an assemblage of exterior regulations uselessly imposed, whose letter, in the absence of the spirit, kills, [1] but that each law may become truly a means of acquiring supernatural virtue and that those who are bound to use these means may conceive an ever greater desire of sanctity and may employ every effort, after the example of the Apostle St. Paul, for the salvation of their brothers.

[1] Cf. 2 Cor. 3:6.

But this necessity of adapting to the progress of the manners of the present does not at all mean for souls consecrated to God that they should lend themselves, in any way whatsoever, to the exigencies of the world, and to its foolish seductions and its appeals. Rather, it is their duty to serve as example to all men by the integrity of their lives; to use, as far as this is possible, all the progress in knowledge and techniques for the advantage of religion. Let the dangers and the trials which today overwhelm the human race seem to religious as so many means of bringing back the souls of the faithful to the practice of the precepts of the Gospel; let them show that they are capable of responding to the multiplicity of their needs and, as We have just said recently in Our exhortation *Menti Nostrae* to the clergy, [2] to fulfill their offices let them rely above all on the means which will be indicated to them by bishops and by their superiors; let them regard these means as the most opportune, the most effective and the most useful, as much for the safeguarding of sacerdotal dignity as for the observance of religious discipline.

[2] September 23, 1950, AAS, 42, 657.

ADAPTATION AND RENEWAL
OF CONSTITUTIONS

Rev. Elio Gambari, S.M.M.

The Council repeatedly insisted that every religious family should strive to be what it is supposed to be—in other words, as God willed it—and to renew itself in an unbroken rhythm of absolute fidelity to the task assigned it by the Lord.

This Council directive is valid for the Constitutions, too, so that by their light every religious can take stock of his own faithfulness.

The Constitutions favor personal contact with God through Christ in the Church, while also opening the religious out to his neighbor. Thus, they give first place to the spiritual life, which alone can provide a divine, apostolic meaning to external activities.

The Gospel and the following of Christ in accord with the Gospel have to appear in the Constitutions as the source and reason for all the rest that is contained therein. Everything in the Constitutions is to flow from the Gospel and to lead back to the Gospel.

It is desirable for Constitutions to make use of Scriptural references in a solid, appropriate manner, exactly and surely interpreted.

The second guide line to follow in revision work is a "feeling with the Church," that is, stress on the place which the institute holds by special title in the mystery of the Church. This must uphold, vivify, and pervade the Constitutions.

The norms for implementing the Decree on Renewal—*Ecclesiae Sanctae,* n. 16—insist on a sharing in the mystery of the Church as the basis of renewal, adding that this participation must be promoted in every way. Now one of the most suitable ways is to see to it that the Constitutions are alive with this "feeling with the Church."

Just as the documents of the Council blossom from a vivid understanding of the mystery of the Church and lead right back to this mystery, likewise will the Constitutions prove to be a great help if they keep religious close to this mystery—indeed, immersed in it.

A third guideline in the renewal of a Congregation's rules is the recall and application of its own special charism, which characterizes the theology, spirituality, apostolate and tenor of life of a religious family.

We have already spoken of the need for dynamic fidelity to this charism. In the concrete, this means continually returning to the inspiration, spirit, mind and directives of the Founder, for these treasures are a heritage valid for all time. And this heritage gives its particular note to the various aspects of the institute's religious life, enlivening the whole.

In the present climate of renewal, the Sacred Congregation of Religious makes it a practice and considers it useful to recommend that principles of spiritual life, of religious life, find their place in

Constitutions. These should be put briefly and should be especially such as will define, confirm or strengthen, and apply to various cases the spirit proper to the Congregation. On the other hand, wordy instructions of an ascetic or mystical nature should not be included, nor too lengthy spiritual exhortations.

Moderation in the use of Scriptural, theological and spiritual maxims will prove advantageous to their depth and effectiveness; they will be more likely to impress the religious and guide them.

Another factor in renewal of Constitutions is the apostolic dimension. Stress and importance must be given to the apostolic potential of religious life and its various elements. Here we refer both to the apostolate in general and to specific apostolates—educational, missionary, social service, etc.

I believe this to be one of the renewal principles desired most of all by institutes which are especially apostolic by nature. Religious life must be presented as the nourishment, support and strength of the apostolate, and the apostolate in turn must be—and evidently so—the expression of religious life, its very nourishment and support (cf. n. 8 of *Perfectae Caritatis*).

Since the Constitutions must be a code of life, it is both right and essential that they help religious to achieve unity in their lives.

Coming now to specific criteria for the work of adapting Constitutions, we name first of all the need for conformity to the Council directives. Revision and correction must be effected so that whatever is contrary to the norms of the Council documents and the Instructions following them is eliminated. For example, provision must be made for the continuation of formation after the first Profession, according to n. 18 of *Perfectae Caritatis* and n. 33-38 of the Motu Proprio, *Ecclesiae Sanctae,* II.

With regard to elimination of obsolete elements of the Constitutions, it should be said that prescriptions are not to be considered obsolete, even though they are no longer practiced, if they are still reasonable or even demanded by the "prophetic" function or witness of religious life. Nor is something obsolete in the Council sense just because it fell out of use through laxity or abuse.

At times, it might be the manner or means prescribed for practicing a directive that is now obsolete, not the content or purpose of the directive itself. A case in point could be various exercises of penance or mortification. New ways should then replace the old, but the penitential content must remain.

Paragraph 17 of the Moto Proprio reminds us that in suppressing the obsolete elements, we must never go so far as to remove all that distinguishes religious from the other faithful in their way of living and acting, just for the sake of novelty.

A religious is to be a "sign" and so he must offer his own dynamic witness by means of something which sets him apart from others. By his splendid and striking testimony, he must stimulate his brethren, showing them how to act in their own sphere of life (*Lumen Gentium,* 13 and 31).

From: *"Renewal in Religious Life,"* (Daughters of
St. Paul, Boston, Mass. 02130)

THE RELATIONSHIP OF RELIGIOUS
TO THEIR CONSTITUTIONS

Rev. Elio Gambari, S.M.M.

Religious have duties toward their Constitutions, just as they have duties toward the Congregation in which they made their Profession. It is especially important to recall these duties in our times, when so much criticism is being levelled at Constitutions.

Faithfulness to duties will be the measure of the effectiveness of the Constitutions in our lives. The Constitutions should be lived by religious through the power of conviction and spontaneous dedication to their directives.

The Constitutions represent a substantial synthesis of a program of life. Therefore, only an in-depth study of them, attentive, diligent and continual, will allow us to get to the heart of them—without, however, ever pretending to have exhausted them. All too often, only the surface is scratched; the real wealth of the Constitutions is never touched.

Knowledge must be followed by respect, both for the law of the Lord in general and for the law which the Lord has given our institute.

From this respect will spring love for our Constitutions. Did we not entrust ourselves to them as to the very hand of God holding us up? This hand of the Lord must be loved, desired and followed. It is our support and our strength in facing the weakness and instability of the will. The more the Constitutions are loved, the greater will be their freeing power. And the more demanding they are, the better it is. This is the norm for judging Constitutions.

Let love for the Constitutions be both affective and effective, which means a love resulting in loyal, prompt and complete execution of rules contained therein. Such a love, moreover, requires that our very lives, not merely our actions, be conformed to the contents of the Constitutions or Rule.

In this conformity lies the expression of personal freedom and the perfection of one's personality.

From: *"Renewal in Religious Life"*

CONFORMITY TO OUR CONSTITUTIONS

Very Rev. James Alberione, S.S.P., S.T.D.

Once one is professed, there is only one road to sanctity, the road of observance! There is no better way—*it is the best!* It may happen at times that in order to observe the Rule, one seems to be doing less good to his neighbor. The fact is, however, that true good, the greater good, is always to be found in observance, in obedience. Besides, the purpose of the Rule is to keep us from being undecided about what should be done. Advice given us, as well as all inspirations, ideas or thoughts that come to mind, should always be harmonized with the directives of the Constitutions, which must determine our decision. Each rule serves to indicate God's will to us in the various situations that arise. In following what the Rule directs, therefore, we are certain of doing what is best.

Hence we have to reflect and meditate on the Constitutions a great deal. After the Bible, they are the first book to be used for spiritual reading and asceticism.

One might say, "Things are different in this country or in this diocese or in this parish." Things may be different, yes, but the Congregation is the same everywhere. The Constitutions were intended to be the same for all.

God's will for us is to be found in the Constitutions. A confessor may have the Carmelite, Franciscan, Dominican, or any other spirit, but each community has its own, and should keep to it. Its spirit is its treasure. A confessor or retreat master may give the members of a community many excellent thoughts which, however, do not conform to their spirit. These instructions are to be received reverently, but they are not to be considered when making resolutions, nor should they become a source of confusion. It is the Congregation's own spirit which nourishes its members.

The Constitutions point out the sure and essential way to sanctity. It has happened that religious going to one confessor or another begin to say, "My confessor is giving me devotion to the Holy Spirit, or devotion to the Infinite Love. . . ." What is to be said to these religious? Simply this: Keep to your own spirit, and no other! Do you want to reject your own? There are some priests who go a little too far with so-called spiritual direction, and the result is spiritual deviation. Your direction is provided by your Generalate; it is already determined by your Constitutions.

No matter who it is who preaches to you or gives you various kinds of advice, even if it be someone in authority, always check to see if his advice conforms to your Constitutions and to the spirit of your Institute.

One of the evils of our day is the lack of upright, enlightened consciences. There is talk of situation ethics and of morality of convenience. We are reminded of Pope Pius XII's words on the need to form an upright conscience. An upright conscience is one conformed to moral theology, to Scripture, and in general, to the Church's teachings.

Our conscience has to regulate our whole lives. The Constitutions and the directives issued by the General Motherhouse are to be followed. Today, with all these "theories of convenience," the line between good and evil may become more and more hazy, and one may gradually develop a false conscience.

Many, indeed, interpret "aggiornamento" as meaning that one need no longer do what she was always taught. They think they can act as they please, excusing this conduct in the name of personality, which more often than not, comes down to plain queerness, to eccentricity! There is no personality except that which leads us to live in Christ. Our personality must become one with the Divine Personality. For religious, this is the only personality. In what must our "aggiornamento" consist, then? In conformity to our Constitutions.

May our lives comply with the Rule! Then we shall be making our contribution to religious life. We shall be contributing our share of prayer, of apostolate, of financial support, of good example, of work in various duties, etc. And it is right that we do so. Yet at times some have only claims to make on the Congregation. The meaning of "Congregation" has to be well understood: it is synonymous with "religious family." And in a family, all have to do their share; if they want to enjoy good things, they have to help earn them. So it is with our Congregation.

Do we feel the need of peace in a community? Then let us contribute toward that peace by not offending others, by not making life difficult for those around us! Let us do our share for peace, for a good life together, for happiness and holy joy in our lives. Let us make our contribution of thought, of activity, of good judgment, throughout the day.

In contrast to those who show thoughtfulness in speech, there are some who are ruthless when they talk. They judge and condemn others from morning to night and meanwhile they do not make their own contribution in accordance with the Commandments. They do not contribute, in other words, to the betterment of the community, or of the Congregation as a whole. This is truly injustice! By the natural law, the members of a society must give if they want to receive.

Let religious become up to date with their Congregation; let them keep up with their Constitutions, so as to live well. The highest compliment—an all-inclusive one—that can be paid a religious is that he is observant.

So let religious strive to conform their lives to their Constitutions. Let them hold them in great esteem, be familiar with them and practice them faithfully. Their own progress and the well-being of the entire Congregation depends in great part on this loyalty. It is not the fear of punishment that should induce everyone to observe them exactly, faithfully and constantly, but rather the desire for their own sanctification, the love of Jesus Christ, our Divine Master, and the love of the Congregation. They are always to remember the divine promise: "You who have left all and have followed Me shall receive a hundredfold and shall possess life everlasting" (cf. Matt. 19:28-29).

REVISING AND ADAPTING
COMMUNITY PRAYER MANUALS

Rev. Elio Gambari, S.M.M.

The criteria for proceeding with the renewal and adaptation of prayer manuals and ceremonials are to be found in the Constitution on the Sacred Liturgy and the Instruction on the Liturgy and are recalled in other documents.

The Constitution requires that a liturgically-based spiritual formation be given religious, and that their devotions be imbued with the spirit of the liturgy (n. 17).

The Apostolic Letter, *Ecclesiae Sanctae,* in its norms for implementing the Decree on the Adaptation and Renewal of Religious Life, spells out these criteria more thoroughly (n. 20, 21). These norms give us two principles which will be of valid help in revising prayer manuals and practices. Number 20 is concerned with making it possible to aim at a more intimate participation in the liturgical life of the Church. To this end it invites institutes to adopt the Divine Office either in whole or in part, in place of another Office.

Paragraph 21 is even more detailed and important: "a larger place should be given to mental prayer instead of a multitude of prayers"—which often lack a sense of unity—"retaining, nevertheless the pious exercises commonly accepted in the Church."

The recommendation that revision of prayer customs not neglect the pious exercises which are a part of the common heritage of the Church or of an institute is the application of what we read in the Constitution on the Liturgy (n. 13): "Popular devotions of the Christian people are to be highly commended, provided they accord with the laws and norms of the Church." One of these exercises is the Rosary.[1]

The Constitution goes on to say that these devotions should be so drawn up "that they harmonize with the liturgical seasons, accord with the sacred liturgy, are in some fashion derived from it, and lead the people to it, since, in fact, the liturgy by its very nature far surpasses any of them."

---

[1] In his encyclical *Rosaries to the Mother of Christ*, Pope Paul VI wrote: "The Second Vatican Ecumenical Council clearly referred to the Rosary, though not in express terms, when it reminded all the faithful that "practices and exercises of devotion towards her (Mary), recommended by the teaching authority of the Church in the course of the centuries, are to be held in high esteem.' As the history of the Church so frequently testifies, this duty of prayer, so abundant in its fruits, is efficacious in averting evils and calamities and greatly fosters Christian living. 'Above all, it nourishes the Catholic Faith which, by timely meditation on the sacred mysteries, gains new strength, and it lifts the mind, to the contemplation of divinely revealed truths.'

Referring to the Dogmatic Constitution on the Church, Pope Paul recently stated, "We find in paragraph 67 of Chapter VIII of the now renowned council constitution *Lumen Gentium*, on the Blessed Virgin, the following principle stated, 'Let the faithful remember that true devotion consists neither in fruitless and passing emotion, nor in a certain vain credulity. Rather, it proceeds from true faith, by which we are led to know the excellence of the Mother of God, and are moved to a filial love toward our Mother and to the imitation of her virtues.' We believe that this is the good way, the only safe way, to promote our devotion, our spirituality in regard to our Lady Most Holy."

The same principles hold for religious institutes, as is explicitly declared in the Instruction on the Liturgy (n. 17): "Exercises of piety, arranged according to the laws or customs of each place or institute, shall be held in due esteem. Nevertheless, care should be taken, especially if these exercises are celebrated in common, that they be in harmony with the sacred liturgy . . . and that they be related to the seasons of the liturgical year."

From: *"Renewal in Religious Life"*

The
Religious Habit

*The religious habit, an outward mark of conse-
cration to God, should be simple and modest, poor
and at the same time becoming. In addition it must
meet the requirements of health and be suited to
the circumstances of time and place and to the
needs of the ministry involved. The habits of both
men and women religious which do not conform to
these norms must be changed.*

Decree on the Adaptation and Renewal of Religious Life, n. 17

"A SIGN OF CONSECRATION"

And now, speaking of the religious habit, choose one which will be the expression of interior unaffectedness, of simplicity, of religious modesty; then it will serve to edify all, even modern youth.

Pius XII, Address to the International
Congress of Teaching Sisters, September 13, 1951

*

A word on the question of clothing: the religious habit must always express consecration to Christ; this is what all expect and desire. For the rest, let the habit be suitable and in keeping with the requirements of hygiene. We could not but express Our satisfaction when, in the course of the year, We saw that one or another of the Congregations had already drawn some practical consequences on this point. To sum up: in non-essentials adapt yourselves as far as reason and well-ordered charity make it advisable.

Pius XII, Address to Superiors General
of Women's Orders and Institutes, September 15, 1952

*

Beloved daughters, even outward appearance itself has some influence on the safeguard of a true and authentic Religious life. Since the pontificate of our predecessor Pope Pius XII, appeals have been addressed to the women's institutes urging them to adopt a habit that is dignified and at the same time in keeping with the requirements of hygiene and the conditions of modern life. These appeals were received in different ways by your Religious families: reactions ranged all the way from those who showed a certain diffidence towad this updating of the habit to those who allowed themselves to be tempted by an excessive "worldliness" ("mondanisation").

Modifications are undoubtedly necessary. Yet care should be taken not to go from one extreme to the other. And care should be taken that the Religious habit by its simplicity and modesty always remains, in accordance with the long traditions of the Church and the wise prescriptions of the conciliar decree, a "sign of consecration"—a visible sign recognizable by all of the state of life embraced by the consecrated virgin.

Pope Paul VI, Address to International Union of Superiors General of Religious Congregations of Women, March 7, 1967

MOTIVES BEHIND RENEWAL

Richard Cardinal Cushing

On the twenty-sixth day of May, 1967, I shall be forty-six years a priest. During all that time I have tried to help everyone, especially you and yours.

Permit me then to ask you to comment on the following questions. Do not answer me. Answer your own conscience. I have had enough of the questionnaires prepared by sociologists. All I want from you is to answer during meditation for your spiritual welfare the following:

1. Women need to watch their motives closely. Why does "renovation" or "renewal" almost immediately take the form of designing clothes? Women's natural vanity? Women's natural desire for fashions?

2. Are the changes being advocated in many cases actually for the good of the Church? Or for our own ease?

3. Will a letdown make you saints? Or more selfish? Or more sensual?

4. Will a closer relationship between laity, priests and sisters help you draw souls closer to God? Or plunge us into conflicts natural to creatures composed of body and soul?

A Sister from the far west said to me: "I think you are giving us religious very much by your writings. Articles by you published in periodicals Sisters read can bring to us the mind of the Church. We are ready to trust you. We have been confused and, indeed, battered by radicals from every side—radicals who later leave the Church or their consecration. I am willing to let the battle rage. You are far from me. I speak for Nuns because you love them. You want nothing—you have nothing—tell me, please what we should do?"

UPDATING AND THE HABIT

Very Rev. Anastasio of the Holy Rosary, O.C.D.

The Council's Decree on the Adaptation and Renewal of Religious Life confirms the validity of the religious habit, as well as its function as a witness and a sign. At the same time it removes it from the influence of specific times and tastes—which in one detail or another reminds one more of the past than of the present.

There is no exhortation to abolish the religious habit. On the contrary, the exhortation is to defend it. For that reason, it is to be adapted in accord with reasonable requirements and proper modern day thinking, so that it can be aptly defended.

Address to Superiors and Mistresses of Novices,
under the auspices of the Sacred Congregation of Religious

Renewal and
the Apostolate

Religious communities should continue to maintain and fulfill the ministries proper to them. In addition, after considering the needs of the Universal Church and individual dioceses, they should adapt them to the requirements of time and place, employing appropriate and even new programs and abandoning those works which today are less relevant to the spirit and authentic nature of the community.

The missionary spirit must under all circumstances be preserved in religious communities. It should be adapted, accordingly, as the nature of each community permits, to modern conditions so that the preaching of the Gospel may be carried out more effectively in every nation.

Decree on the Adaptation and Renewal of Religious Life, n. 20

CONCILIAR DIRECTIVES
ON THE
EXERCISE OF THE APOSTOLATE

All religious have the duty, each according to his proper vocation, of cooperating zealously and diligently in building up and increasing the whole Mystical Body of Christ and for the good of the particular churches.

It is their first duty to foster these objectives by prayer, works of penance and the example of their own life for which this sacred synod strongly urges them to increase their esteem and zeal. With due consideration for the character proper to each religious community, they should also enter more vigorously into the external works of the apostolate.

Decree Concerning the Pastoral Office
of Bishops in the Church, n. 33

Religious priests are by consecration assumed into the responsibilities of the presbyterate so as to become themselves the prudent cooperators of the episcopal order. Today they can be of even greater help to bishops in view of the greater needs of souls. Therefore, they can be said in a real sense to belong to the clergy of the diocese inasmuch as they share in the care of souls and in carrying out works of the apostolate under the authority of the prelates.

Other members of religious communities, both men and women, also belong in a special way to the diocesan family and offer great assistance to the sacred hierarchy. With the increasing demands of the apostolate, they can and should offer that assistance even more and more.

Decree Concerning the Pastoral Office
of Bishops in the Church, n. 34

In order that the works of the apostolate be carried out harmoniously in individual dioceses and that the unity of diocesan discipline be preserved intact, these principles are established as fundamental:

All religious should always look upon successors of the Apostles, with devoted respect and reverence. Whenever they are legitimately called upon to undertake works of the apostolate, they are obliged to discharge their duties as active and obedient helpers of the bishops. Indeed, religious should consider it an honor to respond promptly and faithfully to the requests and desires of the bishops and in such a way they may assume an even more ample role in the ministry of human salvation. This they should do with due respect for the character of their institute and in keeping with their constitutions which, if needs be, should be accommodated to this goal in accord with the principles of this conciliar decree.

Especially in view of the urgent need of souls and the scarcity of diocesan clergy, Religious communities which are not dedicated exclusively to the contemplative life can be called upon by the bishops to assist in various pastoral ministries. They should, however, keep in mind the particular character of each community. Superiors should encourage the work to the utmost, by accepting parishes, even on a temporary basis.

Religious engaged in the active apostolate, however, must always be imbued with the spirit of their Religious community, and remain faithful to the observance of their rule and spirit of submissiveness due to their own superior. Bishops should not neglect to impress this obligation upon them.

Decree Concerning the Pastoral Office
of Bishops in the Church, n. 35

The institute of exemption, by which Religious are called to the service of the supreme pontiff or other ecclesiastical authority and withdrawn from the jurisdiction of bishops, refers chiefly to the internal order of their communities so that in them all things may be properly coordinated and the growth and perfection of the Religious common life promoted. These communities are also exempt so that the supreme pontiff can dispose of them for the good of the universal Church and any other competent authority for the good of the churches under its own jurisdiction.

This exemption, however, does not exclude Religious in individual dioceses from the jurisdiction of bishops in accordance with the norm of law, insofar as the performance of their pastoral office and the right ordering of the care of souls requires.

All Religious, exempt and non-exempt, are subject to the authority of the local Ordinaries in those things which pertain to the public exercise of divine worship—except where differences in rites are concerned—the care of souls, the sacred preaching intended for the people, the religious and moral education of the Christian faithful, especially of the children, catechetical instruction and liturgical formation. They are subject to the local Ordinary also in what pertains to the decorum proper to the clerical state as well as in the various works which concern the exercise of the sacred apostolate. Catholic schools conducted by Religious are also subject to the authority of the local Ordinaries for purposes of general policy-making and vigilance, but the right of Religious to direct them remains intact. Religious also are bound to observe all those things which councils or conferences of bishops shall legitimately prescribe for observance by all.

A well-ordered cooperation is to be encouraged between various religious communities and between them and the diocesan clergy. There should also be a very close coordination of all apostolic works and activities which especially depend upon a supernatural attitude of hearts and minds, rooted in and founded upon charity. The Apostolic See is competent to supervise this coordination for the universal Church; sacred pastors are competent in their own respective dioceses: and patriarchal synods and episcopal conferences in their own territory.

For those works of the apostolate which Religious are to undertake, bishops or episcopal conferences, religious superiors or conferences of major religious superiors should take action only after mutual consultations.

In order to foster harmonious and fruitful mutual relations between bishops and religious, at stated times and as often as it is deemed opportune, bishops and religious superiors should meet to discuss those affairs which pertain to the apostolate in their territory,

Decree Concerning the Pastoral Office
of Bishops in the Church, n. 35

Since the particular church is bound to represent the universal Church as perfectly as possible, let it realize that it has been sent to those also who are living in the same territory with it and who do not yet believe in Christ. By the life witness of each one of the faithful and of the whole community, let the particular church be a sign which points out Christ to others.

Furthermore, there is need of the ministry of the word, so that the Gospel may reach all. The bishop should be first and foremost a herald of the Faith, who leads new disciples to Christ. In order that he may properly fulfill this noble task, let him thoroughly study both the conditions of his flock, and the private opinions of his countrymen concerning God, taking careful note also of those changes which urbanization, migrations, and religious indifferentism have introduced.

The local priests in the young churches should zealously address themselves to the work of spreading the Gospel, and join forces with the foreign missionaries who form with them one college of priests, united under the authority of the bishop. They should do this, not only with a view to the

feeding of the faithful flock, and to the celebrating
of divine worship, but also to the preaching of the
Gospel to those outside. Let them show themselves
ready, and when the occasion presents itself, let
them with a willing heart offer the bishop their
services for missionary work in distant and forsaken
areas of their own diocese or of other dioceses.

Let religious men and women, and the laity,
too, show the same fervent zeal toward their countrymen, especially toward the poor.

Decree on the Mission Activity of the Church, n. 20

Man must respond to God Who calls, and that
in such a way, that without taking counsel with
flesh and blood (Gal. 1:16), he devotes himself
wholly to the work of the Gospel. This response,
however, can only be given when the Holy Spirit
gives His inspiration and His power. For he who
is sent enters upon the life and mission of Him Who
"emptied Himself, taking the nature of a slave"
(Phil. 2:7). Therefore, he must be ready to stay at
his vocation for an entire lifetime, and to renounce
himself and all those whom he thus far considered
as his own, and instead to "make himself all things
to all men" (1 Cor. 9:22).

Announcing the Gospel to all nations, he con-
fidently makes known the mystery of Christ, whose
ambassador he is, so that in him he dares to speak
as he ought (cf. Eph. 6:19; Acts 4:31), not being
ashamed of the scandal of the Cross. Following in
his Master's footsteps, meek and humble of heart,
he proves that His yoke is easy and His burden

light (Matt. 11:29ff.). By a truly evangelical life, in much patience, in long-suffering, in kindness, in unaffected love (cf. 2 Cor. 6:4ff.), he bears witness to his Lord, if need be to the shedding of his blood. He will ask of God the power and strength, that he may know that there is an overflowing of joy amid much testing of tribulation and deep poverty (2 Cor. 8:2). Let him be convinced that obedience is the hallmark of the servant of Christ, who redeemed the human race by His obedience.

Decree on the Mission Activity of the Church, n. 24.

UNITED FORCES

Pope Paul VI

It is of the greatest concern to Us that the work of the members of Religious Institutes should go along harmoniously with the norms established by the Sacred Hierarchy. As a matter of fact, the exemption of Religious Orders is in no conflict whatsoever with the divinely given Constitution of the Church, by force of which every priest, particularly in the performance of the sacred ministry, must obey the Sacred Hierarchy. For the members of these Religious Institutes are, at all times and in all places, subject principally to the Roman Pontiff, as to their highest Superior (Canon 499, p. 1). For this reason, the Religious Institutes are at the service of the Roman Pontiff in those works which pertain to the welfare of the universal Church. With regard to the exercise of the sacred apostolate in various dioceses, Religious are also under the jurisdiction of Bishops, to whom they are bound to give assistance, always without prejudice to the nature of their proper apostolate and the things that are necessary for their religious life. From all this, it is quite evident how much the allied and auxiliary ministry of the Religious given to the diocesan clergy conduces to the good of the Church, when their united forces result in more vigorous and more effective action.

Address to All Religious,
May 23, 1964

HOW GREAT ARE YOUR ACCOMPLISHMENTS

Pope Paul VI

We must tell you how much the Church esteems you and loves you. Hearing the call of Our Lord, you have generously left your homes and families to follow Him, to minister to His needs in the schools, in little children, in the sick, the aged and the infirm, and to dedicate lives of prayer to Him and His Church.

In the name of Jesus Christ and of the whole Catholic Church, We thank you for all that you do for Our blessed Savior and for His Mystical Body. How great are your accomplishments, how high your merit! God will repay you, for His fidelity endures forever.

Be faithful to your vocation; be generous in every sacrifice necessary to protect and foster it. Be holy; yet be also of good heart in your vocation; be cheerful and smiling, so that all may see the great happiness you feel in the unselfish imitation of Our Lord and His blessed Mother.

We pray for you, and for all those entrusted to your care, in schools, hospitals, and other institutions of charity and mercy. We beg a remembrance in your prayers for Us in the fulfillment of Our universal Fatherhood. And We lovingly impart to you, to your pupils, patients, helpers and benefactors, Our special paternal Apostolic Blessing.

To Sisters in Bombay, December, 1964

RELIGIOUS LIFE IS APOSTOLIC
BY NATURE

Rev. Anastasio of the Holy Rosary, O.C.D.

The roots of the essentially apostolic nature of religious life are not to be found in the sum total of the activities set forth in specific rules. Rather, these roots spring from the fact that by means of the religious bond, the development of Baptism reaches such an extent as to make our participation in and communion with the mystery of Christ and the Church to be of the fullest measure. Hence, the action of Christ and of the Church binds consecrated souls. These souls are apostles not because of what they do, but first of all because of what they are.

From: *"La Vita Religiosa nella Chiesa"*

The Various Forms
of Religious Life

THE CONTEMPLATIVE LIFE

Communities which are entirely dedicated to contemplation, so that their members in solitude and silence, with constant prayer and penance willingly undertaken, occupy themselves with God alone, retain at all times, no matter how pressing the needs of the active apostolate may be, an honorable place in the Mystical Body of Christ, whose "members do not all have the same function" (Rom. 12:4). For these offer to God a sacrifice of praise which is outstanding. Moreover the manifold results of their holiness lends luster to the people of God which is inspired by their example and which gains new members by their apostolate which is as effective as it is hidden. Thus they are revealed to be a glory of the Church and a well-spring of heavenly graces. Nevertheless their manner of living should be revised according to the principles and criteria of adaptation and renewal mentioned above. However their withdrawal from the world and the exercises proper to the contemplative life should be preserved with the utmost care.

Decree on the Adaptation and Renewal of Religious Life, n. 7.

Papal cloister should be maintained in the case of nuns engaged exclusively in the contemplative life. However, it must be adjusted to conditions of

387

time and place and obsolete practices suppressed. This should be done after due consultation with the monasteries in question. But other nuns applied by rule to apostolic work outside the convent should be exempted from papal cloister in order to enable them better to fulfill the apostolic duties entrusted to them. Nevertheless, cloister is to be maintained according to the prescriptions of their constitutions.

Decree on the Adaptation and Renewal of Religious Life, n. 16.

THE CLOISTER OF NUNS

The papal enclosure of monasteries must be considered an ascetical institution closely joined to the special vocation of nuns. The enclosure is a sign, safeguard and special expression of their withdrawal from the world.

Nuns of the Oriental rites should observe their own cloister in the same spirit.

This enclosure should be arranged in such a way that material separation from the outside world is always preserved. Individual Religious families, according to their own spirit, can establish and define in their constitutions particular norms for this material separation.

Minor enclosure is abolished. Nuns, therefore, who by their rule are devoted to external works should define their own enclosure in their constitutions. However, nuns who, although contemplative by their rule, have taken up external works, after a suitable time which is granted them to deliberate, should either retain the papal enclosure and give up their external works or, continuing these works, should define their own enclosure in their constitutions, retaining their status as nuns.

Ecclesiae Sanctae, on No. 16 of the Decree Perfectae Caritatis

THE CHURCH TODAY STILL
NEEDS CONTEMPLATIVES

The Church today still needs this form of religious life; the world today needs it.

Yes, the Church and the world, for different but converging reasons, need the contemplative to withdraw from the ecclesial and social community, and seclude herself in her retreat of solitude and silence.

We need to hear the enchanting strains of her calm and recollected prayer. We need her to draw and invite us to the doorstep of her cloister; to present us with the design of a workshop of "divine service," with the miniature of an ideal society, in which love, obedience, innocence, the freedom of things and the art of using them, the primacy of the spirit, in a word, peace . . . the Gospel . . . , have final dominion.

The contemplative serves in the world today by helping us recuperate our personal lives. Excitement, noise, haste, exteriority, the crowd, threaten the interior life of man. He is in want of silence with its genuine interior word, order, prayer, peace.

Pope Paul VI, 1965

❋

Of those who live in the silence of a cloister, and particularly of them, the Church expects a great deal. Like Moses, (Ex. 17:11) they keep their arms raised up in prayer, knowing full well that in this attitude of supplication, victory is obtained. They are in the midst of the world as a testimony: they bear witness to the transcendence of God.

Pope John XXIII, 1961

*

What we have called the spirituality of the wilderness, that form of contemplative spirit which seeks God in silence and detachment, is a deep prompting of the Spirit which will never cease as long as hearts can be found to listen to His voice.

The *love* of God—not fear, not repentance, not mere prudence—causes the solitudes of monasteries to be populated.

What a victory of the Almighty, what a glory for the Savior that, in the midst of great modern cities, in the wealthiest countries, as also in the plains of the Ganges or the forests of Africa, there are souls capable of being content for their lifetime with adoration and praise, who voluntarily dedicate themselves to thanksgiving and intercession, who deliberately pledge themselves to the Creator for mankind, to the heavenly Father as protectors and intercessors for their brothers.

Pope Pius XII, 1958

"YOU ARE CHOSEN SOULS, BUT NOT SEPARATED"

Pope Paul VI

Dearest daughters, you could not come to me, and therefore We say again, as We have said in other circumstances, I come to you, for no one in the Church should be excluded or hindered from having such direct and loyal contact with the Head of the Church.

That courageous, heroic act of yours in detaching yourselves from the world and the social community in order to enter what is called "cloister," has enclosed you herein and keeps you from those contacts which are normally offered to other communities of the faithful. While visiting Santa Sabina, I thought it well to pay a little call on you, too, precisely so that you may be persuaded that your cloister is not a prison and does not segregate you from the communion of Holy Church.

And in greeting you, happy to see that your home has been so well restored, that your community is large, and that you are glad to welcome Us, what shall We say? Only two thoughts. And the first is your relationship with the Church.

THE CHURCH IS LOOKING TO YOU

From an outside view, it would seem that you have been segregated. You are not to be seen in the processions of all the other faithful, nor are you present at those wonderful gatherings in which all the other faithful sing and mingle to form but one heart and soul before the altar of God. You are set apart, secluded.

Does this material, exterior, social seclusion separate you from the Church? I have come to tell you: be convinced that the Church thinks of you—you have not been forgotten—and therefore the separation which would be the gravest of all, the spiritual separation, is non-existent. Why? Because you are the object of particular attention and remembrance. Shall we say more? The Church looks to you, who have given yourselves to this type of life in order to converse unceasingly with the Lord: you have made this rapport between heaven and earth the sole program of your life. The Church sees in you the highest expression of herself; in a certain sense, you are at the summit.

For what is the Church trying to do in this world if not to unite souls to God, if not to make it possible for them to say "Our Father," to talk with the Lord, to converse intimately with God? And what does the Church wish to do other than render every soul receptive to the word of God? You know that our whole salvation comes from listening to the word of God. For faith comes from it, and from faith, all else. Why does the Church preach, speak, work? Why is it missionary and pastoral? It wants souls to open up and receive God's word, His message, His Gospel—and receiving, believe, and believing, order their lives as God wills and thus be saved.

With no reservations, you have given your entire existence to this listening and responding to the word of God. You have forgotten all else in order to have this opportunity in all its intensity and in greater measure and thus it is that the Church sees in contemplative souls, persons who fulfill its purpose—partially, it is understood, but nevertheless in the highest form. You are at the summit of that religious life which the Church wishes to foster among men.

If you are thus upon the mount of the Transfiguration, that is, conversing with God in a very clear vision of His true reality, His Divinity, and His humanity, you are not thereby dispensed from thinking of the infinite number of souls you have behind you.

You are chosen souls, but not separated. You are among those called to carry on a dialogue with God, but not for yourselves alone; you, too, have a mission which transcends your own individual souls and the little cloister of this community. You are at this level of the religious life not only for your own well-being, your own advantage and your own sanctification, but also for the Church, and therefore the spiritual ties—nonetheless real—which form the Communion of Saints, have not been severed; rather, they become more evident and have more strength with regard to you, just as, when a sail is hoisted, the fibers which compose it become taut and exert more force. So it is that you, having been called to dialogue with the Lord, feel the tension of the entire secular world behind you, of the unbelieving world, of a world both sinful and good and of the Church, which is on her way up but has to struggle and needs someone to give her a hand, joining forces with her. She needs your prayer, your sacrifice, your example and your closeness to God.

And, coming among you, I would truly like to recommend this: do not forget the Church, do not make your community your only world. The entire world belongs to you, daughters; the entire Church is yours, and therefore the remembrance of what Saints Peter and Paul said of our great Catholic community ought to live in your hearts.

PRAY

Pray for the missions, pray for the dying, pray for the sick, for sinners, for priests, for children, for other religious vocations, for all those who are on the march toward the kingdom of God. This ought to be your thought, your preoccupation. It must move you, fire you, and make your prayer ardent, almost passionate. One cannot approach the Lord in prayer as tranquilly as if one were taking part in a friendly little conversation. You must carry the world's passion in your heart: "I have withdrawn in order to unite myself; I have withdrawn in order to offer myself; I have withdrawn in order to suffer; I have withdrawn in order to become a victim of expiation for others, to obtain the graces which will pass through me to sweep over the entire world."

You must have a profound sense of this spirit of solidarity with the whole Church. And here we would have great things to tell you. You know that the Church is suffering. You know that the Church meets obstacles in many places, being unable to speak or spread herself. You know that there are still many Christians, many religious, too, who cannot profess their faith or vocation because the conditions of the world about them do not permit. You should bear this suffering of the Church in your heart and be crucified yourselves, as the Lord is crucified in these souls who are suffering the passion of the world for His glory and His name. Isn't it true that this comes first? Let us forge a link between you and the entire Church—are we agreed?

LET RELIGIOUS COMMUNITIES BE PERFECT!

The second thought? You could voice the second thought yourselves. It is this: is your relationship with your community as I wish it to be? To become religious in order to be imperfect would be foolishness. If you have come here, it is because you want to seek and attain to perfection; you do not come to quarrel over things of secondary importance, but truly to embrace the program prescribed by your Rule and adhere to it with joy and perfection, seeking moreover to make this execution of your law resplendent. There are many ways of doing things! One may do them any way or, on the other hand, one may do them with attention, good spirit, good example, gentleness and joy. When something does not go well, say, "Lord, here I must show myself heroic in both a small and great way." You will never have tremendous opportunities to perform deeds of physical or moral heroism as do soldiers, fliers, or sailors. Your heroism is your Rule and you should strive to observe it well.

I repeat, We want all religious communities—and especially yours, which are meant to be more demanding—either to be perfect, or nothing—isn't it so?

Last summer in the American city of Denver, there was a great gathering of Sisters from all the American religious communities. At this meeting, one of the sisters said, "We must be in the front lines." Well said! The Church takes you at your word; you religious must be in the front lines in example, in adherence to the Gospel, in ability to follow your plans in their fullness, and let the world see that truly you do wish to be exemplary.

Perhaps at this point an observation is in order, since you might say: Exemplary? How can anyone see or know what we do here within these thick walls? Do not deceive yourselves. The world knows very well whether you are good, tepid or imperfect. I don't know how it is, but there is a certain transparency by which the world knows if a community is good, perfect and truly borne along by the warmth of chairty or if on the other hand it is tepid and behaves more like some professional society.

As a consequence of this little visit of mine, promise to live up to your definition of contemplative nuns faithful to the Church, all tending toward that great, unique, summarizing virtue which embraces everything in this life and in the next—charity.

Address to Camaldolese Nuns, March 23, 1966.

COMMUNITIES DEVOTED TO THE
APOSTOLIC LIFE

There are in the Church very many communities, both clerical and lay, which devote themselves to various apostolic tasks. The gifts which these communities possess differ according to the grace which is allotted to them. Administrators have the gift of administration, teachers that of teaching, the gift of stirring speech is given to preachers, liberality to those who exercise charity and cheerfulness to those who help others in distress (cf. Rom. 12:5-8). "The gifts are varied, but the Spirit is the same" (1 Cor. 12:4).

In these communities apostolic and charitable activity belongs to the very nature of the religious life, seeing that it is a holy service and a work characteristic of love, entrusted to them by the Church to be carried out in its name. Therefore, the whole religious life of their members should be inspired by an apostolic spirit and all their apostolic activity formed by the spirit of religion. Therefore in order that their members may first correspond to their vocation to follow Christ and serve Him in His members, their apostolic activity must spring from intimate union with Him. Thus love itself towards God and the neighbor is fostered.

These communities, then, should adjust their rules and customs to fit the demands of the apostolate to which they are dedicated. The fact however that apostolic religious life takes on many forms requires that its adaptation and renewal take account of this diversity and provide that the lives of religious dedicated to the service of Christ in these various communities be sustained by special provisions appropriate to each.

Decree on the Adaptation and Renewal of Religious Life, n. 8.

APOSTOLIC ENERGY AND LOVE COMES FROM PRAYER

Pope Paul VI

Now a question about zeal for souls, with which your entire society is on fire: Has it seemed necessary, for the sake of giving increased effectiveness to your work, to depart from so many usages related to spiritual and ascetical practice and training, as if they no longer helped and so prevented a freer and more personal expression of your pastoral concern?

Perhaps some are misled into thinking that to spread the Gospel of Christ it is necessary to adopt the methods of the world, its way of thinking, its profane understanding of life. They have judged the morals of this age by the accepted ideas of naturalism.

In this matter, too, they forget that the apostolic confrontation of the messenger of Christ with men to whom he would give the message of Christ cannot require such an assimilation that the salt would lose its sharp taste, that the apostle would be despoiled of his proper character.

Yes, those clouds have darkened the sky. But in the deliberations of your general convention they have mostly vanished. For, as we have learned with no small pleasure, you with that strong uprightness

that has always guided your wills, after carefully
studying your history, your task and your experience—you yourselves have decided to stay firmly
in your original ways. You did not set aside your
tradition, which at all times has been strong among
you with a present effectiveness and vigor.

The Council's Decree on the Renewal of Religious Life not only allows but encourages changes
in the rules of Religious. By introducing special
changes into your rules, you in no way violate the
sacred law whereby you are religious and members
of the Society of Jesus. Rather you have remedied
your regulations wherever they were pressed down
by the weight of past times; and you have discovered new resources for your future undertakings.

So now this favorable result stands out among
the decisions that you have made in your hard-
working discussion. It is a result, we affirm, in
which it happens that not only the body of your
society but also its spirit is really preserved and
extended by unquestionable additions.

As for that spirit, we earnestly exhort you not
to depart from the beneficial regulations of your
predecessors, but in the future to give a foremost
place in your life to prayer. For how except by
divine grace, which, as it were, like living water
flows to us through the earthly conduits of prayer,
of conversation with God, and especially of the
sacred liturgy—how will the individual Religious
imbibe heavenly guidance and strength to reach his
supernatural sanctification?

Where will the apostle get the energy, direction, power, wisdom and perseverance in the contest

that he must wage with the world, the flesh and the devil? Where will he develop the love that cherishes souls for the sake of their salvation? How build the Church except with laborers who have been commissioned to the work of that mystical building, the Church, as their office and conscientious duty?

Be glad, dearest sons. That is the way, both old and new, of the Christian economy. That is the form which makes a true Religious the disciple of Christ, the apostle in His Church, the teacher of his brothers, or of believers, or of others. Be glad. Our good wishes—more than that, our spirit—communes with you, comforts you, and is present to you.

So your particular sessions which concern the training of your scholastics; the reverence to be given to the teaching and ruling authority of the Church; the rules of religious perfection; the guidelines by which apostolic action and your supporting pastoral works are rightly directed; the true interpretation of the decrees of general Councils; the sure way by which they will be made effective; and others of this kind—they should be considered as answers to our inquiry.

Yes, indeed. The sons of St. Ignatius, who glory in the name of members of the Society of Jesus, still stand true to themselves and remain the trusted ones of the Church. They are ready and strong. Rejecting worn-out and less effective means, they handle new arms with the same obedience, the same eagerness to devote themselves, the same will to produce spiritual victories.

At this solemn, historic hour, you do state and ratify in new regulations that you will be most tena-

cious of your institute. In the age when the renewal
work of the Council of Trent pulsated, your society
gave itself to the service of the Catholic Church.
Therefore it pleases us graciously to repeat the
words and deeds of our predecessors in this age—an
age indeed different but no less outstanding as a re-
newer of the Church, following as it does the Second Ecumenical Vatican Council. It gratifies us to
state that this Apostolic See, and surely with it the
Church, cherishes your society, so long as the society aims to invest its potentiality in sound doctrine
and holiness of the religious life, and gives itself as
a mighty force for the protection and spread of the
Catholic faith.

What was the secret reason why your society
spread so far and enjoyed such prosperity, except
your unique school of spirituality, your *esprit de
corps*, and canonical structure? If that school and
structure remain the same, and if they flourish with
a new vigor of virtues and works, it is no idle hope
that you will steadily grow and enjoy a lasting effectiveness in proclaiming the Gospel and building the
human society of our times.

The structure of your evangelical and religious
life, your exemplary history and organization—are
they not your best defense and recommendation?
Do they not form a strong argument to have faith
in your apostolate? Is not this spiritual and moral
steadiness respecting the community of the Church
the basis of trust in your work, and the assister of
that work?

Allow us to say, at the end of this address, that
we place a great hope in you. The Church needs

your aid, and it is happy and proud to get it from such sincere, dedicated sons as you are. The Church accepts the help that you promise, and more so the life that you offer. And since you are soldiers of Christ, the Church now calls on you and urges you to undertake hard sacred battles in its name.

Do you not see how much defense the faith needs in these times—how open an assent, how clear a statement, how ceaseless a preaching, how wise an explanation, how loving and generous a witness?

We trust in you as the able witnesses of a belief that is one and the same.

Do you not see the opportunities that the modern ecumenism of the holy Catholic Church gives to the servant and apostle: to establish successfully the basic lines with others, to sow prudently the seeds of dialogue, to offer explanations patiently, to widen the room of charity?

Who are better fitted than you to bring together these investigations and labors with the intention that brothers still separated from us will know and acknowledge us, will hear us, and will share with us the glory, joy and companionship of the mystery of unity in Christ the Lord?

Are there not among you able men, prudent, vigorous, well experienced at penetrating the world of this age with Christian principles, as is described in the pastoral constitution [on the Church in the Modern World] that begins with the words "*gaudium et spes*" [joys and hopes]? Do you not still have in your homage for the heart of Jesus a most effective devotion to renew the minds and morals of

the world, in keeping with the exhortations of the
Second Vatican Council, and to carry out produc-
tively the task entrusted to you, which is your own
commitment to work against atheism?

Will you not engage with a fresh dedication in
the training of young people in church and public
secondary schools and universities, with the same
plaudits and reputation that you earned before? You
must remember how many tender souls are confided to you, souls that some day can bring a high
usefulness to Church and human society if they are
trained under the right guidance.

What can we say about the missions? The missions, where so many of your members admirably
labor, sweat, bear sorrow, and make the name of
Jesus shine as the sun of salvation: have they not
been entrusted to you as they were once entrusted
to St. Francis Xavier by the Apostolic See? The
Apostolic See does so because it considers you to be
sure preachers of the faith, daring, on fire with a
charity that your dedication renders inexhaustible,
full of consolation, effective beyond words.

Now to end. What must be thought about the
world—about the world, we say, which as it were
presents two faces: one meaning the conspiracy of
all who oppose light and grace, the other meaning
the great human family for which the Father sent
the Son and the Son sacrificed Himself?

This latter world that now is so powerful and
weak, so hostile and open—does it not summon you
and us to itself with pleading and urging to perform
our duty? Does not this world, as if roaring and
throbbing, cry out to you all in this spot in the sight

of Christ: "Come, come." It waits for you, as we may say, with the need and hunger of Christ. "Come, it is time"?

Most loved sons, surely it is time. Go trustful and eager. Christ chooses you, the Church sends you, the Pope blesses you.

Address to the 31st general congregation of the
Society of Jesus, November 16, 1966

THE SOUL OF THE APOSTOLATE

Very Rev. James Alberione, S.S.P., S.T.D.

Your fidelity to the devout life is the guarantee and measure of your effectiveness and power in the apostolate. Prayer life is the soul of the apostolate, and an apostolate without a soul is dead, profiting neither the one who performs it nor the one to whom it is directed. All the persuasive power of an apostle, all his success and effectiveness depend on his own dependence on God. It is union with God which makes for a successful apostle. The apostolate must be continually fed by piety, and every means should be taken to keep alive the fervor of the community. Where religious are truly devout, they are also more generous, more supernatural and more efficient as apostles.

THE MONASTIC LIFE

The principal duty of monks is to offer a service to the divine majesty at once humble and noble within the walls of the monastery, whether they dedicate themselves entirely to divine worship in the contemplative life or have legitimately undertaken some apostolate or work of Christian charity. Retaining, therefore, the characteristics of the way of life proper to them, they should revive their ancient traditions of service and so adapt them to the needs of today that monasteries will become institutions dedicated to the edification of the Christian people.

Some religious communities according to their rule or constitutions closely join the apostolic life to choir duty and monastic observances. These should so adapt their manner of life to the demands of the apostolate appropriate to them that they observe faithfully their way of life, since it has been of great service to the Church.

Decree on the Adaptation and Renewal of Religious Life, n. 9

RELIGIOUS LIFE
A FOLLOWING OF CHRIST

Pope Paul VI

First of all We have to re-affirm the true and genuine meaning of religious life as a *following of Christ*, in accordance with His words and example: "If any man wants to come after me, let him deny himself, take up his cross and follow me." As if to comment on these words, St. Augustine traces out the ideal of a life consecrated to Christ in his own inimitable and fascinating style, by placing these words on the lips of the Divine Savior: "This is the way: walk humbly so that you may reach eternity. I have given you an example: I was hungry, I was thirsty, I was tired, I slept, I was taken prisoner, I was beaten, I was crucified, I was killed."

"I have spurned all earthly goods to show that they ought to be spurned; and I have put up with all earthly evils which I commanded people to put up with: so that you might not seek happiness in the former, nor be afraid of unhappiness in the latter. . . . And I who created all things became poor too; so that no one who would believe in me would dare to accept praise for earthly riches. I did not want men to make me a king; because, with humility, I was pointing out the path to the lowly whom pride would have separated from me: even though each and every creature attests to my never-ending kingdom. I who feed all was hungry, I who created all drink was thirsty— I, who am the spiritual bread of those who hunger, and spiritual font of those who thirst."

Poverty, humility, mortification: this is the unwavering line of the Savior's life; this is His daily bread, to do the will of God; and this is the line that must be embraced by anyone who wants to follow Christ more faithfully and more closely in religious life.

This calls for a profound spiritual life, steadily cultivated in silence, in detachment from the world, in meditation, in study, in prayer. It calls for an effective practice of the Gospel counsels, as they are proposed by the age-old religious and monastic rules of poverty, chastity and obedience. To quote the wise words of the Dogmatic Constitution *De Ecclesia* of the Second Ecumenical Council of the Vatican: "For these counsels, voluntarily accepted according to each one's personal vocation, contribute greatly to the purification of the heart and to spiritual liberty. They never cease to stir up the fervor of charity. And, in particular, they are able to bring the Christian into fuller conformity with the life of virginity and poverty which Christ the Lord chose for Himself and which His Virgin Mother also embraced" (n. 46).

EXTENDING CHRIST'S PRESENCE IN THE WORLD

This voluntary imitation of Christ should be the aim and purpose of a humble and punctual observance of the Rule, which should be authoritatively brought back to its spirit, and reaffirmed and modified as the times require. The *aggiornamento* called for by the new demands of the times ought to make it easier in our day for individual Religious to conform in this way to their divine Model. It certainly is not a question of an *aggiornamento* that aims at catching up with the secular world. Rather, it is a sincere and loving pursuit of anything that will be of help and encouragement to a more faithful extension in the world of Christ's presence, His example, and His sacrificial life that was expended for the glory of the Father and the salvation of the brethren.

This is the main thing that the men of today want from Religious, over and above their stern demands, over and above their criticisms, even over and above their opposition; and it must be said that some people's hostility may well be the unconscious complaint of one who, along his earthly path, has met a soul consecrated to God and could not see Christ in him, as he longed to do from the bottom of his heart.

With such an aim in mind, you have to have a sense of the true wants, the expectations, the necessities of the world—not of its ways and its mentality—if you are to give better thought and consideration to how Religious can serve its redemption and its prosperity. It is clear that temporal prosperity must not be looked upon as the supreme good in life; and, in this regard, the Religious has the great responsibility of showing the world the ideal of evangelical poverty, the model of a perfect Christian, the eschatological anticipation of the Kingdom of God on earth. As a matter of fact, man's hope must not be avidly and greedily rooted in time; instead the transcendent hope of the ultimate end must be pursued, in search of that which remains definitively above and beyond the frail and perishable things that pass away.

A "SIGN" VALUE TO THE WORLD

This seems to Us to be the most urgent and up-to-date "sign" value that religious life is called upon to offer the community of the faithful. For if the profession of the evangelical counsels stands at the high point of the practice of the Christian life which is planted in germ form in Baptism and developed through the sacramental organism and through fidelity to the grace of God, then it is clear that all those who consecrate themselves to that profession ought to shine forth before their brethren for their total detachment from earthly realities, for their cheerful and unselfish adherence to the obligations taken on in Baptism and Confirmation, and for the living testimony they give to Christ and His Kingdom of truth, holiness and love.

This is a shining teaching of the Sacred Council: "The People of God have no lasting city here; they look forward to one that is to come. Since this is so, the religious state, giving its members greater freedom from earthly cares, more clearly reveals to all believers the heavenly benefits already present in this world. It also bears witness more clearly to the new, eternal life won by Christ's redemption and more clearly foretells the future resurrection and the glory of the heavenly kingdom" (Constitution on the Church, n. 44).

Of course this does not mean that the Religious forgets about the world or is indifferent to the world's anxiety and suffering and eagerness for greater justice and freedom and charity. Once again the Council points this up: "For even though they sometimes do not have direct contact with their contemporaries, they are present to them in a deeper way in the heart of Christ, and they cooperate with them spiritually, so that the building-up of the earthly city may always be grounded in the Lord and directed toward Him" (Constitution on the Church, n. 46).

This mature awareness of the place that the Church assigns to Religious in the world and the task that she entrusts to them, of being the vigilant spokesmen before God for spiritual and material needs and the sentinels watching for the dawning of eternal light, ought to make you ever more sensitive to the grandeur, the responsibility, the elevating task involved in your vocation.

PROFOUND ADHERENCE TO HOLY MOTHER THE CHURCH

The final thing We expect of you is that together you will succeed in deepening your sense of the Church, as the Ecumenical Council has presented it in brilliant synthesis and as We Ourself have been trying to describe it and convey it to all the priests and faithful who have come to Our general audiences over the years.

We know that We will meet with a most frank and open response from you sons and heirs of St. Augustine in this important and delicate matter. As We stressed at the beginning, the Augustinian Order has shone through the centuries because of its fidelity to the Church, which it has venerated and praised as a mother. It is the spirit of the founder that still teaches with tremendous vigor: "Love the Catholic Church, love the Church of Christ, and, in loving the Church of Christ, you will receive the Holy Spirit, if you are united in charity, if you rejoice in being called a Catholic and possessing the faith of a Catholic."

"Love the Lord thy God, love His Church: the former as a Father, the latter as a mother. . . . Let no one say: I commit no sins; but still I am not in the Church. What good is it to you not to have offended the Father, if you claim to have offended the mother? What good is it if you profess the Lord, honor God, preach Him, acknowledge His Son, profess that He is sitting at the right hand of the Father and still blaspheme His Church?"

If you are to have this delicate, filial disposition, you must profess loyalty to the thought and the rules of the Church, and avoid certain critical attitudes that want reform of traditional doctrines, venerable customs, or fundamental and august structures of the ecclesiastical body; and also avoid certain presumed returns to the fonts, as is claimed, which seek to justify a spirit intolerant of discipline, to undermine the teaching of the Church, or to support certain naturalistic orientations that empty souls and institutions of the genuine spirit of Christ.

We are sure that your Order will not only succeed in staying clear of these dangerous attractions, but that it will root its own adherence to the Church ever deeper in the light of the Augustinian teaching and in the spirit of its Rules, and that it will make this adherence its model program, its constant concern, its proud banner before the whole world. May the moving hymn of St. Augustine that contains within it the whole of his soul, aflame with love for the Church, rise to your lips: "O Holy Catholic Church, true mother of Christians, . . . thou art the temple of the eternal king which is in unity: not going to ruin, not torn to pieces, not divided. Thy stones are living stones, God's faithful, and the link between thy living stones is charity."

Address to the 88th General Chapter
of the Augustinians, August 30, 1965

SECULAR INSTITUTES

Secular Institutes, although not Religious institutes, involve a true and full profession of the evangelical counsels in the world. This profession is recognized by the Church and consecrates to God men and women, lay and clerical, who live in the world. Hence they should make a total dedication of themselves to God in perfect charity their chief aim, and the institutes themselves should preserve their own proper, i.e., secular character, so that they may be able to carry out effectively everywhere in and, as it were, from the world the apostolate for which they were founded.

It may be taken for granted, however, that so great a task cannot be discharged unless the members be thoroughly trained in matters divine and human so that they are truly a leaven in the world for the strengthening and growth of the body of Christ. Superiors, therefore, should give serious attention especially to the spiritual training to be given members as well as encourage their further formation.

Decree on the Adaptation and Renewal of Religious Life, n. 11

A CRY IN THE WILDERNESS

Rev. Thomas P. McCarthy, C.S.V.

The associations of consecrated lày-men and women who have dedicated themselves to follow Christ have been called Secular Institutes by Pope Pius XII. These are societies composed of priests, laymen, or laywomen who have bound themselves under vows, oaths, or promises to practice the evangelical counsels of poverty, chastity, and obedience for the purposes of increasing their own personal sanctification while exercising an apostolate of love for Christ within the world.

In the words of Father Stephen Hartdegen, O.F.M., General Secretary of the Total Dedication Conference, "Secular Institutes have a very important role to play in witnessing to the neo-pagan civilization the Christian impact of love and marriage. Their dedicated chastity and virginity is a cry in the wilderness calling men back to their Christian heritage. Here are men and women who have a full and complete grasp and control of themselves, who have liberated themselves from the dominance and slavery of passion so as to be able to give themselves freely and generously in genuine love. The more each Secular Institute member appreciates this, the more fruitful will be his witness of dedicated chastity."

PERFECTION TO BE EXERCISED AND PROFESSED IN THE WORLD

Pope Pius XII

In achieving this raising up of societies of the faithful to the superior status of Secular Institutes, and in the ordering ... of all such Institutes, it must always be borne in mind that the proper and peculiar character of such Institutes, namely, that they are secular—and in this lies the whole reason for the existence of such Institutes—must stand out clearly in everything. Nothing of the full profession of Christian perfection, solidly based on the evangelical counsels and truly religious as to its substance, will be withdrawn, but this perfection is to be exercised and professed in the world; and consequently this perfection must be adapted to secular life in all such things as are lawful and not opposed to its duties and exercise.

Moto Proprio, *Primo Feliciter*, March 12, 1948

LIVING IN CHRIST
AND OF CHRIST
Very Rev. James Alberione, S.S.P., S.T.D.

It is an error to equate a Secular Institute with "Pious Union" such as an organization of cooperators or auxiliaries. On the practical level, it is just as erroneous to display expansive zeal for Catholic Action groups while remaining totally indifferent to religious Congregations and Secular Institutes. To discourage people from entering a religious community or Secular Institute, considering their members as failures, is a grave mistake. However, it is just as mistaken to impose the obligation of entering a Community or Secular Institute indiscriminately on all those who have a serious desire for personal sanctity.

To enter a Secular Institute a person must have a vocation. In this regard it should be noted that entrance into a state of perfection is not a question of generosity but of a divine calling. The call to profess the evangelical counsels imposes heavy renunciations because of which the Gospel event of the rich young man may be re-enacted today, either by laity or clergy: " 'If you will be perfect. . . .' When the young man heard the saying, he went away sad . . ." (Matt. 19:22).

Religious perfection is not just a lovely dream. It demands a deep spirit of piety, recollection, mortification and continual generosity. One has always to resist the world, the flesh and the ego. Thus it can be easily understood why constant spiritual direction is necessary. This is even more true for members of Secular Institutes, who live in contact with the world, in continual danger, arising from their apostolic activity itself, while at the same time they lack those spiritual aids which abound in the strictly religious Institutes.

This spiritual direction must be firm and permit no mediocrity. The spiritual directors need to be demanding rather than indulgent, infusing courage in the face of difficulties and especially when confronted by misunderstanding. They have to educate members to loyalty and fidelity to their Constitutions and to their superiors.

With the establishment of Secular Institutes, for both clergy and laity, a new field of action has been opened to all priests, just as new problems and needs have emerged. Right judgment and prudence alike are needed. The number of members is not as important as the quality. Let us make sure the two requirements established by Pope Pius XII are met: that the candidates have a burning love of God and transform their whole lives into an apostolate. In a word, the members of a Secular Institute, living in Christ and by Jesus Christ both in the privacy of their interior lives and in their apostolic work, sanctify themselves and sanctify their fellowmen, revealing thereby the grandeur and power of apostolic grace.

**Vocations
to the
Religious Life**

VOCATIONS TO THE RELIGIOUS LIFE

Priests and Christian educators should make serious efforts to foster religious vocations, thereby increasing the strength of the Church, corresponding to its needs. These candidates should be suitably and carefully chosen. In ordinary preaching, the life of the evangelical counsels and the religious state should be treated more frequently. Parents, too, should nurture and protect religious vocations in their children by instilling Christian virtue in their hearts.

Religious communities have the right to make themselves known in order to foster vocations and seek candidates. In doing this, however, they should observe the norms laid down by the Holy See and the local Ordinary.

Religious should remember there is no better way than their own example to commend their institutes and gain candidates for the religious life.

Decree on the Adaptation ond Renewal of Religious Life, n. 24

CONCILIAR DIRECTIVES FOR VOCATION RECRUITMENT

ENCOURAGING VOCATIONS

The duty of fostering vocations pertains to the whole Christian community, which should produce such vocations through the living of a full Christian life. Thus the principal contributers are the families which, animated by a spirit of faith and love and sense of duty, become a kind of initial seminary. Next in importance is the parish in whose rich life the young people take part. Then it is the teachers and those who are in charge of the training of youths, especially the leaders of Catholic associations who should carefully guide the young people entrusted to them to recognize and freely accept a divine vocation. Finally, all priests must manifest an apostolic zeal in fostering vocations and attract youths to follow in their footsteps through the example of their own life and their happy spirit.

Decree on Priestly Training

VOCATION WORK MUST BE PLANNED

The synod, moreover, orders that the entire pastoral activity of fostering vocations be methodically and coherently planned, and with equal prudence and zeal, fostered by those organizations for promoting vocations which, in accord with the ap-

propriate pontifical documents, have already been
or will be set up in the territory of individual dioceses, regions or countries."

Decree on Priestly Training

PRAYER FOR VOCATIONS

The sacred synod commends, first of all, the
traditional means of common effort, such as urgent
prayer, Christian penance and a constantly more in-
tensive training of the faithful by preaching, by
catechetical instructions, or by the many media of
social communication that will show forth the need,
the nature, and the importance of the priestly
vocation.

Decree on Priestly Training

Let all Christian people be taught that it is
their duty to cooperate in one way or another, by
constant prayer and other means at their disposal,
that the Church will always have a sufficient number of priests to carry out her divine mission.

Decree on the Ministry and Life of Priests

VOCATIONS MUST BE SPOTTED

This voice of the Lord calling, however, is
never to be expected as something which in an extraordinary manner will be heard by the ears of the
future priest. It is rather to be known and understood in the manner in which the will of God is daily
made known to prudent Christians. These indications should be carefully noted by priests.

Decree on the Ministry and Life of Priests

TEACHERS AND VOCATIONS

Parents and teachers and all who are engaged in any way in the education of boys and young men should so prepare them that they will recognize the solicitude of Our Lord for His flock, will consider the needs of the Church, and will be prepared to respond generously to Our Lord when He calls, saying, "Here I am Lord," (Isaia 6:8).

Decree on the Ministry and Life of Priests

THERE ARE STILL VOCATIONS
IN OUR CENTURY

Pope Paul VI

On the second Sunday after Easter, inspired by the Gospel of the Good Shepherd, the Church—the entire Church—observes the World Day of Prayer for Vocations.

The word "vocation" actually has a very broad connotation, and applies to all humanity called to Christian salvation (cf. Conc. Ec. Gravissimum, proemio; Gaudium et Spes: 13; 19; 21). But it becomes specific when it refers to those particular attitudes and those particular duties which determine the choice everyone makes to give his own life a perfect meaning. Every state of life, every profession, every dedication may be called a vocation, which confers upon it a higher dignity and a transcending value.

However, the word vocation acquires its full significance, which at the same time tends to become specific and perfect, if not exclusive, precisely where it is a matter of a doubly special vocation. This is so because it comes directly from God, like a ray of light penetrating the most intimate and deepest recesses of one's conscience; because it expresses itself practically in the total giving of a life to the one and highest love, to the love of God and to that which flows from it and makes us one with the first of brothers.

In this special sense, a vocation is such a unique and delicate fact, one so sacred, that it cannot be separated from the Church's intervention. The Church studies it, the Church encourages it, the Church guides it, the Church verifies it, the Church solemnly takes it upon herself.

Why does the Church manifest so much interest in vocations? Precisely because of the extraordinary value each holy vocation carries within itself. How could the Church be indifferent, or negligent—the Church who is mother and teacher of souls—in view of such a spiritual phenomenon, in which the most priceless virtues of a soul manifest themselves and in which the grace of the Holy Spirit is actualized in admirable ways and degrees.

We recall, in this connection, the parable of the precious pearl (Matt. 13:46). We recall the admonition of the (Second Vatican) Council which fixes the sanctifying function which is proper to bishops in relation to the encouragement they must lend to vocations.

Each vocation toward God's worship and toward service of the Church deserves the most lively attention on the part of those who cultivate, or who watch over the garden of souls. A vocation brings to reality in an eminent degree the flowering of God's kingdom in the world, whether in the Church or in the world as a whole. It is a sign of the presence of Love that comes from above; it is the beginning of a dialogue between the living Christ and the people—the family, the parish, the diocese—from whose bosom the chosen one is called. A judgment of values obliges the Church to concern itself with vocations.

But there is more. A judgment of necessity doubles such an obligation. Vocations are the hope of the Church where its constitutional solidity and its spiritual effectiveness are concerned. The Church, such as Christ wanted it to be, does not live without ministers. Evangelization requires them; the Gospel will be spread in proportion to the number, activity and sanctity of the ministers, called and consecrated to the most sublime, the most indispensable service—that of salvation.

We recall vividly the descriptive words of St. Paul: "For whoever calls upon the name of the Lord, shall be saved. How then are they to call upon him in whom they have not believed? But how are they to believe him whom they have not heard? And how are they to hear, if no one preaches? And how are men to preach unless they are sent" (Rom. 10:13-15)?

The need for a ministry qualified to irradiate the truth and grace brought by Christ in the world could not be expressed in more positive terms. And here is the drama! The Church does not send forth paid mercenaries; the Church does not organize a network of professional propagandists. The Church sends forth volunteers. She sends forth men who are free and who surely are not paid for what is required by their work in terms of labor, risk and merit.

The Church sends forth particular men—poor and generous, free from every compulsion, and bound within by the most sacrosanct of bonds, that of unique, chaste, perennial, consecrated love.

The Church sends forth followers of Christ who give their all to Him. The Church sends forth young men filled with ardent fervor and imagination, who have had an insight into the highest definition of life: an undertaking of divine love.

The Church sends forth humble heroes who believe in the Holy Spirit, and who, like Christ, are ready to give their life for the Church of Christ: "Christ... loved the Church and delivered Himself up for it" (Eph. 5:25); thus are the chosen, those whom the bishop welcomes, tests, instructs and then "ordains," in other words, charges with a sacramental efficacy of power and of tremendous and ineffable gifts, and then sends forth. He sends them forth to God's people; to children, to the poor, to those who suffer, to the weary, to the disciples of the Kingdom, and to the missions, to those far removed, to all! And they go forth. How marvelous!

But where are these chosen ones? Where are the ones who are called? Which are they and how many are they? Ecclesiastical sociology shows, here and there, some statistics which at times are distressing! Where are such vocations which appear to decide the fate of Christianity in our world and in our times? The drama is this: Jesus Himself gave warning of it: "The harvest indeed is great, but the laborers are few" (Matt. 9:37).

But, indeed, there are still vocations in the Church in our century. Our seminaries are rejoicing. Often a singularity of vocations substitutes for number. There come young men who already have a conscientious awareness and who are mature men. They know what they are choosing.

At this point, we would like to send to all those who are called to the priesthood and to the religious life: men and women (and what a discourse the women who are "called" would be deserving of!), we would like to send to all of them our affectionate greeting. May all seminarians, may all students with adult vocations, may all novices (men and women) of the religious families know that the Pope stands with them, prays for them, and, with tears of joy and hope, blesses all and each of them in the name of the Christ whom they go to meet.

Nevertheless, our heart still is not free from great anxiety: there are too many empty places in the framework of the services which the Church has need of: the number of vocations is too scanty in proportion to the needs. And we will go further, they are too scanty in proportion to the possibilities for the ministry. At times, this or that community of the faithful appears too indifferent to the problem of recruitment and formation of the clergy for our hearts to be placated.

We wish we could reach the doorways of the homes of many Christian families with a discreet, but frank, word: Do you have any vocations among your children?

We wish we could reach every pastor, every spiritual teacher: Are you watchful to discover the signs of a divine calling among the persons entrusted to your care?

We would like to thank and encourage the superiors and teachers of our seminaries and to tell them of the merit of their great solicitude.

And then, like the messengers of the Gospel word on the roads of the world, (we would like to) say to youths, among all the rest: Do you know that Christ needs you? Do you know that His call is for the strong; that it is for those who rebel against mediocrity and the cowardice of a comfortable and insignificant life; that it is for those who maintain an understanding of the Gospel and feel the duty to regenerate the ecclesiastical life with their own personal contribution and by bearing the cross?

Would that our cry be heard! But, meanwhile, we ask all, yes, all of you members of the holy Church of God, to welcome our invitation and to do at least one thing: do what Christ Himself commanded: "Pray . . . the Lord of the harvest that He send forth laborers into His harvest" (Matt. 9:38). We will point out that prayer is an essential part of this divine "economy." And it is precisely to prayer that the "Day" invites the clergy and the faithful throughout the world: to prayer for vocations.

Letter on the World Day of Prayer
for Vocations, March 5, 1967

FOUR POINTERS ON RECRUITMENT

Pope Paul VI

Considering all the efforts and undertakings demanded by our time for the desired renewal of the Church, it must surely be admitted that the work of priestly and religious vocations claims the primary place. Indeed, an effective, stable, and properly planned pastoral activity can scarcely be understood that does not devote its chief care to recruitment of religious candidates.

However, since We are speaking to men of outstanding experience in this field of the sacred apostolate, We need not remind you of the gravity of the questions and difficulties that demand solution in these days; how, alas, in so many areas the apostolate is handicapped by a scarcity of sacred ministers, which compels Us sadly to repeat the words of Christ our Lord: "The harvest, indeed, is great, but the laborers are few" (Luke 10:2).

Nor do we wish on this occasion to tackle the grave and complex questions concerning the right training of candidates for the priesthood. Important documents have been published by the Apostolic See on this matter on many occasions, and the Ecumenical Council itself gave wise rules that will be a great help in fulfilling this task properly and fruitfully.

It is rather Our concern at the moment to touch upon certain points regarding the psychology of youths called by a heavenly inspiration to take up the sacred ministry. This divine vocation, as you know, depends entirely on the secret counsel of God, according to the statement of our Divine Redeemer: "You have not chosen me, but I have chosen you" (John 15:16). However, God expects that a man will respond to His invitation by the free assent of his will; in other words, the divine call asks for man's hearing. Accordingly, we must see to it that the minds of the faithful—and of youths in particular—enjoy suitable aids by the help of which they may be able to hear the divine word, and when He invites them to Himself to answer in the words of the young Samuel: "Speak, Lord, for your servant hears" (1 Kings 3:9).

Now of all the aids by which young minds are disposed to hear the word of God, the most important is recollection which affords the chance of fostering interior silence. Today through sight and sound there bursts upon the minds of children and adolescents such an enormous number of distractions, often empty of solid content and sometimes even evil and pernicious, that these youths are prevented from considering and understanding the perfect way of life, its excellence and beauty. Accordingly, in a wise education they should be given certain moments for silence and recollection, especially moments in which a careful self-assessment can be made. Such could be the time in which they give thanks to God after Holy Communion, or it could be at a fixed period for meditation on eternal truths. Under such conditions youthful minds, being united in prayer to God, can converse with Him as with a Father. Then God Himself gradually will reveal His secret designs and expectations, and the youths will come to understand whether they are called to the priesthood or committed to some other service.

FAMILIARITY WITH SCRIPTURE

Another aid, which should be considered of great value and importance, is developing in youths an assiduous familiarity with God's words contained in Holy Scripture. This is best done according to the norms of "active" instruction, which has become prevalent in our time, demanding the mutual work of teachers and pupils. This means that the pupils read certain passages of the Gospel, discuss them, perceive the solemn and sacred force of Christ's words, and then try through their own effort and ability to comprehend the life and actions of our Divine Savior. For such spiritual formation, as all know, it is most important that we inform youths regarding the place and authority that Christ holds in their souls, and that we speak of Him as He is known from the Gospel sources. This explains the Church's concern in the matter, as given in the Decree on Priestly Training of the Vatican Council, "*Optatam totius*", n. 8: "Let them be taught to seek Christ in faithful reflection on the word of God; to seek Him in an active sharing in the mysteries of the Church." For on the minds of those young men who have developed this familiarity with Christ—a familiarity that comes not only from the study of books but more especially from the soul's intimate converse with Him and from a profound piety—an impression is made, which can never be effaced.

EXPERIENCE IN THE LIFE

Still another help to youths to hear the voice of God is to know by experience the active life of the Church. All who work for an increase of ecclesiastical vocations should be eager to have youths share in the needs of those laboring for the Gospel, in the hardships of the poor, and in the circumstances of a Christian community that is outstanding for its virtuous life. It is especially important that boys know the seminary where young men grow and develop in the future service of the Church. Such youths should be encouraged to their own potential in carrying out such works. Moreover, from their earliest years they should be accustomed to taking an active part in the liturgical rites, since nothing more powerfully moves souls to piety than familiarity with the sacred mysteries. This familiarity has the power to fill youths deeply with a kind of sacred inspiration, and to inflame them with the desire to follow in the footsteps of Christ.

SPIRITUAL DIRECTION

Finally, to insure that a vocation to the Church should in the end happily flower forth, it is very necessary for youths to have a chance to approach and listen to a teacher of the word of God—some priest worthy of respect for his sound conduct and

mature counsel, who can, like a father, receive the
secrets of their hearts, and assist them as teacher,
guide and friend. It often happens, in fact, that a
vocation to embrace the priestly life does not manifest itself spontaneously, but is like the jewel in the
Gospel, which is hidden in the field and has to be
discovered. God, Who reserves to Himself the calling of His elect, yet asks for the help of sacred ministers in order that youths may become aware of the
action of heavenly grace and bring to maturity the
divine seed planted in their souls. For sacred vocations, therefore, there should never be lacking the
friendly conversation of the priest, his fatherly advice, and above all his spiritual direction. All should
be provided in such wise as to preserve due respect
both for the action of God and the freedom of the
candidates for the priesthood.

These are the points which We have thought
fit to propose for your consideration, and We commend them to your concern and your zeal for religion. All that remains for Us is to exhort you earnestly to carry on the work of your holy apostolate
with unshaken confidence. For though you are
meeting with great difficulties, it must never on any
occasion be thought that God is not providing for
the needs of His Church and is not now, as in the
past, calling to Himself countless numbers of generous, strong, sound and pure youths, who will obey
the voice of Christ and conceive the desire of dedi-
cating themselves to the Church. Never cease to
put before these chosen ones the lofty ways of the
sacred apostolate and of Christian holiness. Ceaselessly show them the needs of souls, inflame their

hearts to follow in the footsteps of Christ, and they will follow you generously!

We commend these our prayers to Almighty God, and that they may be effectively realized, We lovingly impart to you and your collaborators, as a pledge of Our fatherly kindness, the Apostolic Blessing.

Address to the European Congress of National
Vocation Directors, December 3, 1966

HOW TO PRESENT RELIGIOUS LIFE

Pope Paul VI

The religious life in this twentieth century presents itself thus: where now are the religious vocations inherited or following family traditions, or, on the other hand, vocations reserved to the weaker or disabled persons, incapable of facing the duties and vicissitudes of a secular profession or of marriage, or again, blooming in confined environments abetted by an acquiescent timidity on the one hand, or by an authoritarian oppression on the other?

Tell the souls that are avid for perfection and open to the idealism of the Gospel that still sparkles among our youth, what a religious vocation really is, a vocation to which the Church adds strict sup-

porting rules of ascetical practice and opens wide
the horizons for the most enrapturing ascent of the
spirit.

Tell the value of a life on which love, in its
purest and strongest expression—love of God, inflicts its delightful torment and confers its joy, a
continuing joyfulness.

Tell what mission there can be in a life that
immolates itself with Christ in a sacrifice that has
no return and which assumes in the Church and in
the world a significance and strength in the redemption of others.

We trust, beloved daughters in Christ, that
this purified and shining concept of the religious
life and particularly of yours, will be presented once
more to God's People and to modern society by virtue of the Council and through you who follow in
its footsteps.

Then, newly idealized by its genuine content
of Christian perfection in charity, we trust that such
a concept may regain, in reference to spirit of
choice, its original and mysterious power of attraction, as though echoing completely the sweet and
mighty voice of Jesus: "Come and follow me!"

We hope that vocations will thus increase in
number, since many institutions are suffering at
present from a lack of such vocations. We cannot
foresee whether the Lord will grant this mutual
wish. We are certain, however, that vocations will
increase in quality, if not in number.

However, this new and yet traditional presentation of the religious ideal requires precisely the

very renewal, both in spirit and form, which you are seeking.

It remains only for us to encourage the updating which you are promoting with the guidance of teachers and ecclesiastical superiors and under the impulse of your fervent chapters.

Address to Major Superiors of Women's Religious

Institutes of Italy, January 12, 1967

INDISPENSABLE FOR SPIRITUAL TRAINING

Pope Pius XII

In truth, if priests are ordained for men (Cf. Heb. 5:1), it is for men of our time. Consequently, there must be a certain flexibility and adaptation in the training given to the candidates. But at no period can anything be substituted for the fundamental requirements laid down by Christ: "If any man will come after me, let him deny himself, and take up his cross daily, and follow me" (Luke 9:23). The urgent warning of Paul to Timothy has its real echo in every generation: "Be thou an example of the faithful in word, in conversation, in charity, in faith, in chastity" (1 Tim. 4:12). And your deliberations concerning the spiritual training which is indispensable for those who are beginning the religious life, will provoke, as they always do, that renewal of fervor in everything, which is so necessary for spiritual and religious men.

WHY THE VOCATION DECLINE?

Very Rev. Godfrey Poage, C.P.

Director, Pontifical Office for Religious Vocations

One of the questions posed most frequently by recruiters and religious superiors visiting the Pontifical Office for Religious Vocations is: "How can you explain the present decline in numbers of candidates for the seminary or novitiate?"

Now before venturing a reply we admit a familiarity with the many answers offered in Catholic newspapers, religious reviews, and vocation meetings. At one extreme is the claim that today's youths are too soft, too spoiled to undertake the rigors of a life dedicated wholly to God. At the other extreme is the presumption that the life of a priest, brother or sister is no longer relevant and so offers no challenge. In between are arguments that the drop-off is due to the poor image of the priest or religious . . . or to the changing patterns of family life . . . or to secularization and urbanization. Others claim that the problem is a consequence of public criticism of seminaries and religious institutes, and of the uncertainties caused by the current furor over defections and the problem of celibacy.

In reply we are willing to admit some truth in all these explanations. We also note that there are today more opportunities than ever before for zealous youths to serve the Church without changing their status. For example, they can teach religion and even get a doctorate in theology. They can go on the missions and engage in all the corporal works of mercy. In short, they can do just about everything that was once reserved to priests and religious. So, except for the obvious honor of being able to confect the Sacraments, teenagers today ask: "What is the special advantage of tying oneself down by sacred orders or religious vows?"

Here possibly is the crux of the vocation problem. Never before have there been so many Catholic boys and girls with the mental and physical qualifications for the priesthood or religious life. Never have so many youths been without canonical impediment and with every moral endowment for the life. So why are there so few accepting what they admit is "the highest possible vocation"? It is simply that they lack the desire for such a life. They don't want it!

In the [preceding] address of the Holy Father, we were given four specific recommendations for eliciting the desire for the priesthood or religious state in youths. . . . Where such recommendations have been followed, vocations are increasing—not declining!

THE VOCATION PROBLEM
DESERVES FIRST PLACE

Very Rev. James Alberione, S.S.P., S.T.D.

A decisive commitment to the recruiting and formation of vocations is necessary first of all. This matter does not depend only upon the Superior; it concerns and obliges all; it depends upon everyone. One brother, for instance, has twenty-five vocations to his credit so far; these young men are already professed and out on their missions. Much depends upon the grace of God, but much also depends upon one's zeal. And this is one of the clearest signs of love for one's Congregation.

How necessary it is to form Christians! And how much more necessary it is to form souls consecrated to God, since they will better promote God's glory and the salvation of souls.

To give God all we have is sanctity: "Well done, good and faithful servant; because thou hast been faithful over a few things, I will set thee over many" (Matt. 25:21). The Divine Master praised the widow who donated two small coins, because that money was all she had to live on, in contrast to others who contributed large sums which did not constitute all they had.

Moreover, giving souls to God is the sublimest type of parenthood. Do we or do we not feel our fatherhood or motherhood? Let us carry in our

hearts the many souls whom God calls and awaits—
souls who are often confronted with many difficulties. Threatened vocations! The majority are smoth-
ered in their social-educational environment; often
they are suffocated in the home itself. The devil is
battling to snatch these elect souls from Jesus: "Sa-
tan has desired to have you, that he may sift you as
wheat" (Luke 22:31). Let us have compassion on
these souls, whom we may be able to help with our
prayers or actions.

The vocation problem deserves first place
among all works of zeal. Jesus did not initiate his
public ministry with preaching; He began by choosing disciples. He sought them along the lakeshore;
He called them. And James, John, Andrew, Peter,
Philip, and others, responded. Then when these
men witnessed the miracle at Cana—the changing of
the water into wine—they believed: "And his disciples believed in him" (John 2:11).

If we truly love our neighbor as ourselves, we
will want many others to possess the great good
which is ours: the vocation. If we are happy with
the grace we have received, we will want many
others to share it, too. If we have our sights set on
sanctity, we will want others, also, to live by
this ideal.

May God grant us His wisdom in this matter of
vocations. We cannot expect candidates to be without any failings or weak points. We all have weak
points, more of them than virtues. But what we have
to require is good will, which brings results, in
emending and striving for perfection, which is the
true ideal of the religious.

In the first place it is necessary to look for vocations and to recruit a good number of them so that
a choice can be made. If there are ten in the young-
est group of aspirants, how many will reach profession or ordination? From among His *many* followers, Jesus named twelve to be His apostles, to live
with Him and understand what He was teaching, to
imitate His all-holy examples, so that they might re-
late later what they had seen and heard: "You shall
be witnesses for Me" (Acts 1:8).

Let us call upon the Divine Master, Who is our
Way in this regard too.

Invocations for vocation recruiters:
O Jesus, our light, show us whom You have
chosen.

O Jesus, our hope, let Your elect hear Your
words, "Be firm and steadfast."

O Jesus, infuse Your grace, so that they will
respond to Your call: "Immediately they left their
nets and their father, and followed him" (Matt.
4:22).

O Jesus Divine Master, You said, "The harvest is great but the laborers are few;" we lovingly
accept Your invitation: "Pray the Heavenly Father
to send forth laborers into His harvest."

O Lord, give rise to a devout crusade for vocations: all the faithful for all vocations. Raise up
more priests, and may they be the salt of the earth,
the light of the world, the city placed on the mountain top, for the salvation of mankind redeemed by
Your Blood. Raise up more religious, both men and
women, to fill the earth with religious houses, which

welcome those you have favored in a special way, and which will be centers of light and warmth; fonts of piety, gardens of saints, singing, "Glory to God and peace to men of good will."

O Mary, God's chosen one, Mother and Guardian of holy vocations, pray with us, pray for us, and for all those called by God.

VOCATION CLUBS —
BEST RECRUITING TECHNIQUE

Very Rev. Godfrey Poage, C.P.

Hardly a day goes by without some bishop, religious superior or recruiter visiting the Pontifical Office for Religious Vocations and asking: "Besides prayer and sacrifice, what is the most effective technique of promoting vocations to the priesthood or religious life?"

That same question is repeated over and over again in daily correspondence. Letter after letter asks: "What would you recommend for increasing interest in the priesthood . . . brotherhood . . . sisterhood? What type of program has been most effective?"

The unequivocal answer is: "Start a Vocation Club!"

The principal source of candidates for a vocation club are the Catholic schools. There are likewise wonderful prospects among the Catholic students in public schools. Other excellent sources are altar boy groups, youth choirs and similar associations. In a word, any place you can find Catholic youths, you can find prospects for a vocation club.

Experience proves that the success of a club is not dependent upon the number of potential candidates in the area, but upon the zeal and competence of the moderator. It is the same with sodalities, mission groups, or parish youth clubs. Such organizations are only excuses to bring the best Catholic youths under the influence of a zealous and competent leader. If the director is active and enthusiastic, there will be great results. If he or she lacks interest and conviction, nothing will be accomplished.

A club can be started by any priest in the parish, a teacher in school, or an interested religious. This recruiter gives a vocation talk at Catechism class or a school assembly.

The boys who are interested in knowing more about the priesthood or brotherhood are told that they can sign an application card and join a special organization devoted to fostering this interest. It will be their own special vocation club. A similar appeal is made to girls interested in knowing more about the sisterhood. In their club they will find out all about the life of a sister.

These boys' and girls' clubs are *always* separate organizations, and the director should remind the youngsters that by joining the club they do not commit themselves to becoming priests, brothers, or sisters. They are only evidencing their interest in finding out more about these vocations. It is always best, too, for a priest or brother to direct the boys, and for a sister to guide the girls.

During the school meetings there are vocation talks, films, slides, and various study projects. When the members meet on their own time, the director arranges some kind of trip or special progam. For the boys there can be a trip to some seminary or religious institute, where they can tour the buildings, see how the religious live and, if there are seminarians or novices present, join them in some games. For the girls there can be visits to different convents, where they can see how the sisters live and the work they do.

In the past twenty-five years these clubs have developed and guided thousands of those who are now priests, brothers, and sisters. Practically all who have had anything to do with the program, either as members or directors of clubs, are most enthusiastic. They realize that the clubs furnish what most of our prospects need: namely, more information, greater inspiration, and regular spiritual direction.

The real secret of the club's effectiveness is that it brings qualified youths under the influence of zealous and capable spiritual directors. The club gives its moderator an excuse to talk about vocations to the priesthood or religious life *at any time*. It makes all the students in a school or parish vocation-conscious and brings the subject out into the open. It also dissipates a great deal of parental opposition, for there is so much talk about the club at home that the parents soon presume on the decision of their son or daughter, even before the matter is discussed.

But by no means is the club a method of cramming vocational instruction into boys and girls. It is simply a program that is interest-creating and encouraging. At best only 20-30% of the youths of a given school or parish will want to become club

members, and of that number you can expect only
from 9-12% to continue with the whole course and
eventually enter a seminary or convent. But don't
forget that the other ninety-some per cent are wiser
and better for their training. Perhaps, in the years
ahead one of their sons or daughters will enter the
religious life. For this, if no other reason, the clubs
deserve recognition.

"Newsletter," Pontifical Office for Religious Vocations,
May, 1964

AN EXEMPLARY RECRUITER

When Sister M. Sophronia, O.S.F., died of cancer, the School Sisters of St. Francis lost one of their best recruiters. For every one of her forty-eight years of teaching she guided at least one girl to the convent and one boy to the priesthood or brotherhood. The last five years of her life, though racked by pain, she managed to stay on her feet and double her yearly average of recruits. Her record is all the more amazing in that Sister Sophronia spent most of her life teaching in little country schools.

Two years before she died, Sister M. Sophronia was induced to explain her recruiting methods, and the following quotations from her letter are most revealing. Reading "between the lines" one realizes that her success was due to zeal, competence, and plain hard work.

"In September," Sister M. Sophronia explained, "I start the first day of school by having the children pray for vocations. The hour we select for this exercise is one o'clock in the afternoon. Then the third week of school I organize a vocation club and pick for chairman one who is a good prospective recruit.

"In October I begin a series of weekly vocation talks. Special time is set aside every Friday for this purpose. Though the talk is only for five or ten minutes, I generally have a pertinent story or some

451

news-item clipped from a paper or magazine to stimulate a short discusssion period.

"In November I start using a Question Box. When there are no spontaneous questions, I have all the pupils think one up. This is my best way of reaching the individuals and their problems. Timid pupils would otherwise never receive help.

"Thus I go on, month by month. As soon as I notice a child developing special interest, I begin the direct approach. I immediately encourage this youth to frequent Communion, then daily Communion. I suggest sacrifices such a one could make, and we make a private novena together. From the moment I become convinced that the youth is qualified and has the desire, I make special efforts to give personal help and encouragement, such as a remark here and there, a fine book or pamphlet, a question as to how the vocation is developing.

"The month of March is the culminating point of my program. I arrange special vocation activities all month and correlate them with every subject possible—posters, book reports, compositions, letters to their patron saints, novenas, and class plays.

"In April I start private interviews, using a little questionnaire I have made up. It takes from thirty to sixty minutes for each child, and when the youngster tells me definitely, "I would like to be a priest (or religious)," I immediately have such a one write to the proper authorities. This requires the parents' approval, and if the youth has not yet spoken to the mother or father, I coach him on how to do so. Then I ask the parents to come to see me. I tell them how God has privileged them and how

He will now bless them for the sacrifice of their child. As a rule the appeal succeeds. The parents are happy to learn that I am so personally interested in their child.

"In May I continue instructions, stories, and the question box as usual. We select a feast of our Blessed Mother and make an act of special consecration to her, adding that we recommend to her special care those of the class whom Jesus has called to His special service. I also provide a day of recollection for the older students.

"Finally, I keep in touch with my recruits during vacation. I encourage them to receive Holy Communion daily and give them certain daily prayers to recite. Occasionally we get together for a talk and I generally arrange some special Latin lessons for the boys who plan to go to the seminary, so they do not have too much difficulty during their first weeks there."

There were many more comments and suggestions that Sister M. Sophronia made. But one thing is evident from what we have quoted. Sister was willing to sacrifice herself for vocations, and her efforts paid off. At her death she could claim almost a hundred priests, brothers, and sisters for whom she had been responsible!

"Newsletter," Pontifical Office for Religious Vocations,
March, 1966

WHAT ONE PASTOR DID!

At the Golden Jubilee of Msgr. J. J. Treanor of Sacred Heart Parish, Waseca, Minn., there were present 17 priests and 70 Sisters whom he had helped to the religious life. His practice was to say a "Pater and Ave" for vocations each time he went upstairs and an "Our Father and Hail Mary for the same intention each time he came down. From the results he figured it "cost" about 5,000 prayers for each of his spiritual children.

"Newsletter," Pontifical Office for Religious Vocations,
March, 1966

EVERYTHING DEPENDS ON THE CHOICE AND FORMATION OF VOCATIONS

Pope Pius XII

So that your Institutes may always respond to the wishes of the Vicar of Christ, act in such a way as to enroll in your ranks only young people who are suitable, that is to say, chosen for their virtue and, in the proper measure, for their intellectual and other qualities. Far from you be that excessive concern to assemble a multitude of subjects who one may fear will prove one day less worthy of your lofty vocation: they will be for the Church neither an adornment nor a benefit, but they will cause her harm and distress. If, on the other hand, faithful to the norms constantly being proposed by the Church, you welcome into your ranks only those who are truly worthy, God will take care to raise up vocations of quality, and the esteem which men will have of your state will prepare the way for divine grace in a great number of souls. Trust God: if you serve Him worthily, He Himself will take care of you and of your Institutes which He will protect and prosper.

Address to Major Superiors, February 11, 1958

POINT OUT THE RENUNCIATIONS

Pope Paul VI

Is it perhaps that the Lord is calling not so frequently or that His voice has become less effective? Certainly not!

It is rather a question of creating conditions, always with great respect for the liberty of souls, in which the divine call can be heard and followed. . . .

To youths, generous and strong by nature, the ideal of the priestly and religious life should be presented in all its completeness. This means pointing out to them the renunciations and abnegations which such a life entails, as well as its significance and value.

Address to Italian Episcopal Conference, June, 1966

MEDIOCRITY, NOT SACRIFICE, REPELS YOUTH

Hildebrand Cardinal Antoniutti

You deplore the lack of vocations, but are you aware of your great responsibility? Have you prayed sufficiently that the Lord will send laborers into the harvest? Have you tried to give an example that will attract and win youths?

The young are not afraid of sacrifice. They are put off only at the sight of mediocrity. Priests and religious who are strong, generous, ardent, humble, devout and charitable always find souls eager to follow them.

When have missionary vocations been most numerous? It has been when tragic news has been received from missionary countries of priests and religious being massacred or thrown out, churches destroyed or profaned, and everything finished. Then youth have been fired with the desire to work in those regions that are most troublesome, among people who are most obstinate, and amid dangers that are gravest.

Address on the Fourth Centennial
of Catholicism, in the Philippines;
from "Newsletter," Pontifical Office
for Religious Vocations

THE "DRIVE" WHICH GOD ALONE GIVES

Most Rev. Fulton J. Sheen

My dear People of God: Vocations are dwindling. We leave to others to seek out the causes of the decline. What is important is not to analyze the chemistry of the waters which flood the sinking ship of vocations, but to refloat it.

Today a thousand devices are used to instill vocations, such as deluging our youth with letters, pamphlets and appeals. But Our Lord gave only one way—and that was *prayer*. He prayed before He chose His apostles; He prayed before He chose His disciples. Then came His words about prayer, "And when He saw the crowds He felt sorry for them because they were harassed and dejected, like sheep without a shepherd." Then He said to His disciples, "The harvest is rich but the laborers are few, so ask the Lord of the Harvest to send laborers into His harvest" (Matt. 9:38; Luke 10:2).

Jesus saw the harvest of souls greater than the reapers. More were ready to be saved than were preachers to save them. Without reapers, the harvest would be lost.

To win these workers, Our Lord said to pray to the "Lord of the Harvest." Who is the Lord of the Harvest? It is the Heavenly Father. "My Father is the Husbandman" (John 15:1). But why did He say pray to the Lord of the Harvest? Because prayer is *desire*. Only the Church which wants priests will have them.

Now here we come to the basic reason for prayer—our English translation of the Bible says that if we pray, God will "send laborers into the harvest." But in the original Greek, the word "ekbalein" meaning to "drive," or to send with haste and urgency, or to compel as if there was always a human unwillingness to be overcome (Exodus 4:10, 13; Judges 4:8; Jonah 1:3).

The same word is used to describe how the Holy Spirit "drove" Our Lord into the wilderness to be tempted and tried in all our human situations. It is always used to indicate the Power of God driving out the devil from those possessed (John 13:31) and the money changers from the Temple (John 2:15), and finally, it is used to indicate the constraint the Good Shepherd used to force a sheep that delays unduly in answering the call of the shepherd (John 10:4).

The conclusion is this:

1) Vocations come from prayers to the Heavenly Father of souls.

2) If we pray, the same God who used His Divine Power to drive out devils and push reluctant sheep to the sheep fold, is the same God who will drive vocations into the hearts of the young.

3) There could be, for example, a hundred thousand young men and women who feel dimly the call of God to serve Him, but, because we do not pray, that extra "push" or "compulsion" or "drive" which God alone gives, is lacking.

WHY THEY COME TO
RELIGIOUS LIFE

Very Rev. James Alberione, S.S.P., S.T.D.

Those who come to religious life come for greater wisdom, life, grace, spirit of prayer, and participation in Christ's life so as to gain a greater reward in heaven. They do not come for a more comfortable life or for greater sense pleasures. He who loves these things seeks not the religious life. He is not following the Divine Master nor has he understood His words: "If anyone wishes to come after me, let him deny himself, and take up his cross, and follow me" (Matt. 16:24).

Neither do they come for honor, glory, or renown. Searchers after fame take another road, one that does not lead to the manger, a road the Master did not take.

In calling a soul to the religious life, the Lord promises more trials, greater sufferings, greater humiliations. Trials, obedience, and mortification constitute our wealth! The Lord has called us to a more abundant life, that is, He wants us to have more grace, which means a closer incorporation in Him. Furthermore, He has given us the power to obtain through prayer what we lack.

Let religious go forward, then, with courage and energy. They have come for the superabundant life, for heaven. Christ said they will receive the hundredfold, and not only in the next life, but the hundredfold in this life, too. In heaven there will be the hundredfold of glory; here on earth, the hundredfold of grace. "We are . . . joint heirs with Christ, provided, however, we suffer with him that we may also be glorified with him" (Rom. 8:17). "This saying is true: If we have died with him, we shall also live with him; if we endure, we shall also reign with him" (2 Tim. 2:11-12).

Here it is the hundredfold of the "enduring" part; in heaven, the hundredfold of the "reigning"; here, the hundredfold of the "suffering"; in heaven, the hundredfold of the "glorification." Here it is the hundredfold of participation in the poverty of Nazareth, the hundredfold of Christ's obedience, of His hidden life, the hundredfold of the humiliations of His public life, the hundredfold of His passion; in heaven, the hundredfold of His resurrection and glory. The measure of our union with Jesus here on earth, of our imitation of Him, will be the measure of our glory in the next life.

The great highway which leads to the "abundance" of spiritual and eternal life is religious life.

From: *"The Superior Follows the Master,"*
Daughters of St. Paul, Boston

Updating and
Religious Formation

Adaptation and renewal depend greatly on the education of religious. Consequently neither non-clerical religious nor religious women should be assigned to apostolic works immediately after the novitiate. Rather, their religious and apostolic formation, joined with instruction in arts and science directed toward obtaining appropriate degrees, must be continued as needs require in houses established for those purposes.

In order that the adaptation of religious life to the needs of our time may not be merely external and that those employed by rule in the active apostolate may be equal to their task, religious must be given suitable instruction, depending on their intellectual capacity and personal talent, in the currents and attitudes of sentiment and thought prevalent in social life today. This education must blend its elements together harmoniously so that an integrated life on the part of the religious concerned results.

Religious should strive during the whole course of their lives to perfect the culture they have received in matters spiritual and in arts and sciences. Likewise, superiors must, as far as this is possible, obtain for them the opportunity, equipment and time to do this.

Superiors are also obliged to see to it that directors, spiritual fathers, and professors are carefully chosen and thoroughly trained.

Decree on the Adaptation and Renewal of Religious Life, n. 18

THE TRAINING OF RELIGIOUS

The training of Religious beginning with the novitiate should not be organized in the same way in all institutes, but the special character of each institute should be considered. In the revision and adaptation of this training an adequate and prudent place is to be given for experience.

Those precepts set down in the Decree *Optatam Totius* (On the Training of Priests), adapted to suit the character of each institute, are to be observed faithfully in the education of Religious clerics.

Further training after the novitiate is to be given in a way suitable to each institute. This training is altogether necessary for all members, even for those living a contemplative life, for Brothers in lay religious institutes and for Sisters in institutes dedicated to apostolic works, such as now exist in many institutes and are called juniorates, scholasticates and the like. This training should generally be extended over the entire period of temporary vows

This training is to be given in suitable houses and, lest it be purely theoretical, should for the sake of the inexperienced be complemented by the performance of works and duties in keeping with the nature and circumstances proper to each institute in such a way that they gradually become part of the life to be lived in the future.

While always maintaining the formation proper to each institute, when individual institutes cannot give adequate doctrinal or technical training this can be provided by the fraternal collaboration of many. This collaboration can take various forms at different levels: common lectures or courses, loan of teachers, associations of teachers, sharing of facilities in a common school to be attended by members of several institutes.

Institutes equipped with the necessary means should willingly assist others.

After adequate experimentation, each institute is to prepare its own suitable norms for the formation of its members.

Ecclesiae Sanctae, on No. 18 of the Decree Perfectae Caritatis

FORMATION FOR INTERIOR LIFE AND APOSTOLIC ADAPTATION

Pope Paul VI

In bringing about this renewal of your Institutes, your primary concern must always be the spiritual life of your members. Wherefore, among yourselves and among all other Religious whose duty it is to devote themselves to works of the sacred apostolate, We would be entirely opposed to see anyone espousing that false opinion which claims that primary concern must be given to external works and only secondary attention devoted to the interior life of perfection, as though this were demanded by the spirit of the times and the needs of the Church.

Zealous activity and the cultivation of one's interior life should not bring any harm to each other; indeed, they require the closest union, in order that both may ever proceed with equal pace and progress. Therefore, let zeal for prayer, the beauty of a pure conscience, patience in adversities, active and vibrant charity devoted to the salvation of souls, increase in union with fervent works. When these virtues are neglected, not only will apostolic labor lack vigor and fruitfulness, but the spirit also will gradually lose fervor. As a consequence, the Religious will not be able to avoid, for long, the dangers which lie hidden in the very performance of the sacred ministry.

With respect to that portion of the apostolate which is entrusted to the care of the Religious, We wish to make some further observations. Religious Institutes should sedulously adapt the work proper to their apostolates to modern conditions and circumstances. The younger Religious, particularly, are to be instructed and educated properly in this matter, in such a way, however, that the apostolic zeal with which they must be inflamed, does not remain circumscribed exclusively by the boundaries of one's own Order but rather opens outwardly toward the great spiritual necessities of our times. Nor is this enough. For while being educated along the lines We have indicated, they should also cultivate an exquisite sensitivity to their duties by force of which, both in words and deeds, they will constantly show themselves as true ministers of God, distinguished by soundness of doctrine and recommended to the people by holiness of life. However, in these matters, let not the Religious be left solely to their own initiative, since their work must always be subject to the vigilance of Superiors, especially if it is a matter of work that has notable relevance to civil life.

Address to All Religious, May 23, 1964

WHAT TODAY'S YOUNG ADULTS WANT

Pope Paul VI

To look back, to remember, is a duty; not only because it is necessary to have an historical knowledge of the environment in which one lives, but because respect for tradition is part of genuine ecclesial pedagogy. The negligent and scornful mentality of a few modern innovators toward the past is not very intelligent. And if it seeks to interpret and second the instinctive and natural detachment of youthful psychology from the manners of living of the preceding generation, it does not always do this with the happy intuition of the heart of the youth. For young people do want to be free of certain restrictions and inhibitions imposed upon them, but they do not want to ignore the good fortune and honor of their origin; they do not want to be egoistic and ungrateful towards those who have loved and educated them; they do not want to base their maturity upon their own inexperience, but rather upon that which the experience of others has prepared and given to them.

FORMATION PERSONNEL

Rev. Elio Gambari, S.M.M.

The obligation to keep updating one's formation is even stronger for those involved in the very delicate and difficult apostolate of forming the institute's personnel. Indeed, formation, which is the source of continual renewal for the Congregation, presupposes unceasing renewing and updating on the part of those who are the institute's "channels." Young people always—but especially today—appear to be in a state of rapid transformation, at times disturbing, in a world whose face is forever changing. It is precisely in this situation that those involved in formation must act in order to prepare the young of today for today's living and tomorrow's.

All this demands not only a sensitive spirit and keen powers of perception, but also a profound awareness of the problems of young people and of modern society. At the same time it requires the ability to make unchangeable, transcendant values and realities acceptable and appreciated, and to see to it that young religious learn to share in the life of the whole Church at the present moment in history.

From: *"Renewal in Religious Life"*

JUNIORATES, OR POST-NOVITIATE FORMATION

Rev. Elio Gambari, S.M.M.

The purpose of the juniorate is to continue and complete the work of formation and to ensure an immediate, practical preparation, through suitable experiences, for the kind of life to which perpetual vows will bind the religious permanently. At the same time, this period of formation provides for a final testing, on the part of both the institute and the religious, of his fitness for the life of the Congregation and of the genuineness of his vocation. Thus, with the juniorate the purpose of the period of temporary vows takes on a more concrete and specific form.

As with formation in general, the juniorate must be functional in terms of the Church and the Congregation. Hence it must respond to the specific spirit and mission of the institute in the heart of the Church.

However, there are elements, norms and needs of a general nature which apply to all institutes, and there are others pertaining to certain kinds of institutes similar in works and activity. Individual Congregations must not neglect to take these into account and welcome them, while making every effort to study and spell out juniorate procedures in keeping with their own needs. Although there is a certain freedom of action in planning the juniorate as to distribution of the programs and content during the time of temporary vows, still there are limits and pointers applicable to all.

In this planning, we have to keep in mind the existence or non-existence of a second year of novitiate, the breadth and degree of formation achieved before entrance into the novitiate, and the apostolic, doctrinal and professional formation needed for the institute's particular activities. Moreover, the religious, spiritual formation must be on the same level as the preparation afforded in the above sectors, if we want to avoid lack of balance in the lives of religious.

From: *"Renewal in Religious Life"*

Conferences of Major Superiors

This synod favors conferences or councils of major superiors, established by the Holy See. These can contribute very much to achieve the purpose of each institute; to encourage more effective cooperation for the welfare of the Church; to ensure a more just distribution of ministers of the Gospel in a given area; and finally to conduct affairs of interest to all religious. Suitable coordination and cooperation with episcopal conferences should be established with regard to the exercise of the apostolate.

Similar conferences should also be established for secular institutes.

Decree on the Adaptation and Renewal of Religious Life, n. 23

ON CONFERENCES OR UNIONS OF MAJOR SUPERIORS OF MEN AND WOMEN

Care is to be taken that the union of superiors general of men and women can be heard and consulted by means of a council established at the Sacred Congregation for Religious.

It is of greatest importance that national conferences or unions of major superiors of men and women cooperate with episcopal conferences with confidence and reverence (cf. No. 35 of the Decree *Christus Dominus;* No. 33 of the Decree *Ad Gentes Divinitus*).

Therefore it is hoped that questions involving both sides be discussed in mixed commissions composed of both bishops and major superiors of men or women.

Ecclesiae Sanctae, on No. 23 of the Decree Perfectae Caritatis

JOINING FORCES

Pope Pius XII

Your Union of Superiors General which was lately set up on your initiative and which continues spontaneously to hold its meetings, has been approved by the Apostolic See as a permanent institution and recognized as a moral personage. This union postulates on your part the determined will to contribute to everything for which the Church desires your collaboration. In fact you have well understood that you all form one single army in which—some as footsoldiers, others as horsemen or archers—all in the last analysis are fighting the same good fight. At a time when the enemy of Christ's name is each day welding his forces into a band which he hopes will be invincible, you have understood that this is the opportune moment, that it is necessary, for you and for all who serve God, to unite your forces, each one at his own post and with his own weapons, with an eye to the same victory.

This unity, to which is opposed the differences in nationality, mind, customs, and other human traits, will still flourish wonderfully if your souls are profoundly impregnated with the true charity of Christ which the Holy Spirit showers on this same unity. Let this supernatural and infused charity find you prompt in response to His action, and it will itself effortlessly untie all the knots of a too narrow predilection, justified but too narrow, for one's own Institute, which insinuates itself little by little because of human weakness. Certainly each one has the duty to love the Institute to which Divine Providence has called him, to mold his mind and his conduct according to the norms of this Institute, to choose and to accomplish up to a certain point the apostolic ministry according to the proper laws of the Institute: but everyone must always turn all things to the sole service of the same Church, Spouse of the same Lord and Savior.

Address to Major Superiors
of Religious Institutes, February 11, 1958

UNIONS OF CHOSEN SOULS

Very Rev. James Alberione, S.S.P., S.T.D.

Let us give thanks to our Lord for having inspired the Unions of Major Superiors. They are veritable alliances of high spiritual powers, directed toward the sanctification of all religious and the service of Christ's Church, of His Vicar, the Pope. We should view these Unions above all as unions of chosen souls, of prayerful souls, as the Holy See views them in urging their formation.

Conclusion

Religious institutes, for whom these norms of adaptation and renewal have been laid down, should respond generously to the specific vocation God gave them as well as their work in the Church today. The sacred synod highly esteems their way of life in povetry, chastity and obedience, of which Christ the Lord is Himself the exemplar. Moreover, their apostolate, most effective, whether obscure or well known, offers this synod great hope for the future. Let all religious, therefore, rooted in faith and filled with love for God and neighbor, love of the cross and the hope of future glory, spread the good news of Christ throughout the whole world so that their witness may be seen by all and our Father in heaven may be glorified (Matt. 5:16). Therefore, let them beseech the Virgin Mary, the gentle Mother of God, "whose life is a model for all," that their number may daily increase and their salutary work be more effective.

Decree on the Adaptation and Renewal of Religious Life, n. 25

Daughters of St. Paul

In Massachusetts
50 St. Paul's Avenue
Boston, Mass. 02130
172 Tremont Street
Boston, Mass. 02111
381 Dorchester Street
So. Boston, Mass. 02127
325 Main Street
Fitchburg, Mass. 01420

In New York
78 Fort Place
Staten Island, N.Y. 10301
625 East 187th Street
Bronx, N.Y. 10458
39 Erie Street
Buffalo, N.Y. 14202

In Connecticut
202 Fairfield Avenue
Bridgeport, Conn. 06603

In Ohio
141 West Rayen Avenue
Youngstown, Ohio 44503
415 Euclid Avenue
Cleveland, Ohio 44114

In Florida
2700 Biscayne Blvd.
Miami, Florida 33137

In Louisiana
86 Bolton Avenue
Alexandria, La. 71301

In Texas
114 East Main Plaza
San Antonio, Texas 78205

In California
1570 Fifth Avenue
San Diego, Calif. 92101
278 - 17th Street
Oakland, Calif. 94612

In Canada
8885 Blvd. Lacordaire
St. Leonard Deport-Maurice
Montreal, Canada
1063 St. Clair Avenue West
Toronto, Canada

In Australia
58 Abbotsford Road
Homebush N.S.W., Australia

In Africa
Box 4392
Kampala, Uganda

In England
29 Beauchamp Place
London, S.W. 3, England

In India
Water Field Road Extension
Plot N. 143
Bandra, India

In Philippine Islands
No. 326 Lipa City
Philippine Islands